ANTI
CAPITALISM

ANTI
CAPITALISM
A GUIDE TO THE MOVEMENT

Edited by Emma Bircham and John Charlton

BOOKMARKS
PUBLICATIONS

London, Sydney

ANTI-CAPITALISM: A GUIDE TO THE MOVEMENT
• •

First published July 2001
Revised and reprinted August 2001

Bookmarks Publications Ltd,
1 Bloomsbury Street,
London WC1B 3QE,
England

Bookmarks,
PO Box A338,
Sydney South,
NSW 2000,
Australia

ISBN 1 898876 78 9

Typeset by Megan Trudell
Design by Noel Douglas (noel@freemachine.net)
Photos by Jess Hurd (reportdigital.co.uk),
Balthazar Serreau and Tom Krusse
Printed by Bath Press
Inside cover photo: 'Teamsters and Turtle kids
together at last'—environmentalists and unionists
at Seattle, November 1999

ANTI-CAPITALISM: A GUIDE TO THE MOVEMENT

First published July 2001
Revised and reprinted August 2001

Bookmarks Publications Ltd,
1 Bloomsbury Street,
London WC1B 3QE,
England

Bookmarks,
PO Box A338,
Sydney South,
NSW 2000,
Australia

ISBN 1 898876 78 9

Typeset by Megan Trudell
Design by Noel Douglas (noel@freemachine.net)
Photos by Jess Hurd (reportdigital.co.uk),
Balthazar Serreau and Tom Krusse
Printed by Bath Press
Inside cover photo: 'Teamsters and Turtle kids
together at last'—environmentalists and unionists
at Seattle, November 1999

ACKNOWLEDGEMENTS
Many thanks to the following people for their assistance in the production of this book:

Christophe Aguiton, Tom Behan, Geoff Brown, Matthew Caygill, Jill Chanter, Judy Cox, Kevin Danaher, Andy Durgan, Peter Dwyer, Bilal El-Amine, Martin Empson, Nick Howard, Olaf Klenke, Paul McGarr, David McNeill, China Miéville, Paul Obermayer, Judith Orr, Kevin Ovenden, Sean Purdy, David Renton, Guy Taylor, Ritch Whyman and Jim Wolfreys.

CONTENTS

ANTI-WEF DEMONSTRATION, MELBOURNE, AUSTRALIA, 11 SEPTEMBER 2000

OUR WORLD IS NOT FOR SALE

I think we are really at war.

We've got an enemy which is the whole corporate system. The objective of that corporate system, whether financial or industrial, is to be able to go where it wants, and produce what it wants, when it wants, for as long as it wants, to make as much money (obviously) as it can, and damn the costs. The goal is profit and anything that enhances that goal is good and anything that goes against that goal is bad.

If the enemy is transnational and is going for total control, then I think it's obvious that the response has also got to be transnational and it's got to be a mix of people. We don't want totalitarianism. That's not our goal. We want international democracy. But if we're to get it we've got to fight for each other. The threat is to all of us. If we're not fighting each-for-all, all-for-each, we're going to be picked off one-by-one.

Now if you're in a war, and I want to convince you that we are in a war, you've also got to think about who your allies are. Are our governments allies? I'm very sorry to say that it's a rare government that's an ally in this struggle. There's a permanent government which is the government of the industrial and financial corporations. And then every now and then we're allowed to elect men in suits (and they mostly are men) who read the script for the permanent government.

The state seems to be accepting its own demise. I don't know what the reason for that is. We struggled with this contradiction during the anti-MAI struggle. Why were our governments prepared to give up so much and get absolutely nothing in return? The only answer I could think of, is contained in a document that's 150 years old which says, 'The state is the permanent committee for running the general affairs of the bourgeoisie.'

We've got to stop and turn around, and we've got to do nothing less than overthrow the permanent government of the transnational corporations.

We can win if we pledge ourselves to each other because history is handing us an enormous opportunity, and we've got to seize it.

—Susan George in Seattle, November 1999

Genoa, July 2001.

Foreword
Emma Bircham

● ● ● ● ● ● ● ● ● ● ● ● ● ● ● ● ● ● ●

We are winning.

As this second edition goes to print, the effects of the demonstrations in Genoa are still reverberating around the globe. The Italian police viciously attacked activists in the streets and shot dead one young protester. The next day hundreds of thousands of people came to Genoa from more than 50 countries to show that we will not be intimidated and we will not be divided. We are growing, strengthening and deepening our resolve.

'You: G8. Us: 6 billion.' This was the slogan of the Genoa Social Forum. The G8 shook hands and posed for photos during a meeting which cost taxpayers three times the annual health budget of Tanzania, and resulted in no new debt cancellation for developing countries. Our leaders accept the statistic that 19,000 children in developing countries die every day so that Western bankers can receive interest on unpayable debts—they are just not prepared to do anything about it. It would seem that the majority of the world's population—1.2 billion of whom live in conditions of severe poverty, according to the United Nations—are not the constituents these politicians desire. When 300,000 of us confront them in the streets, when we hold solidarity demonstrations in 50 other countries around the world, they spend their energy attempting to discredit, divide and destroy us.

In Genoa they did not succeed.

When the first edition of this book went to print we had just witnessed the use of live ammunition against protesters in Gothenburg who had been demonstrating at the European Union summit. Genoa confirmed that this is the deadly direction in which the governments of the world wish to take things. Rather than deal with the issues about which we are protesting, they prefer to attack those who voice their discontent.

'Another world is possible.' When chanted in unison by hundreds of thousands of people in the streets, in many different languages, this is a phrase which begins to take shape, pointing towards a future in which people will be put before profit, human interests before corporate dividends. Capitalism has outlived its usefulness. It has produced inequality on a scale unprecedented in the history of human existence—three individuals now control more wealth than the poorest 43 countries. The redistribution of wealth from the poor to the rich has gone on for too long, and has corrupted and degraded all spheres of society. Another world is necessary.

'This is fun! We've got them on the run,' we shouted in the streets as global policy makers decided to hide in the desert in Qatar for the next WTO ministerial and in the tiny Canadian town of Kananaskis for the next G8 meeting. This is hardly the response of world leaders confident that they are acting in the interests of those they claim to represent. They are corporate lackeys, justifiably scared of the people whose health and welfare they are sacrificing at the altar of profit.

'Solidarity.' Above all, what Genoa demonstrated was that we will not be divided. What the hundreds of thousands of trade unionists, socialists, anarchists, environmentalists, human rights activists, religious campaigners and others showed was that we will be united in action. Genoa was a test for the anti-capitalist movement and we rose to the challenge, emerging more confident than ever. In the afterword to this edition, Tom Behan reflects on the events in Genoa and the way forward for the movement.

The mass demonstrations from Seattle to Genoa reflect a staggering crisis of legitimacy—unequalled since the Vietnam War. The states and corporations which govern in our names have shown themselves to be spectacularly incapable of doing so. We have been forced to come out in the streets to win back our world from those who have so disastrously mismanaged it.

We may feel intimidated and overwhelmed by their sheer size and power, but it is in the essence of capitalism that their power is already ours. We are the ones that create their wealth—we have only to redirect that wealth creation in the interests of all. This is the constructive project that has begun to emerge from the anti-capitalist movement as street protests begin to link up with strikes, mass strikes and occupations from one side of the world to the other. This is the meaning of 'anti-capitalism'—the promise of moving beyond capitalism to a more radically democratic, self-governing, self-sustaining world.

When Tony Benn spoke at the opening rally of the Globalise Resistance conference in London in February of this year, he announced, 'We are no longer on the defensive,' to thunderous applause. That realisation rang true for the thousands of activists in the audience who had worked together and separately through the long, difficult days of the 1980s and 1990s—under the brutal interventions of Thatcherism and the rapid rightward shift of New Labour.

Since Seattle, and reinforced by Genoa, a broader picture has come into view which shows we are no longer alone in our privatised, downsized, deregulated lives—we are part of a movement that is determined to respond, that understands an alternative is possible. We have come to understand that the system which oppresses us in one corner of the world, or in one aspect of our lives, is the same system wreaking its havoc elsewhere. We have realised that a fundamental change in society is required.

The purpose of this book is to give activists from different strands of the movement the knowledge they need to offer informed solidarity to those in other areas of the struggle and in other parts of the world—so that we will remain undivided. It is also intended to help keep up the debate about where we are going and how we will get there—so that we will be united in action.

We have nothing to lose, and so much to gain.

Emma Bircham is the publisher of Bookmarks books.
publications@bookmarks.uk.com

Protesters from a diverse range of organisations attempt to blockade the EU summit, Nice December 2000.

Introduction
George Monbiot

● ● ● ● ● ● ● ● ● ● ● ● ● ● ● ● ● ● ● ●

The neo-liberals' great advantage is that they have only one idea. That idea—that society should subordinate all other concerns to the interests of big business—was conceived and cloned in a Chicago laboratory, then hatched and raised in political incubators all over the world. Uniform, universally applicable, hygienically manufactured, it suffers none of the complexities which trouble the ideas bred in the turbulent womb of the real world.

We, the opponents of neo-liberalism, by contrast, are enfeebled by our greatest strengths. Our creativity, our diversity, our authenticity have encouraged us each to fight their programme in our own tiny and idiosyncratic way. About once a year we come together, demonstrate a formidable collective strength, then disperse and scarcely talk to each other until the following year's event. And in the meantime we are picked off one by one.

We have remained apart for several reasons. We have failed to grasp the idea that all of us—workers, environmentalists, opponents of privatisation, defenders of local amenities, human rights and social justice campaigners—are threatened by the same global forces. We have been divided by our ideological differences and suspicious of each other's tactics. Above all, we have failed to understand how powerful we can be if we work together.

The other side, however, has entertained no doubts about how effective we could become. This is why governments all over the world have been passing pre-emptive laws allowing them to monitor and bug us, to curb our freedoms and criminalise our campaigns. The neo-liberals know that though they have harnessed the wealth and power of the state, they cannot avoid one terrifying fact: we are many, and they are few. We are powerless only because we have behaved as if this were the other way around.

Since the protests in Seattle, however, the thousands of people's movements confronting neo-liberalism have begun to recognise each other's existence, even in some cases to offer each other support.

If the world is not to be offered up for sale, we have to turn this developing mutual respect into a mass mobilisation, operating not for a few days once a year, but continuously, everywhere on Earth

If the world is not to be offered up for sale, we have to turn this developing mutual respect into a mass mobilisation, operating not for a few days once a year, but continuously, everywhere on Earth. It is my belief that Globalise Resistance is one of the first indications that this is beginning to happen.

The meetings we held around Britain in February were the most inspiring I have ever attended. They brought together people who had never spoken to each other before, and in vast numbers. Everywhere we went there was a sense of excitement then of exultation, as people began to recognise their natural allies in campaigns they had formerly disregarded. Few came away from the meetings without the sense that something big, very big indeed, was about to begin. Now we must mobilise this enthusiasm to ensure that no one ever fights alone again. This guide to the movement, *Anti-Capitalism*, will help us to do so.

I don't think I have ever come across a book which contains so many different viewpoints and perspectives and yet such a unity of purpose. Just two years ago it would have been impossible to produce: many of the socialists, anarchists, greens, direct activists, trades unionists, academics and voluntary sector workers who have contributed would never have agreed to be represented in the same pages. But their collaboration is one of the clearest signs that I have seen that the new consensus is here to stay: people are now prepared to put their names, visibly and publicly, to a resistance coalition that involves some of their former opponents.

The range of topics tackled here also shows just how far the movement has progressed in the last two or three years. Let no one accuse us of single issue politics ever again: much of the range of modern human experience is represented in this collection, and each of the authors is plainly aware that her or his topic is not wholly divisible from any of the others.

Holding this immense coalition of interests and ideologies together will not be easy. Divisions will keep emerging, though it's my belief that if we respect each other's positions without having to subscribe to them, the mobilisation itself will resolve many of our differences and even—through the collective genius that always emerges when people freely organise—foment solutions upon which we can all agree.

This book will, I believe, help us both to cement our new unity and to advance our struggle to free the world from predatory corporations and their captive governments. It is time to use our creativity, our diversity, our authenticity, as assets rather than liabilities. If we can do that on a daily basis, then the world will belong to its people once again.

George Monbiot is author of *The Captive State* and a member of the Globalise Resistance steering committee.

ISSUES

The United Colors of Benetton store in central Prague on the morning of the demonstration against the IMF/World Bank meeting, 26 September 2000.

Corporate globalisation
Susan George

● ● ● ● ● ● ● ● ● ● ● ● ● ● ● ● ● ● ●

First, I shall try to describe very succinctly what the international
economic and financial system is, how it works, and to whose benefit. Second, I will suggest ways in which it can indeed be con-
fronted and transformed.[*]

Transnational corporations

The international economic and financial system is dominated by
industrial and financial transnational corporations (TNCs) whose
simple if unwritten programme is based on a trinity of freedoms.
They demand:

- ► Freedom of investment
- ► Freedom of capital flows
- ► Freedom of trade in all goods and all services including
  living organisms and intellectual property

Their ultimate goal is to be free to produce, distribute and
invest what they want, where they want, for as long as they choose,
and to be able to move capital, personnel and goods at will. Sub-
categories of these essential freedoms naturally include massive
privatisation of publicly held companies and public services. Nothing should be excluded *a priori* from the market, neither healthcare
nor education; human body parts or genetic material; food, seeds,

water, air or forests; art, music or sport.

TNCs can usually remain above the law, even when they cause grievous harm and damage to people and the environment. Let us recall the cases of Union Carbide in Bhopal, Shell's actions in Nigeria against the Ogoni people or the recent oil-spill on the French Breton coast as a result of Total-Fina's irresponsibility. These corporations demand deregulation and strict limitations on government intervention, except in the case of corporate welfare such as tax-breaks or publicly funded research support, which should be maintained—although welfare payments to citizens should not. In their view all taxes, particularly those on employment, are bad, except for taxes paid by consumers, salaried employees and wage earners.

TNCs measure their success by profit rates and 'shareholder value', meaning the market price of the company's stock. Some corporations even buy up their own stock to cause the market price to rise. Cost-cutting, especially through massive layoffs, is another way to increase shareholder value, and loyalty to employees or to the communities where they happen to be located is a thing of the past.

The United Nations (UN) claims there are now about 60,000 TNCs with half a million affiliates, but the ones to watch are the top one, two or five hundred. Of the top 100 economic entities in the world, 51 are corporations, only 49 are states. General Motors or General Electric are much larger than Saudi Arabia or Poland, and so on. The top 200 firms are responsible for about a quarter of all the measured economic activity in the world—or gross world product.

All told, the 60,000 TNCs counted by the UN employ only about 60 million people worldwide. Let us generously assume that each of these jobs generates another two jobs somewhere else in the economy: this still amounts to only 180 million people employed by TNCs, or well under 10 percent of the world's available workforce. In the space of five years in the 1990s the top 100 TNCs increased their sales by 20 percent while slightly reducing their total employment.

So TNCs employ relatively few people compared to their size.

They also invest much less in genuine economic activity than most people believe. During the past five years more than three quarters of what the press and the UN label as 'foreign direct investment' was actually cross-border mergers and acquisitions. The TNCs are constantly in search of greater market shares which they can obtain more easily by buying up other companies than by creating new ones.

The UN does not publish figures on financial TNCs—such as commercial banks, insurance companies, pension funds and mutual funds or brokerage houses, even though their turnover is in the billions of dollars and often rivals the sales of the industrial giants. The last reliable figures I know of date from 1995 and were published by the Bank for International Settlements (BIS)—the central bank of central banks in Basle.

At that time banks, insurance companies, pension funds and institutional investors were handling $28 trillion worth of funds, a figure which has quite possibly doubled today. As the BIS notes, the managers of this money routinely display 'herding behaviour', meaning that they all race for the exit as soon as any unfavourable signs are perceived, particularly in fragile, so-called 'emerging markets'. As the BIS further explains, a mere 1 percent shift in the holdings of these giants is equivalent to more than a quarter of the entire stock market capitalisation of all the emerging markets of Asia taken together, and to two thirds of the value of all Latin American equity markets.[1]

So no one should be at all surprised that sudden financial crises have plagued countries such as Thailand, Korea, Indonesia or Brazil. Considering the volume and the volatility of funds floating around the world in search of profits, the miracle is that these crises are not more frequent.

Not just any profit will do: the World Economic Forum—the Davos people—publish an annual competitivity index on which, for example, France and Germany get comparatively low rankings. Why? Because in these countries average rates of return to corporate capital are 'only' about 12 percent. This is not high enough—pension funds and other institutional investors demand rates of at least 15 percent and in some places have been known to garner 23 percent. When capital is rewarded in this way, there is clearly not going to be an enormous amount left over for remunerating labour which has, indeed, seen its share of the pie decline over the past 20 years.

So these are a few characteristics of the giant corporations that make the world economic and financial system go round. They are few in number and they hold, of course, disproportionate power. For this reason, I try never to use the word 'globalisation' without qualifying it: we are living in the era of *corporate-led, corporate-driven globalisation*. Although the TNCs have not yet been able to impose totally their political programme, they are adept at using a variety of official and unofficial instruments to impose the three basic freedoms I alluded to at the beginning: freedom of investment, freedom of capital flows, and freedom of trade of goods and services.

> **The TNCs and their allies, the Fund, the Bank and the WTO, cannot build an inclusive world—their policies are in fact throwing petrol on the fires of inequality**

The IMF, the World Bank and the WTO

The three major *official institutions* helping to push forward the corporate agenda are the World Bank, the International Monetary Fund (IMF) and the World Trade Organisation. The IMF is the architect of so-called structural adjustment programmes in the poorer, highly indebted countries of the South and the East—about 95 countries at the moment. Because of their debt burdens these countries must earn the IMF's stamp of approval in order to receive loans from any source, and to obtain the Fund's approval, they must adopt its neo-liberal views about economic management. These views, taken together, are also sometimes referred to as the 'Washington Consensus'.

Rules of the Washington Consensus and of structural adjustment include strict fiscal discipline, which means limiting budget deficits and reduced government spending on fields such as health, education and infrastructure; tax reform to benefit corporations and higher-income individuals; market-determined interest rates; open borders with regard to capital flows, imports, exports and foreign direct investment; plus privatisation, deregulation and downsizing of civil servants. Basic necessities invariably rise in price because subsidies are outlawed; exports are encouraged at the expense of local production for satisfying local needs. Mass unemployment often results as governments fire employees and small businesses fail due to high interest rates, shedding their personnel. While the IMF may call these measures structural adjustment, ordinary people call them hardship and austerity packages. And many of us sum up this doctrine as *neo-liberalism*.

The World Bank is the world's most important 'development' lender. In tandem with the Fund, it shapes policy in dozens of countries. It cooperates with TNCs not only through procurement but also by its policy choices; for example, it lends 25 times as much to fossil-fuel-based energy projects as to sustainable/renewable energy projects. The Bank also oversees massive privatisation policies from which local and foreign investors profit.

The role of the Bank and the Fund, especially the Fund, in managing recent financial crises in Thailand, Korea, Indonesia, Russia, Brazil and Mexico has been sharply criticised, not just by progressives but by important establishment figures like Harvard economist Jeffrey Sachs and the Meltzer Commission, named by the US Congress.

This group of 11 mainstream economists recommended a much-reduced role for both the Fund and the Bank but the US Treasury so far refuses to follow these recommendations.

The US Treasury recognises, quite correctly, that the combination of debt plus structural adjustment plus massive privatisation is a far more efficient instrument than colonialism ever was for keeping countries in line. The international institutions that implement these policies help both transnational corporations and elites in the poorer countries who profit from structural adjustment because wages are lower. It's worth noting as well that every time a financial crisis strikes, cash-strapped local businesses can be bought up on the cheap. TNCs again benefit from these fire-sale prices, as do local elites.

Perhaps most useful of all to the corporate programme is the World Trade Organisation (WTO) because it is spearheading the drive towards total freedom of trade and its rules are binding. The decisions of the WTO's 'dispute resolution mechanism' (panels of trade experts meeting behind closed doors) are enforceable through sanctions and apply to all 136 member-countries, developed and less developed, soon to be joined by China and others. The WTO's future negotiations will concern not merely the liberalisation of trade in goods and agricultural products but also rules pertaining to intellectual property, investment and government procurement. Through the General Agreement on Trade in Services it is bringing virtually all areas of human existence under its purview, including health, education, culture, the environment, tourism, energy, etc. Its Dispute Resolution Body is proving a highly effective tool for reducing standards of food safety and environmental protection. On the whole the WTO is perhaps the greatest institutional threat to democracy now functioning.

The US Treasury recognises, quite correctly, that the combination of debt plus structural adjustment plus massive privatisation is a far more efficient instrument than colonialism ever was for keeping countries in line

Transnationals are quite naturally interested in the greatest possible freedom of trade since fully one third of world trade takes place between subsidiaries of the same company (eg IBM 'trading' with IBM, Ford with Ford and so on); a further third is trade between subsidiaries of different TNCs (eg Ford trading with IBM). Corporations have shaped the agenda of the WTO from the beginning as the director of the WTO Services Division, David Hartridge, explained:

>...without the enormous pressure generated by the American financial services sector, particularly companies like American Express and CitiCorp, there would have been no services agreement and therefore perhaps no Uruguay Round and no WTO.[2]

Corporate lobby groups

That's a very quick overview of the official instruments transnationals use to further the trinity of freedoms. Let me now turn briefly to some of the *unofficial instruments*, a variety of highly effective lobbies through which TNCs influence opinion-shapers and governments. Most people think of highly visible gatherings like Davos when they think of transnational lobbies. In reality the most important organisations are far more discrete. They include:

- ► The European Round Table of Industrialists (ERT) made up of the chief executive officers of 47 of the largest European TNCs. The ERT works closely with the European Commission and individual heads of states; it has virtually written some of the Commission's most important 'white papers' and has taken primary responsibility for the European Transport Network ('TEN').[3]
- ► The TransAtlantic Business Dialogue (TABD) composed of CEOs from North America and Europe. The TABD holds regular meetings with top politicians and international agency leaders; it strongly influences international trade negotiations and maintains permanent working committees on a variety of topics including standard-setting for goods and services so that products may be freely sold in all markets.
- ► The US Coalition of Service Industries (USCSI) coordinates a wide variety of sectoral service groups; works closely with the US Special Trade Representative in targeting the WTO.
- ► The US Council for International Business was particularly visible during the attempt to establish the Multilateral Agreement on Investment.

With regard to negotiations at the WTO, both the US government and the European Commission have set up TNC advisory groups to guide them. The US Special Trade Representative has established over two dozen committees, by industry, with over 800 people from TNCs represented. When US environmental groups brought a lawsuit against the government because they were not represented in the Wood and Paper Products Committee, a federal judge ruled in their favour. Rather than include the environmentalists, the US government is appealing the decision. The European Commission put together the European Services Forum, chaired by the president of Barclays Bank, and recently called

What some people have built—and it is a construction—others can dismantle

on it to identify the most promising markets and existing trade barriers in the fields of 'education, environmental, health and social services and audio-visual services'.[4]

No other group in civil society has anywhere near the access to political decision-makers that TNCs enjoy.

Confrontation and transformation

After that lightning tour of the world economy, you may have the impression that these actors—the industrial and financial transnationals and their assorted lobbies, plus the Bank, the Fund and the WTO, are simply too powerful to confront, much less transform. Perhaps it's true, as they keep telling us, that corporate-led globalisation is inevitable and we may as well learn to live with it. Conservative American foundations and think-tanks have spent hundreds of millions of dollars over the past two decades to convince us that resistance is vain and, in any case, the system is good for us. Eventually, we are assured, everyone will benefit from globalisation, no one will be excluded, so not to worry.

I want to devote the rest of this piece to showing that all of this is nonsense. In the first place, the ideological arguments of the Washington Consensus and the TNCs are false. Second, corporate-led, neo-liberal globalisation is not a force of nature like gravity. What some people have built—and it is a construction—others can dismantle and put better and fairer rules in place. Third, and finally, significant victories have already been won. They have been, like most victories, partial and they may be fragile, but they are nonetheless signs that times are changing. The Corporate Consensus, however powerful, is running scared and the proof of that is that they are holding one crisis meeting after another and consulting their public relations firms non-stop in an attempt to figure out how they can discredit social movements, how they can cut off their funding or co-opt them.

Challenging neo-liberal ideology

First the ideology. The Corporate Consensus claims that their kind of globalisation is good for everyone. I've already explained that these companies are not employment-friendly or environment-friendly and are interested only in shareholder value. So it is no surprise that neo-liberal style globalisation is not good for everyone. Since the early 1990s, in the US, average corporate profits have increased by 108 percent, the Standard and Poor stock market index has increased by 224 percent and the compensation packages of corporate chief executives have increased by a whopping 481 percent. During the same period average annual wages for workers have risen only 28 percent, just barely ahead of inflation.

> **If workers had been rewarded like their chief executive officers they would be making an average of $110,000 a year, not $23,000, and the minimum hourly wage in the US would be $22, not $5.15**

Indeed, if workers had been rewarded like their chief executive officers they would be making an average of $110,000 a year, not $23,000, and the minimum hourly wage in the US would be $22, not $5.15. In the US, instead, a person working 40 hours a week, 52 weeks a year at the minimum wage earns only $10,700 a year. This is 40 percent below the official poverty line for a family of four.

Furthermore, studies by both UNCTAD and the United Nations University show that inequalities in most countries are inexorably rising, whether in China, Russia, Latin America or the West; 85 percent of the world's population now live in countries where inequalities are growing, not diminishing. Aggravating this situation is Third World debt which continues to rise and creates an unbearable burden.

As for inequalities at the global level, the difference between the top 20 percent and the bottom 20 percent of the world's population stood at about 30 to one at the end of World War Two, about 60 to one in the early 1970s, and is now about 82 to one and increasing. Economics professor Robin Hahnel points out that during the immediate post-war period until the early 1970s—a period that favoured capital controls, restrictions on foreign investment and diverse models of development—growth rates for gross domestic product (GDP) per capita were about twice as high as in the more recent neo-liberal, TNC-dominated era which began at the end of the 1970s.[5]

In any given society globalisation benefits mainly the top 20 percent, and the higher they are on the social scale, the more they benefit. In contrast, the lower they are, the more they lose of the little they have. The TNCs and their allies, the Fund, the Bank and the WTO, cannot build an inclusive world. Their policies are in fact throwing petrol on the fires of inequality.

Social movements

On the second point, neo-liberal, corporate-driven globalisation is not a force of nature and it is not inevitable, although lobbies plus ideological conditioning plus the Corporate Consensus have often made it seem that way. Globalisation as we know it has been put in place particularly since the fall of the Berlin Wall, before most people understood what was happening.

The Third World has been largely silenced because it is indebted and dependent on the IMF/World Bank, and on the goodwill of the North and Southern elites have been largely coopted. As for the elites and the governments of the North, with few exceptions, they are delighted with the status quo—the elites because they have enriched themselves beyond all historical precedent, the governments because they listen chiefly to the Consensus and seem to have acquiesced to the erosion of their powers. The so-called Third Way is a dead end. So who is left? Who might possibly change the current course of globalisation? Isn't it an illusion to believe it can be done?

The answer—the only answer—lies in the citizens' movement,

also known as social movements, or non-governmental organisations (NGOs), or civil society, which has a difficult but not impossible task. Here it is important to remember the successes already registered.

Successes so far

You will recall that one of the freedoms I mentioned in the trinity of freedoms the TNCs demand is freedom of investment. Between 1995 and 1998 they attempted to push through a treaty called the Multilateral Agreement on Investment, the MAI, which would have given them complete control over this vital domain, including the option to sue governments directly if any government regulation or law might impair their expected profits. In spite of the secrecy—the MAI was being negotiated behind closed doors at the OECD—citizens learned about this scandalous treaty and were able to force governments to abandon it.

Some companies that sought to impose genetically modified organisms on consumers have discovered that people-power is not dead. For example, Monsanto's agricultural division is today worth approximately zero dollars. Shell has received very bad publicity because of its oil platforms and its environmental and human rights record in Nigeria. In France, after the devastating oil-spill of the *Erika*, Total-Fina declared that it had played by the rules and was not responsible. Only days later, due to public pressure, the company promised to cough up several hundred million francs to help pay for the damage.

And need I remind you of the Battle of Seattle and of the April demonstrations against the Bank and the Fund in Washington? These highly visible events didn't just happen—they were the outcome of years of patient organising by groups throughout the world.

This movement is international and it is broadly based. The different national coalitions that make up the citizens movement are workers and unions, small farmers and their organisations, consumers, environmentalists, students, women, the unemployed, indigenous people, religious believers. There are some scientists, technicians and other intellectual workers as well, but not nearly enough. These people have widely differing backgrounds, they have set out on this journey from very different places, and most of them didn't even know each other five years ago. Nonetheless, and in spite of the cultural and organisational difficulties, they have arrived at a common analysis and are well on the way to common platforms and common strategies. They are the backlash against corporate-led globalisation and they are not going to go away. Here, in telegraphic style, are a few of the demands they are making:

- ▶ *We need fair trade, not free trade.* Like any other system, the world trading system needs rules, but not the rules now in place at the WTO. Education, health, culture and the environment should not be treated as merchandise, and food security should come before trade in agriculture. The WTO dispute resolution mechanism—its court of law—should be subordinate to international law such as human rights, multilateral environmental agreements, and the core conventions of the International Labor Organisation. The body has already entirely too much power and should not be granted any new ones.
- ▶ *We need to tax international capital.* $1.5 trillion dollars is traded every day on foreign exchange markets alone, and most of it is purely speculative and has nothing to do with the real economy. A 'Tobin Tax'—a very small burden—should be applied to Forex (foreign exchange); one could also tax mergers and acquisitions and TNC sales worldwide. The money should be used for the excluded throughout the world, to abolish poverty and at least begin to reduce the North-South gap.
- ▶ *We need to close down the tax havens.* The criminal economy is flourishing partly because legitimate governments tolerate money-laundering and financial crimes. While we're at it, why not abolish flags of convenience?
- ▶ *We need rules to protect the environment,* starting with the precautionary principle. And poor people must be given material incentives to protect their environment.

World Bank lending to ecologically destructive projects must stop.

► *We need to make corporations both financially and legally responsible for all their actions, that is, for the actions of all their subsidiaries.* No more Bhopals, no more oil-spills.

► And, of course, *we need to cancel Third World debt*, otherwise we are condemning countless millions to continued misery and death.

This is only for starters. Surely we need more diversity and more responsibility at the local level, more democratic national governments, more control over TNCs, but so far we don't have any blueprints, just some guidelines and, frankly, we have been too busy putting out fires. So I don't know about 'global governance', but I'm sure I don't want a single world government. Let's go, rather, for subsidiarity, a complicated name for saying decisions should be taken as close as possible to the people who will be affected by them. Various layers of governance are possible and desirable.

I also speak out for a diversified citizens' movement and I see no reason why we shouldn't win. The Corporate Consensus is not even economically efficient. They may have the money, they may have most of the power for now, but their way is guaranteed to be ecologically unsustainable, culturally homogenised, socially polarising, financially destabilising and democratically unacceptable. On our side, we have the numbers, we have excellent ideas, and we are slowly getting organised nationally and internationally. What's even better is that we are on the right side of the argument because we are fighting for dignity, decency and democracy. I hope you will want to join us.

Susan George is Associate Director of the Transnational Institute in Amsterdam. She is also Vice-President of ATTAC France (Association for Taxation of Financial Transaction to Aid Citizens) and the author of nine books.
www.tni.org/george

Notes

* A version of this article entitled 'Confronting and Transforming the International Economic and Financial System: A Succinct User's Guide' was originally delivered as a speech to the International Network of Engineers and Scientists for Global Responsibility (INES) in Stockholm, 14 June 2000.

1 Bank for International Settlements, 68th Annual Report (Basle, 8 June 1998), ch 5 and p90.

2 David Hartridge, Director of Trade in Services Division, WTO, 'What the General Agreement on Trade in Services (GATS) Can Do', Clifford Chance conference on 'Opening Markets for Banking Worldwide', www.1999.cliffordchance.com/library/publications/wto/section3.html

3 See Corporate European Observatory (CEO), *Europe, Inc* (Pluto Press, 1999).

4 Robert Madelin, DGI, Directorate M, to Andrew Buxton, Chair of the ESF, 24 January 2000.

5 Hahnel gives full figures in his commentary of 8 April 2000 for the ZNet network (a subscriber service). Only Asia grew slightly faster in the second period compared to the first, and that growth fell drastically after the 1997-98 crisis.

Protecting the neo-liberal agenda, Czech riot police defend the IMF/World Bank meeting, Prague, 26 September 2000.

Massive demonstrations saw water privatisation successfully beaten back in Bolivia, 2000.

GATS
Barry Coates

● ● ● ● ● ● ● ● ● ● ● ● ● ● ● ● ● ●

Opposition to the capture of rule-making by corporate interests is at the heart of the international movement that is challenging globalisation. International institutions are heavily influenced by corporate lobbies, either directly or through compliant governments, and the resulting rules serve the interests of a few corporations, rather than the majority of the world. A new assault on local and domestic regulation is under way. Governments and industry lobbies in the rich world are using every possible mechanism to strip away the remaining impediments to the creation of global markets.

The spotlight was turned on the World Trade Organisation (WTO) at Seattle in 1999, as one of the most powerful mechanisms to elevate profits for multinationals over a fair deal for all. Despite the earnest calls for reform by politicians, the trade system has not only survived intact but, if the European Union has its way, will be massively extended.

Perhaps the most grotesque example of what is wrong with the WTO is now under negotiation—the General Agreement on Trade in Services (GATS). Service industries as defined under the WTO now comprise most of the world's economic activity, and the current round of negotiations in GATS would give major new rights to transnational corporations, while removing discretionary powers of governments.

As citizens concerned about retaining the rights for democracies to act in the public interest, we must not only challenge the underlying principles of the WTO, but focus on specific agreements, pay attention to the rights that are about to be lost, and campaign for a better system.

GATS locks countries into a system of rules that means it is effectively impossible for governments to change policy, or for voters to elect a new government that has different policies

GATS is vulnerable. Even seasoned negotiators realise that it has escaped the attention that has been focused on other agreements. This has been a serious oversight, since GATS covers most of the world's economy and creates sweeping new rights for corporations. GATS must be fundamentally changed to protect public services and prioritise the needs of the poor, the environment and the rights of workers, consumers and vulnerable members of society.

What's at stake?

Imagine a nightmare scenario: governments handing over the few remaining public services to rapacious companies—health, education, social services, local authority services, etc—removing regulation on the delivery of services that are vital to the poor and disadvantaged groups; giving multinationals the right to freely come and go without restrictions; subjecting laws that aim to protect the environment, human rights and the vulnerable to the challenge of an international tribunal if they are deemed unnecessary or if they restrict trade; and rendering democratic elections powerless to reverse these policies. In essence, these are the aims of GATS. It aims to remove barriers to the global service industries, to ensure they are not hampered by 'unnecessary' regulation and to protect the interests of the multinationals by making GATS effectively irreversible.

This last point is crucial. A number of governments around the world are handing over public services to the private sector and removing regulations on corporations. Faced with increasing evidence of the shambles that often results (railways in the UK,

28

electricity in California, water in New Zealand) it is inevitable that future governments will wish to strengthen regulation and take back management control, or even ownership into the public sector. But GATS locks countries into a system of rules that means it is effectively impossible for governments to change policy, or for voters to elect a new government that has different policies. GATS has a one-way ratchet mechanism. There are obligations to open up more services to multinationals and deregulate more, but new restrictions on those multinationals are all but impossible.

An even more dangerous scenario is being played out across the developing world. Many of the poorest nations have been subjected to over a decade of structural adjustment programmes, as a price for having their debts rescheduled by the IMF, World Bank and richer nations. During the past 20 years, during which structural adjustment has been the dominant policy instrument, many of the world's poor have been made even poorer. For example, over the period 1980 to 1998 the people of sub-Saharan Africa have become 15 percent poorer, and growth rates in South Asia and Latin America have stagnated while inequality has risen dramatically. The promises that globalisation would create endless riches for all have been exposed as a sham. The reality is that most of the world's population are struggling to survive in a world whose rules are shaped by and for the large corporations and elites.

Under structural adjustment, countries have been forced to privatise key industries and public services, remove business regulation, charge user fees for health and education services, cut subsidies on things that the poor need, reduce tariffs and trade barriers, lower corporate and income taxes, and sack government employees. Ninety developing countries have been subjected to some or all of these policies under programmes mandated by the IMF and the World Bank. The economies of these countries—more than half of the countries in the world—have been run effectively from Washington DC. The results are abysmal, except for the opportunities afforded to a small groups of elites and the multinationals to asset-strip and buy cheap public state enterprises.

Social resistance to these policies has escaped the attention of the global media. The report *States of Unrest*[1] documented over 50 protests in a year, involving more than a million people. Privatisation of public services was one of the dominant issues that sparked protest.

Endless research reports, lobbying, determined campaigning by groups in the South, and the growing public movement against structural adjustment finally forced changes. After two decades the illegitimacy of government from Washington DC has become too apparent. As a result, structural adjustment policies have been renamed and rebranded. Now the poorest countries are allowed to have a say in the policies that their governments implement. The new Poverty Reduction Strategy Papers are meant to be prepared with civil society involvement. The reality, however, is that the World Bank and IMF retain veto power. Even so, there are signs that some developing country governments are starting to question the liberalisation model. In some countries there is even discussion of alternative policies in the political mainstream.

The promises that globalisation would create endless riches for all have been exposed as a sham

Faced with a possible restoration of democracy, industry lobbyists have become aware that decades of privatisation and liberalisation in developing country economies could be reversed. GATS is one of the mechanisms that would ensure that this could never happen. As the WTO secretariat states, the real value of GATS is that it locks in the gains from liberalisation and makes them effectively irreversible.

So what exactly is GATS?

GATS stands for the General Agreement on Trade in Services. (These three or four letter acronyms used by the WTO seem designed to hide what they are doing behind a facade of legal complexity, apparently far too technical and difficult for ordinary people to understand. Actually, the agreements and the principles behind them are very simple.)

GATS is a trade agreement, establishing rules to govern

Bolivia

An example of the vital importance of democracy to reverse bad decisions was shown in the case of water privatisation in Bolivia. In 1998 the water supply of Cochabamba, the third largest city in Bolivia, was privatised at the insistence of the World Bank. A British company, owned by the US multinational Bechtel, was given effective monopoly over their water supply. In order to make quick profits they raised prices to the point where some users were paying double the previous price and spending more on water than food. The company's monopoly even meant that it prohibited the collection of rainwater in roof tanks.

Not surprisingly there were protests—repeated mass demonstrations on the streets. The government appeared to back down but then clamped down on the demonstrators. But that wasn't the end of it—the demonstrators went back and they continued to demonstrate.

People were killed, including a 17 year old boy who was shot in the face. The Bolivian government was forced to reverse the privatisation, and now the city has started experimenting with local water supply schemes.

The important lesson from the Bolivian experience is that the democratic process must be allowed to take decisions on vital issues of service delivery, particularly if the services are essential to the poor. Under GATS that kind of reversal of government policy would not be allowed to happen.

international trade in services. GATS was signed in 1994 at the conclusion of the last round of trade negotiations (the Uruguay Round). GATS is a far-reaching agreement that would create new rights for multinational companies. They were deeply involved in the negotiations. As the director of the WTO Services Division, David Hartridge, commented, 'Without the tremendous pressure exerted by the American financial services industry, particularly companies like American Express and Citicorp, there would have been no services agreement.'

> **'When the Death Star of the WTO exploded with the protests in Seattle, GATS was the hatch pod in which Darth Vader made his escape'**
> — Rob Newman

The 1994 GATS set up the framework, but was not fully operational. As the comedian Rob Newman said in an article in the *Guardian*, 'When the Death Star of the WTO exploded with the protests in Seattle, GATS was the hatch pod in which Darth Vader made his escape.' The current negotiations, called GATS 2000, would extend GATS to a wide range of sectors and make it fully operational. The negotiations are under way and are likely to last several years. However, some of the crucial decisions on what sectors to liberalise will be made in 2001.

At its heart GATS aims for the progressive liberalisation of all service industries. Trade in services is not subject to high external barriers, unlike some products such as agricultural commodities. Therefore, unlike other trade agreements that focus on removing external tariffs and import quotas, GATS targets domestic barriers to trade. These cover a huge range of government laws, regulations and policies. GATS aims to remove any impediments to foreign companies (those supplying from abroad or investing domestically) or any measures that discriminate against them. These may include any grants to local companies and subsidies to domestic enterprises (which may include public-funded service providers); nationality and residency requirements, licensing standards and qualifications, and registration procedures; fishing, hunting, logging and other natural resource licenses; requirements for companies to benefit the local economy, use local suppliers, hire local people or train workers; and preferences for types of service suppliers (such as local not-for-profit health trusts, rather than foreign multinationals).

What services would be covered by GATS?

Under the precise definition of the WTO a service is 'anything you can't drop on your foot'. Some examples of services are water supply, healthcare, public health, education, public transport including railways, postal communications, broadcasting, audio-visual, culture, entertainment, tourism, and finance. That is just part of a list of 160 service sectors. The one service sector not included is defence. Perhaps this is because the massive subsidies that governments provide to defence companies would be threatened under GATS.

There have been assurances from the government that public services will not be included in GATS, since the agreement excludes public services supplied 'in the exercise of government authority'. But the agreement then says that public services would be included if there is any part of those services which is being delivered commercially or in competition with the private sector. It is hard to come up with examples of public services that would not be included. For example, the British government is increasingly involving the private sector in healthcare provision, extending beyond ancillary services to running hospitals and clinical services. In education, fees charged by universities could be defined as commercialisation of the service, and private schools are in competition with state schools. The WTO secretariat prepared a list of the public services that would definitely not be included under GATS. Their very short list comprised social security and central banking. They could have added international trade negotiations. The GATS negotiators will presumably manage to retain their public sector jobs.

Economic activity in the form of services now makes up more over two thirds of most economies. The problem for the multinationals is that most of it is provided by domestic firms. That is what GATS is aiming to change. For example, the US multinationals are targeting education and health sectors in the EU for GATS negotiations, while the EU is targeting the publicly-owned water supply in developing countries. These priorities reflect the interests of the multinationals in being able to access new markets.

GATS is, as the European Commission's website says, 'first and foremost, an agreement for the benefit of business'. It is a vital piece in the 'globalisation project' since the expansion of services trade is predicted to dwarf international trade in products. GATS also extends beyond the external barriers to trade into the heart of government policy-making. In addition to the obvious coverage over trade policy and corporate regulation, there are few laws or policies that GATS may not potentially affect—including those on public services, the environment, social welfare, human rights, working conditions, consumer protection, government procurement and local planning laws. As such, GATS creates new precedents in international trade agree-

Banana wars

We can learn a lot from looking at one of the cases that has already been decided under GATS. Many people have heard of the WTO dispute on bananas. The US government brought a case against the EU's support for small banana growers in the Caribbean, who supply around 9 percent of bananas to the EU versus over two thirds supplied from Latin America by the big multinational companies. The US case was launched within a day of the chief executive of the biggest multinational, Chiquita, donating half a million dollars to the US Democratic Party. But the surprising thing about the case is that the US doesn't grow bananas.

This was a case taken under GATS. The US government argued that Chiquita was a services company that distributed bananas and so it was covered under GATS. This shows that GATS is already starting to bite in ways that were quite unexpected. Experience of WTO dispute panels, and the far-reaching GATS provisions, means that a wide range of domestic and international laws and policies will be challenged or prohibited.

ments. Because of its huge coverage and its far-reaching provisions, GATS has been called by the WTO secretariat 'probably the most important agreement signed since 1948'.

The devil is in the detail. Faced with the start of a campaign on

GATS, there has been an attack on non-governmental organisations (NGOs) by the WTO, the British government and industry lobbies. Their response has been full of half-truths. For example, they insist that governments have 'the right to regulate', omitting to explain what is meant by the GATS provisions that aim to prohibit 'unnecessary barriers' on trade in services. Their own internal papers contain damning evidence of a mechanism that would elevate the interests of foreign companies above all public interest. What it actually means is that any regulation on services would be subjected to two tests: (1) is it a necessary regulation? and (2) is it an unnecessary burden on foreign service providers? The decision about what is necessary will be up to the WTO, not the governments that are charged with the responsibility of regulating in the public interest. The criteria will be whether the regulations restrict foreign multinationals from providing services. Of course there are other rules that could be applied, such as a test of whether any regulation promotes access for the poor to public services. But GATS rules prioritise the interests of multinationals above all else.

Why should the aim of international rules on services be to remove any barriers to foreign corporations? Why shouldn't the objectives be to promote universal access to basic services?

What is the UK government doing?

In 1999 the government circulated a survey to big service companies in the UK and asked what services around the world they wanted to have liberalised. They promised that responses to the consultation would be kept confidential. So British multinationals responded that they wanted services in other countries to be liberalised, particularly services such as finance and banking, insurance, telecommunications, electricity and gas. The government's position has been that a major expansion of sectors under GATS would be in the interests of British business. Other considerations, such as the impact on the environment, poverty, or human rights, were not researched or given proper consideration. Developing countries have been promised a proper impact assessment of services liberalisation since 1994—it has still not been undertaken.

Meanwhile, Pascal Lamy, the EU commissioner for trade (who negotiates on behalf of the UK on most services issues), has acknowledged that something has to be sacrificed in these services negotiations. The EU will need to allow access to its own service sectors, particularly to US multinationals, and has stated that no service sector in the EU is non-negotiable. The US is specifically targeting healthcare and education in the EU—the position of US multinationals is that public sector provision of these services is getting in the way of business opportunities. Over the next year it will become apparent if the EU is prepared to give rights of access to sensitive public services. So far, the British government has undertaken no research on the domestic impacts of GATS, including how it will affect workers, the environment, access to public services for the poor, and the powers of local authorities.

There are alternatives

Politics at the international level is ruled by the tired Thatcherite notion of TINA—'There Is No Alternative'. The only international institutions with the power of enforcement are those with a liberalising/deregulatory agenda, most notably the WTO, and

NAFTA and the WTO

An indication of some of the likely impacts of GATS can be seen through experience with similar provisions in NAFTA—the North American Free Trade Agreement. In a recent judgement a US company called Metalclad was awarded £12 million after the Mexican state of San Luis Potosi had stopped it from opening a hazardous waste-processing plant. The designation of the site of the plant as an ecological reserve had, the arbitration tribunal ruled, been a ploy to stop the waste processing.

Meanwhile, the WTO dispute panel has ruled that ten out of 11 regulations are 'unnecessary' barriers to trade, including rules to stop the by-catch of dolphins, protect turtles and restrict cigarette imports. GATS contains new provisions that allow challenges to such 'unnecessary' regulations. It is likely that GATS will threaten a wide range of policies designed to reduce poverty or protect vulnerable people and the environment.

therefore the only rules on services deemed to be possible are those that regulate governments from regulating corporations. It is time these assumptions were questioned. Why should the aim of international rules on services be to remove any barriers to foreign corporations? Why shouldn't the objectives be to promote universal access to basic services? Or promoting the development of domestic service businesses, especially in poor nations and communities? Or promoting ecologically sound development?

There is a vacuum at the heart of the global economy. There are new rights being given to corporations but not enforceable responsibilities towards societies and communities where they operate. International rules on services should start by regulating the multinational services companies. For example, the *Economist* magazine reports that Rupert Murdoch, the media mogul, made £1.4 billion in the UK since 1987. How much tax did he pay? Zero. There are no international laws on monopolies or cartels. There are no international laws to prevent multinationals from using their global influence and power to cross-subsidise in order to drive small companies out of business, allowing the big to get bigger.

The corporate giants use tax shelters and tax havens, free trade zones and incentives, government subsidies and powerful PR companies to influence the laws in their favour, and they hire lobbyists to shape international rules through the WTO. The ranks of GATS lobbyists were strengthened recently when Sir Leon Brittan, the former EU trade commissioner and strong proponent of GATS, became a lobbyist for the financial services industry. The revolving door between trade negotiators and lobbyists is well-oiled.

Increasingly in the global economy all of the advantages are being given to the foreign corporations and none of the burdens. Small domestic companies face anything but a level playing field. Yet agreements such as GATS give even more rights to multinationals. The presumption seems to be that the corporate giants are being victimised and driven out of business. In reality, the merger and acquisition boom and the increasing concentration of markets is evidence that the largest global corporations benefit from advantages and rights that are not available to smaller local companies.

Can GATS be reformed?

Is it possible to rewrite a few paragraphs and have a better GATS? Can the negotiations be made fairer to developing countries? The problem is more fundamental. The aim of GATS is to remove barriers to the cross-border supply of services (even if those barriers aim to promote the public interest). This aim must not be allowed to take precedence over all other goals of societies. The interests of multinationals to remove restrictions on their profit-seeking behaviour is not a valid goal for individual societies or the international community. Along with other WTO agreements, members of the public should reject the attempt to elevate corporate profits over the interests of people. A new approach to international rule-making is required.

What can we do?

There are already strong social movements in the South as well as the North challenging specific policy changes at the local and national level, whether they are abuses of workers' rights, destruction of the environment or exclusion of the poor from public services. It is important that the international campaign on GATS works with and supports these actions. It is also important to recognise that GATS represents a structural threat. In future, governments will be able to wash their hands of decisions on the delivery of services by arguing that their hands are tied by agreements already signed. GATS poses a major threat to democratic choices for generations to come. It is the basic right of people in a democracy to use the political process to influence government policies that are most at risk under GATS. The most important message is that GATS can be stopped. We can organise, we can network and we can activate.

The roots of the GATS campaign must be networking across those active in social justice, the environment and corporate responsibility. Increasingly members of the public are aware that governments are giving away rights to corporations, and are ready to join a campaign that will oppose GATS and propose fairer rules.

In the UK the World Development Movement launched the campaign 'Stop the GATSastrophe' last November at a meeting

MAI campaign

In 1995 governments started negotiations of the Multilateral Agreement on Investment (MAI), a draft agreement on foreign investment in the OECD (the rich nations' club) that contained many similar provisions to GATS. Campaigners were pessimistic about launching a public campaign to oppose the MAI—like GATS, it was a little known and complex international agreement. But through meetings in towns and cities across Europe and North America people started hearing about the MAI and understanding that it was a corporate charter.

Like GATS, the MAI would have given sweeping new rights to corporations but no responsibilities. When the campaign started we would draw an audience of 30 or so, but the word started to get around and the numbers grew to 50 people and to 200 people. By the time the negotiations collapsed there were a surprising number of people across the developed world who understood the principles of the MAI and its likely impacts.

It was a campaign that involved trade unions, local authorities, women's groups, churches, a huge array of NGOs, activists of all types—it was a really powerful coalition.

The internet was vital for international communication and for circulating a joint statement, which was signed by over 500 organisations from 70 countries.

addressed by Naomi Klein (author of *No Logo*) and George Monbiot (author of *Captive State*) to an audience of 1,000 people. Thousands of letters and cards have already been sent to constituency MPs. A motion calling for proper scrutiny of GATS attracted over 250 MPs in Westminster and a majority of MSPs in Holyrood. Some media articles have started to question the approach under GATS and a number of public meetings have been held across the UK. A recent seminar brought together academics, researchers, NGOs and trade unions concerned about the impacts of GATS in the UK.[2] There are now GATS campaigns growing in most countries in the developed world, and starting in many developing countries.

There is time to build a strong campaign on GATS. For those concerned about its impacts, the most important starting point is within your sphere of influence. This may be through student groups (People and Planet is playing a major role in the GATS campaign), local trades union branches, campaign groups, local authorities, political organisations or religious gatherings. A simple action is to call on them to sign a resolution against GATS and tell their membership. And the multiplying effect is powerful. Tell your friends and colleagues about it, encourage them to read some of the basic briefings and, in turn, tell others. Many of the people you know probably work in the public sector, are dependent on essential public services, and are likely to be affected by GATS. And be prepared to enter into debate with politicians or economists who may not understand what they mean when they recite empty slogans about free trade and the benefits of unregulated markets. GATS is one of the issues that can help to make the link between the issues at home and the impacts on the world's poor, between social/environmental/corporate issues and between politics and democracy.

The campaign to stop a new round of trade negotiations that culminated in Seattle in November 1999 was a landmark. But the people who were on the streets of Seattle were dwarfed by the hundreds of thousands who have expressed concern over the unfairness of trade rules and the millions who are engaged in campaigns over issues related to structural adjustment policies. It is very possible to build a campaign that will stop negotiations on the GATS agreement— and perhaps even to start the process of regulating global corporations and putting people before profits.

Barry Coates is Director of the World Development Movement (WDM), a democratic membership network of individuals and local groups, campaigning to achieve justice for the world's poor.
wdm@wdm.org.uk

: Notes

1 World Development Movement, *States of Unrest*, July 2000.
2 As with other research reports and briefings, it is available on WDM's website www.wdm.org.uk

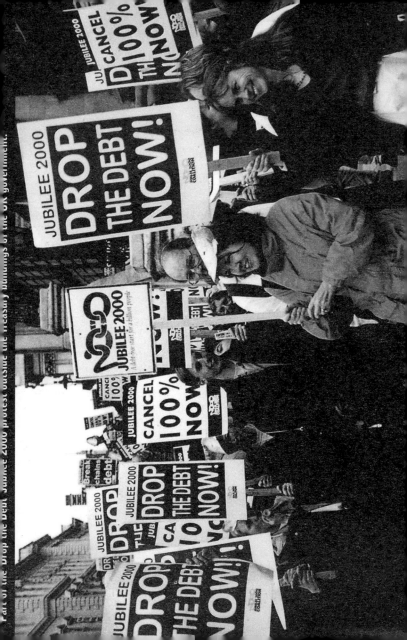

Part of the Drop the Debt Jubilee 2000 protest outside the treasury buildings of the UK government.

Debt
Ann Pettifor

● ● ● ● ● ● ● ● ● ● ● ● ● ● ● ● ● ● ●

We live today in a global economy once again dominated, as in the 1920s, by international finance capital. According to one estimate, before 1970 some 90 percent of all international transactions were accounted for by trade, and only 10 percent by capital flows. Today, despite a vast increase in global trade, that ratio has been reversed, with 90 percent of transactions accounted for by financial flows not directly related to trade in goods and services.[1] Most of these flows have taken the form of highly volatile stocks and bonds, investment and short-term loans. By 1992 financial assets from the advanced nations of the OECD totalled $35 trillion—twice the economic output of the OECD. McKinsey and Company projected that the total financial stock would have reached $53 trillion by the year 2000—'triple the economic output of the OECD economies'.[2]

These changes to the global economy—the shift from the dominance of industrial capital to finance capital—did not come about 'naturally' or spontaneously. They are the result, as Eric Helleiner has shown, of deliberate policy-making, driven first by the City of London and the British government, and later by Wall Street and the US government.[3] Both governments use the International Monetary Fund (IMF) as an agent for implementing effectively deflationary policies, whose ultimate purpose is not to reduce poverty—preserve us from the hype of the Poverty Reduction and Growth Fund!—but always, and only, to protect the value of creditor assets.

In the 1920s similar deflationary economic policies were applied to justify the dismissal of public servants, to suppress wages and keep unemployment high. The most important of these policies was the stabilisation of currencies, fixed in terms of gold, to guarantee debt service to foreign bondholders. Much the same happens today. Instead of the gold standard we have dollarisation and currency boards. Currencies are stabilised to guarantee and uphold the value of creditor assets—in particular, the value of debt service payments to foreign bondholders and other creditors. The IMF, agent of all international creditors public and private, intervenes in the market and imposes a range of policies (known as structural adjustment programmes) on debtor nations. The real purpose of these policies is (a) to defend the value of the assets of international creditors and investors, and (b) to allow foreign investors, creditors and speculators to transfer and extract assets from debtor nations.

> **Debt acts as the key mechanism for the transfer of wealth from weak to strong, from debtor nations to international creditors, from taxpayers and wage earners to the holders of paper claims**

Central to our *planned* global economy dominated by finance capital is the powerful lever of debt. Debt acts as the key mechanism for the transfer of wealth from weak to strong, from debtor nations to international creditors, from taxpayers and wage earners to the holders of paper claims, from productive to financial activity.[4] Without the leverage of debt, IMF policy makers would not be able to intervene in the economies of poor nations and impose deflationary policies and the deregulation of capital markets— essential to ensure such transfers.

Debt as a constant threat to economic stability and human rights

As the year 2000 drew to a close, the world of international finance held its breath, concerned that Argentina would default on its short-term debt, thereby precipitating what the *Financial Times* euphemistically called 'a general loss of confidence'.[5] By the spring of 2001 Argentina had effectively defaulted, using smoke and mirrors to disguise the reality of partial default. Argentina's predicament is dire, despite her government's widely acknowledged achievement of fulfilling creditors' conditions. On the advice of creditors, represented by the IMF, Argentina's currency, the peso, is artificially inflated and pegged to the value of the US dollar—thereby maintaining the value of creditor assets, while impoverishing Argentinians. Goods and services cost the same in Buenos Aires as in New York or London, even though Argentinians earn a great deal less than New Yorkers or Londoners.

The *International Herald Tribune* noted in November 2000 that Argentina's 'various misfortunes...are not of its own making'.[6] Investors have been eager to lend, greedy for the high rates of return on their investments. The Argentinian government, while perhaps not always acting wisely, has faithfully followed the advice (and interests) of her creditors, and maintained a permanently fixed exchange rate against the dollar, securing stability for investors who wish to remove their funds. Exports (which raise revenues for debt repayments) are growing rapidly. Inflation is low and government debt and the budget deficit are only 50 percent and 1.9 percent of national income respectively.

But Argentina now has foreign debts in the order of $125 billion, denominated in dollars, and so with each ratcheting up of the value of the US dollar, the cost of the debt rises, tightening the noose around the necks of the public and private sector, strangling the economy, and bleeding Argentineans of their precious export and scarce tax revenues. Social tensions are rising, and workers in Argentina have organised general strikes to protest the impact of the debts on the economy—in particular, the deflationary austerity conditions set by foreign creditors, represented as always by the IMF.

Anarchy parading as prosperity

Here in Britain there is very little mention of Argentina's crisis—the British public have little awareness of the huge dangers lurking in the global economy—because the anarchy of the international financial system currently parades as prosperity and freedom, as Peter Warburton so rightly argues.[7] Absorbed by our highly demanding rates of consumption—and cushioned by levels of affluence unprecedented in history—we in the West care little for what is happening in the enchanted forest of international finance.

But there are spooks in the anarchic global financial forest, a forest that has been carelessly if deliberately cultivated, deregulated and then allowed to run riot by respected central bankers like Hans Tietmayer, Eddie George and Alan Greenspan. The spooks attack like bolts of lightning, unexpectedly and out of the blue. No one, except perhaps for one or two very brave economists, predicted Japan's descent into an economic morass. Nobody predicted the South East Asian crisis. And no one—least of all the Nobel Prize economists running the Long Term Capital Management Fund—predicted Russia's default in 1998.

And no one at the beginning of the new millennium knows what to do about economies that are currently spooking the global economy—Turkey, Pakistan, Argentina and Indonesia. But those who are in the know are also aware that the unsustainable debts of these economies pose a major threat to all of us—particularly those who are lending, investing, consuming and speculating on *borrowed money*.

Structural imbalances and instability

Japan in the 1980s, like Britain today, wallowed in the sort of consumption levels we now enjoy, with investors recklessly chasing rising asset values higher and higher—all on borrowed money.

The parallels between Japan then and Britain and the US today are, in my view, disturbing. Here we are living through a classic asset bubble, particularly in London, and, as record surges in mortgages show, people are borrowing, often way beyond their means, to finance the purchase of assets. It was just this process of over-borrowing and over-consuming that led to the build-up of unpayable debts in Japan, and caused deep pain and personal loss when the deflation of asset values led banks and companies to collapse because of large debts. Unemployment rose, incomes fell and the economy stagnated.

But while there are parallels between Japan and Britain and the US—especially in the reckless lending and borrowing that central banks unleashed to finance such consumption and to fuel the asset bubble—there is one big difference. Japan has a trade surplus, and can largely finance its own consumption. Both Britain and the US are running historically high trade *deficits*—each day the US consumes $1 billion more in imports than it produces in exports—and on the eve of the 2001 general election Britain announced an extraordinarily high trade deficit—$7.7 billion—of a kind that once lost Harold Wilson a general election. And yet news of that announcement, and of the instability and imbalances that it represented, was greeted with a yawn by economic and political commentators.

Britain and the US are mobilising—through borrowing—two thirds of the world's savings to finance their growing habit of living beyond their means. The US, which according to the latest census has a population of just 280 million people, has foreign liabilities of about $3 trillion. The whole of the developing world, including China, Brazil and India, with populations of 6 billion people, have foreign debts of only $2 trillion.

Money rights before human and democratic rights

At the end of the year 2000, and again quite unnoticed by the rest of the world, 3,000 employees of the Thai Petrochemical Industry (TPI) disrupted a meeting in Bangkok. Foreign creditors were due to have obtained 75 percent of the equity in TPI and effective control of this key Thai industry. These creditors included the World Bank's International Finance Corporation, Chase Manhattan and the US government's EXIM Bank. Protesters carried placards with slogans such as 'World Bank No Thanks' and 'Yankee Go Home'.[8]

Simultaneously in Africa the Zambian finance minister, Mr Katele Kalumba, was protesting at a proposal for debt 'relief' negotiated by international creditors under the IMF and World Bank's Highly Indebted Poor Country (HIPC) initiative. After the 'relief' offered by her international creditors, the World Bank predicted that Zambia would transfer $235 million in the year 2002 in debt repayments to her creditors, nearly $100 million more than she can currently afford to pay.[9] Zambia is a country in which four fifths of the population live on less than $1 a day; 1 million of the 9 million inhabitants suffer from HIV/AIDS; life expectancy is only 40 years, and 13 percent of children are orphaned—the highest rate in the world.[10]

In 1999 the Zambian government spent $123 million a year on the health of its people. In contrast, and in the same year, $137 million of Zambia's precious, scarce resources were transferred to much richer foreign creditors.

These examples demonstrate the extraordinary power of foreign creditors over poor sovereign debtors, power that deprives nations of independence and autonomy while transferring real resources from the poor to the rich. Because of high levels of debt, governments are forced to ignore the human rights of their people—and to subordinate local needs and mandates to the interests of foreign creditors and capital markets. Indebted governments are required by their creditors, regardless of democratic mandates, to prioritise foreign debt service payments over domestic spending on, for example, health, clean water and sanitation. The US's creditors, mainly Japanese foreign bondholders, have no such grip over their client state—thanks to the dominance of the US dollar.

Debt bondage, ethics and Jubilee 2000

In the West concern about the domination of finance capital over poor countries has been growing, amplified by the international Jubilee 2000 movement. The campaign's guiding principles were grounded in Judaic and Christian biblical ethics on human rights, opposition to usury, and the need for periodic correction to imbalances—the Sabbath and Jubilee principles. The campaign drew on what Ched Myers called the 'Hebrew Bible's vision of Sabbath economics (which) contends that a theology of abundant grace and a communal ethic of redistribution is the only way out of our slavery to the debt system, with its theology of meritocracy and private ethic of wealth concentration'.[11] These principles and ethics have, in turn, resonated with Muslims and other peoples of faith, and with those of no faith at all.

The link between debt bondage and ethics—as an issue of public as well as private morality—is, of course, ancient; laws have throughout our history been promulgated against usury. In England a series of post-Reformation usury laws set maximum rates of legal interest for money lending which in 1713 finally settled at 5 percent. The limitation on interest was to remain operative throughout the early industrial period, being finally abandoned only in 1854.[12] A loan which fell foul of the usury law was unlawful and unenforceable by the lender. Adam Smith did not consider that free market notions justified the lifting of this 'prudent fetter on cupidity'.[13] Until quite recently it was possible for usurers to be excommunicated by the Catholic church, and usury is still a crime that can be fiercely punished under Islamic *sharia* law. Attempts over the centuries to legislate against usury reflect ethical concerns about the exploitation of weak and vulnerable debtors by the collective actions of much richer, more powerful creditors.

Punishment through usury is one form of discipline over lenders and borrowers; market forces are another. Within the framework of the current international financial system, sovereign debtors are invariably disciplined for reckless borrowing. International lenders, investors and speculators, on the other hand, are protected by a state-owned, Soviet-style bank—the IMF—from risk, and from the wrath of market forces.

Protecting creditors, speculator and investors from market forces

Despite widespread criticism of the way in which reckless lenders were protected from risks and from bad judgements during the South East Asian, Russian and Brazilian crises of 1997 and 1998, G7 finance ministers have set up another fund, the so-called $90 billion 'precautionary fund' under IMF stewardship.[14] The purpose of this fund, according to finance ministers, is to deter 'financial turbulence spreading from country to country in a contagion process...to send a clear message to speculators that they may be taking big risks if they (short) sell a nation's currency'. However, as Michel Chossudovsky has pointed out, such a plan achieves just the opposite: 'Rather than "taming the speculator" and averting financial instability, the existence of billions of dollars stashed away in a "precautionary" fund is likely to entice speculators to persist in their deadly raids on national currencies'.[15] Such trenchant criticism and calls for tougher action on creditors forced the IMF to respond—albeit timidly.

In October 1999 Ecuador became the first ever country

to default on so-called Brady Bonds—private sector bonds that repackaged debt from the Latin America crisis of the 1980s. The default was rather dramatically announced at the IMF annual meetings that year, with Fund staff making clear, for the first time, that the institution was now reluctant to bail out investors.

While Ecuador's bond-holders were disciplined, there has been no indication as yet that the IMF will treat other international creditors in the same way. Nor is there any sign that the 'precautionary fund' has been wound down. So

> **Reckless and greedy lenders and investors will continue to be rescued; while debtor governments will be placing the burden of losses and liabilities on local taxpayers, in particular the poor**

reckless and greedy lenders and investors will continue to be rescued, while debtor governments will be left with a heavy burden of new debt, and with some obligation to clear up after the crisis. They will do so, ultimately, by placing the burden of losses and liabilities on local taxpayers, in particular the poor. This invariably results in the denial of human rights to such people.

Transformation of global structures

In its latest Trade and Development Report 2001, the United Nations Conference on Trade and Development (UNCTAD) calls for radical restructuring of the international financial architecture, to ensure an independent process for sanctioning the right of debtor nations to take emergency action to suspend debt payments. The Report notes that 'there is strong resistance by some major creditor countries as well as private investors to a mandatory stay on creditor litigation on the grounds that it would give rise to debtor moral hazard and weaken market discipline.' However, the report notes that this is not the view of the deputy governor of the Bank of England, who has said:

> A well-articulated framework for dealing with sovereign liquidity problems should reduce the inefficiencies and inequities of the current unstructured approach to standstills... It would be no more

likely to induce debtors to default than bankruptcy law is used to induce corporate debtors to default.[16]

UNCTAD argues that since standstills and exchange controls need to be imposed and implemented rapidly, the decision should rest with the country concerned, subject to a subsequent review by an international body. Clearly for the debtor to enjoy insolvency protection, it would be necessary for such a ruling to be legally enforceable in national courts. This would require the backing of the IMF.

'However,' argues UNCTAD:

> ...the IMF is not a neutral body and cannot therefore be expected to act as an independent arbiter...moreover, since the Fund itself is a creditor, and acts as the authority for imposing conditionality on the borrowing countries, there can be conflicts of interest *vis-à-vis* both debtors and other creditors. An appropriate procedure would thus be to establish an independent panel for sanctioning such decisions. Such a procedure would, in important respects, be similar to GATT/WTO safeguard provisions that allow developing countries to take emergency actions when faced with balance of payments difficulties.[17]

The report argues that the rationale and key principles for an orderly debt workout can be found in domestic bankruptcy procedures. The aim is to share the adjustment burden between debtor and creditors and to assure an equitable distribution of the costs among creditors.

The Jubilee International Movement for Economic and Social Justice (JMI) has long called for an independent, transparent and accountable process of arbitration for settling the debt repayments of effectively insolvent countries.[18] We insist that such a process must be accountable to civil society in debtor nations as well as OECD creditor nations. In debtor nations, key stakeholders must have a say in the process of arbitration. Only through such an open process will sovereign debtors be restrained from reckless, and often corrupt, borrowing. And only by imposing the discipline of losses and liabilities on creditors, will Western governments and financiers be restrained from corrupt lending, and from extracting and transferring precious, scarce resources from poor to rich. Under such a process human rights could once again take precedence over money rights.

Conclusion

There is a growing consensus that countries with huge populations like Argentina, Turkey, Indonesia, Nigeria and Zambia need an orderly process for managing unsustainable debt. This consensus is not shared by those usurers who collectively benefit from the vulnerability of these debtor nations. However, there is much less public awareness of the enormous threat posed to the stability of the global economy by the activities of undisciplined, protected and greedy creditors and investors. On the contrary, their activities are veiled in secrecy and protected by highly respected central bankers. In the 1920s central bankers protected the interests of creditors and investors over the interests of millions of ordinary people by upholding the gold standard even as the world plunged into crisis.

Today central bankers and the IMF are once again engaged in protecting the interests of a small number of foreign creditors and investors over the human rights of millions of people. There is now an urgent need for this protectionism to be ended, and for a return to discipline, order and regulation in the international financial system.

If we are to prevent another economic crisis on the scale precipitated by the deflationary policies of the 1920s, then it is time to end the domination of money rights over human rights.

Ann Pettifor is Programme Coordinator for Jubilee Plus at the New Economics Foundation in London.
www.jubileeplus.org/www.neweconomics.org

Notes

1   In James A Kelly, 'East Asia's Rolling
    Crises: Worries for the Year of the
    Tiger' (Center for Strategic and
    International Studies (CSIS), Pacific
    Forum, Pacnet 1, 2 January 1998),
    quoted in 'Asian Financial Crisis: An
    Analysis of US Foreign Policy Interests
    and Options'.
2   From William Greider, *One World,
    Ready or Not* (Simon & Shuster,
    1997), p232.
3   The role of British and US policy in
    freeing financial markets from national
    control is documented in a study by
    Eric Helleiner, *States and the Re-
    emergence of Global Finance: From
    Bretton Woods to the 1990s* (Cornell
    University Press, 1994).
4   Polanyi Levitt, quoted above.
5   *Financial Times* editorial, 18
    November 2000.
6   *International Herald Tribune*, 21
    November, 2000.
7   Peter Warburton, *Debt and Delusion:
    Central Bank Follies That Threaten
    Economic Disaster* (Allen Lane, the
    Penguin Press, 1999).
8   *Financial Times*, 17 November 2000.
9   OXFAM report, 2000.
10 Jubilee 2000 press release, 21
    November 2000, and World Bank
    HIPC documents on Zambia,
    September 2000.
11 'Jesus' New Economy of Grace: the
    Biblical Vision of Sabbath Economics'
    (second of two parts), *Sojourners*,
    July-August 1998.
12 From W R Cornish and G de N Clark,
    *Laws and Society in England 1750-
    1950* (Sweet and Maxwell, 1989),
    p227.
13 Adam Smith, *Wealth of Nations*
    (Penguin, 1976), pp356-358.

- 14 G7 communique, 30 October 1998; *Financial Times*, 31 October and 1 November; David Snager, 'Wealthy Nations Back Plan to Speed Help to the Weak', *New York Times*, 31 October 1998.
- 15 Michel Chossudovsky, 'The G7 "Solution" to the Global Financial Crisis—a Marshall Plan for Creditors and Speculators' (Department of Economics, University of Ottawa, Canada).
- 16 Trade and Development Report, UNCTAD 2001, pp149-150.
- 17 Ibid, p134.
- 18 See Ann Pettifor and Jo Hanlon, *Kicking the Habit* (Jubilee 2000 UK 1999), available on the Jubilee Plus website: www.jubileeplus.org

ATTAC Sweden on the EU summit demonstration, Gothenburg, June 2001—part of the carnival atmosphere that was disrupted the next day as three demonstrators were shot by police.

Protesters in Germany block railway lines to halt cargos of nuclear trains.

Environment
Ronnie Hall

● ● ● ● ● ● ● ● ● ● ● ● ● ● ● ● ● ● ● ●

It's easy to think of conflict between trade and the environment as something rather technical, something important but maybe not quite as urgent as other pressing concerns—like restrictions on access to essential medicines for people with HIV in Africa. But trade's impact on our environment is in fact critical. Our health and well-being depend upon our environment. We rely on it for the food we eat, the water we drink and the air we breathe. Natural resources are our ultimate building blocks. Every single thing we use and trade has been fashioned from or made with natural resources of one kind or another—oil, metals, wood, sunlight.

So surely it's a matter of common sense to maintain a healthy and resource-rich environment, both for ourselves and our children? Why then do we find ourselves living in a surreal world in which we're using up precious natural capital like there's no tomorrow?

Forests are being clear-cut, minerals strip-mined and fossil fuels exploited at completely unsustainable rates to provide natural resources for the global economy. At this rate, we would need eight planets to provide the resources required by the 10 billion people who are expected to be alive in 2050—assuming they will all be consuming at the same rate that people living in the UK do now.

The United Nations Environment Programme has confirmed that tropical forests and marine fisheries have been seriously over-exploited and that globalisation is also leading to species invasion.[1] The global marine catch nearly doubled, for example, between 1975 and 1995, and over-fishing for export-led development now means that 60 percent of the world's ocean fisheries are at or near the point at which yields start to decline.

This rapid destruction of the planet's resources is matched by growing inequality, as the gap between the haves and the have-nots gets wider and wider. With 1.2 billion people still living in severe poverty[2] even the United Nations has commented that 'The imbalances in economic growth, if allowed to continue, will produce a world gargantuan in its excesses and grotesque in its human and economic inequalities'.[3]

It's generally the rich, industrialised countries of the North that consume the most. Consumption in some other countries—including those who need to consume more—is going down. In Africa, for example, consumption has decreased by 20 percent since 1980 and basic needs, such as adequate nutrition, literacy and information, aren't being met.

The irony is that many of the resources consumed in the North actually come from the poorer countries of the South. In fact, the global North, using the resources of the global South at rock-bottom prices, has incurred an ecological debt to those countries. Yet it's still impoverished Southern countries that find themselves compelled to play the neo-liberal game—exporting more and more—in order to pay off the only debts that seem to count: the financial ones. This leads to oversupplied world markets, falling commodity prices and decreasing returns on Southern exports. These worsening terms of trade make it ever more difficult for the South to pay its financial debts.

▶ Global wood production has increased by 36 percent since 1970[4] and a recent study by the International Union for the Conservation of Nature and Natural Resources[5] found that over half the 10,000 tree species looked at were globally threatened.

▶ Over-fishing for export-led development means that 60 percent of the world's ocean fisheries are at or near the points at which yields start to decline.[6]

► In the 1960s the Philippines was one of the top four timber exporters in the world. In the process 90 percent of its forests have been lost. The country is now a timber importer with 18 million impoverished forest dwellers, an external debt of nearly $40 billion (up from $17 billion in 1980) and over one third of the population still living below the poverty line.

► In 1995 the average amount of paper consumed by a person living in an industrial nation in 1995 was 78.2 kilograms. In sub-Saharan Africa it was just 1.6 kilograms.

Impacts on food, health and the environment

Sadly, the impacts of international trade on resource use and distribution are not the end of the story. In fact, the trade system, its rules and its institutions have an extremely wide range of additional impacts on food, health and the environment—all of which concern Friends of the Earth.

Agriculture—in terms of livelihoods, access to land and the production of healthy and nutritious food—has to be at the top of this list. The increasing emphasis on international as opposed to local and national trade is having an extremely severe impact. Small farmers are being displaced (and at best taken on as smallholders in poor conditions, with unfair contracts and without compensation) as cheap, subsidised imports undercut production, land is turned over to production for export and farms merge to cut costs and compete. Crop diversity is being lost and traditional foods are being replaced with imported products. The impacts are undoubtedly worst in developing countries, where over half the population may be involved in agriculture, but farming is also in crisis in the North. In the US, for example, small farms are disappearing at the rate of 30,000 per year.

The World Trade Organisation (WTO) Agreement on Agriculture (AOA), established during the last Uruguay Round of trade negotiations, has exacerbated this problem, because it unashamedly pits small farms against larger, more 'efficient' agribusinesses in both the North and the South. Furthermore, at the end of the Uruguay Round governments agreed to compensate 'net food importing' developing countries for losses they would incur as cereal prices went up—a promise that they subsequently singularly failed to deliver on.

More international trade also means more road and air transport, with knock-on effects for health, habitats and the stability of our climate. Already, nearly 3 million people around the world die from air pollution every year. Yet it's been estimated that truck transportation in North America, for example, is likely to increase sevenfold between 1995 and 2005 as a result of the North American Free Trade Agreement (NAFTA). It has also been suggested that the proposed Trans-European Network of roads will threaten the social integrity of 1,000 small villages throughout Europe.

> **'Globally there is enough food to feed the world. But, to our shame, we live in a world where food rots and people starve'**
> —Jacques Diouf, director general of the UN's Food and Agriculture Organisation (FAO)

In terms of health, WTO agreements also discourage governments from providing cheap drugs, banning imports of genetically modified (GM) foods, and introducing strict health and safety laws that might be considered 'barriers to trade'. In fact, any national legislation that governs import standards—the quality of food or the pollution efficiency of petrol engines, for example—is dictated by two of the WTO's most (un)memorably named agreements, the Technical Barriers to Trade agreement (TBT) and the Sanitary and Phytosanitary agreement (SPS).

These two agreements restrict governments' ability to opt for high standards based on the precautionary principle (which is not explicitly recognised by the WTO) or consumer or ethical concerns. Take GM foods, for example. If governments can't prove there's a problem with GM food, they can't impose a permanent ban on imports. They can't say no to it on the basis of consumer objections either.

The same sort of restrictions operate at the international level too, although they've never been tested out in quite the same way (there have already been several inter-government disputes about national environmental and health legislation concerning imports of beef produced with growth hormones, and asbestos, for example). Key multilateral environmental agreements (MEAs)—governing trade in ozone-depleting substances and hazardous wastes, for example—conflict with WTO rules. So far, however, governments have refused to agree that these vital MEAs must take precedence over trade.

There are also clear links between neo-liberal economics and the troubled but vital Kyoto Protocol which is intended to reduce emissions of climate-changing gases. The prevailing ethos is that free trade and free markets bring benefits to all and thus trade barriers have to go. As part of this process companies have to compete on the global market and cut their costs—in government-speak they have to be 'internationally competitive'. This means that costly standards or regulations are frowned upon even if effective. Market-based solutions, such as tradeable emissions permits systems (which could allow energy-efficient countries and companies to sell rather than use emissions permits) are the order of the day. As always, trade and profits come first.

- ▶ Trade liberalisation of maize could jeopardize up to half a million livelihoods in the Philippines and between 700,000 and 800,000 in Mexico.
- ▶ In the last 30 years land devoted to soya exports in Brazil jumped from 200,000 to 2 million hectares.
- ▶ Indonesia plans to increase land under palm oil development from 2.5 million hectares to at least 7 million.

Neo-liberal economics is out of date

How on earth have we arrived at this grim state of affairs? How did we come to have an economic system that is both completely unsustainable and ignores the needs of the poor and disenfranchised of the world? There are two key reasons.

Firstly, neo-liberal economics—free trade theory—is just plain out of date. However, it still sounds convincing at a superficial level—and how many people have time to go deeper than that? As a result governments are still getting away with promoting free trade as a sustainable win-win system even though it's already been shown to be nothing of the sort.

Basically, the theory states that nations should specialise in producing what they're best at and then trade with each other (known as comparative advantage theory). Borders should be opened and companies should compete with each other and become more efficient. This will generate wealth, which will 'trickle down' to the rest of the population, who will in turn have more money to spend and go out shopping. Demand will go up and companies will make more money. A neat and virtuous circle that benefits everybody. No wonder governments like it.

Sadly, this is not what happens in reality, as we've seen above, and there are a number of reasons why not. The three most important have a direct bearing on equity, sustainability and quality of life.

Firstly, comparative advantage theory was developed at a time when capital was firmly anchored in domestic economies. Today, with new and powerful information technology and open borders, capital can be moved around the world virtually instantaneously. As a result it is increasingly difficult for those countries that don't hold the winning cards (such as a stable economy, low costs and good infrastructure) to retain or attract internationally mobile investment capital. In other words, the system is not a win-win one at all, but a win-lose one. Some countries and many millions of people are losing out altogether.

Secondly, neo-liberalism is unsustainable. Those who first proposed free trade as a solution to the world's economic problems were unaware that heightened demand for the world's finite resources would be a significant limiting factor in the 21st century. As a result, our current economic model is based on increasing and unsustainable rates of resource use. Governments have yet to recognise that there is no 'invisible hand' guiding the market towards sustainability.

Thirdly—and importantly—the way we measure our economic well-being is flawed. The 'freeing of trade' has been accompanied by global economic growth (although not very evenly distributed) as measured by gross domestic product (GDP). However, GDP is a seriously deficient measure of 'social welfare' or 'development' because it reflects people's income rather than their real quality of life.

For example, GDP counts the cost of healthcare, pollution clean-up and the renovation of habitats as positive contributions to the nation's wealth, even if they are the result of a rapidly deteriorating environment. On the other hand, important social roles, including both the care of children and the elderly and household work are ignored (unless they're paid for). Overall, GDP can continue to rise even when people's quality of life is deteriorating. This helps to explain the apparent contradiction of rising GDP in many countries and the sharp increase in criticism being leveled at the WTO.

Corporate globalisation—the real name of the game

So why do governments continue to promote an irrational economic model in the face of mounting opposition? The influence of transnational corporations (TNCs) plays a significant role. They are the principal winners in this win-lose system known to many as corporate globalisation and they expend a great deal of effort promoting free trade.

TNCs—cutting costs, merging, shedding jobs and growing more powerful by the day—need access to new markets and cheap resources to keep generating profit for their shareholders. Current trade rules and negotiations are helping them do just this. Trade negotiators in Geneva, for example, are at this moment negotiating further liberalisation of trade in services under the General Agreement on Tariffs and Trade (GATS) and it looks as if two of the outcomes could well be dramatically increased exploration and drilling for oil and new markets across the world for companies that build and sell incinerators.

Corporations are able to influence governments precisely because those governments either believe in or find it convenient to profess belief in the tenets of free trade (as described above), including the myth that wealth generated by companies will trickle down to the rest of the population—it doesn't—and that what's good for companies is automatically good for the rest of us—it isn't.

TNCs have built on this by banding together to form highly

influential 'corporate lobby groups' to lobby governments. Organisations such as the International Chamber of Commerce (ICC), the Transatlantic Business Dialogue (TABD) and the European Round Table (ERT) are able to meet frequently with trade officials to press for their concerns—and the environment is often high on their list of targets. The ERT, for example, is currently calling for 'removal of environmental and food safety non-tariff barriers' to be one of a handful of topics to be negotiated in a 'focused' new round in Qatar.[7]

▶ The total income of the ten largest TNCs is now greater than that of the world's poorest 100 countries, and many TNCs have greater sales than the GDP of some developed countries. For example, General Motors is more powerful in pure economic terms than Thailand or Norway.

▶ In 1997 total world cross-border investment flows amounted to over $40 billion. Short-term, often speculative capital now totals more that $2 trillion annually.

Towards sustainable economics

Governments constantly point out that there's no alternative to globalisation, but this simply isn't true. One can certainly argue that there's no going back on globalisation in general, with its many different political, social, cultural and technological ramifications, but it's absurd to argue that specific neo-liberal policies, that governments themselves chose to implement, are the only choice we have. It's simply a convenient myth perpetuated by those that benefit from corporate globalisation.

What goverments have failed to grasp is that whilst they may be able to deal with, contain or deny the negative impacts of corporate globalisation at the moment, this state of affairs is most unlikely to continue. Opposition is already mounting as increasing numbers of people feel the downside of neo-liberalism, but the the real challenge for humanity will be providing a decent quality of life for a predicted population of 10 billion people in 2050. Current global policies, that favour rich people, countries and companies using natural resources at completely unsustainable rates, simply cannot do this. Right now governments need to set aside short-termism and think about our future. There have to be—there are—alternatives.

> **'Free trade theory is arguably the single most powerful insight in economics'**
> —WTO

Friends of the Earth believes that economics needs to be brought into the 21st century—it needs to be flexible, fair and sustainable, and about more than money, profits and growth. Governments need to agree new goals for sustainable economies in the form of a coherent and internationally-agreed set of social, economic and environmental principles.

The inappropriate one-size-fits-all neo-liberal mentality needs to be replaced with an understanding of the benefits of economic diversity—both in terms of countries and peoples having the freedom to choose appropriate economic strategies and in terms of promoting diversity within countries and sectors (meaning no monopolies).

Economic subsidiarity also needs to be introduced, so that decisions about economics can be taken at the most local level possible. At the same time, decision-making on the environment and sustainability needs to be strengthened at the international level.

Critically, local economies and communities need to be strengthened and protected, resources need to be husbanded and shared fairly, and communities' rights to make decisions about their local, traditional resources need to be recognised. Export-led development, which tramples on the needs of millions of subsistence farmers (and has a particular impact on women responsible for growing food for their families), has to go. All in all, economics needs to be opened up and democratised so that people can know about, understand and be able to influence the development of their economies. All these things are possible.

> **'They have suppressed recognition of the fact that the empirical cornerstone of the whole classical free trade argument, capital immobility, has crumbled into loose gravel'**
> —Herman Daly and John Cobb, 1989

In the short term there are a number of thing governments could do to start to turn trade around. Firstly, they should reject the European Unions' proposal for a new round of trade negotiations, on the basis that it would take us further and faster down the wrong road. Secondly, they should act to reverse the impact of the last Uruguay Round of negotiations on farming and food by dismantling the disastrous Agreement on Agriculture. Thirdly, they should commission an independent review of the Uruguay Round to assess the social and environmental impacts of all the other WTO agreements agreed to in Marrakech.

Finally—and most importantly—they can and must establish processes that will make corporations fully and fairly accountable to local communities and elected governments. Corporate globalisation must stop.

The failure of the WTO's Seattle Ministerial in 1999 was a highly significant first step in the right direction, with people from all walks of life coming together to voice their opposition to neo-liberal economic globalisation. Since then that voice has been growing louder and louder around the world, but still the process drags on. How can we finally bring it to a halt?

For us, the answer—the card that hasn't been played yet—is to break the taboo on speaking out against free trade. Free trade is a myth—it's illogical and out of date and you don't have to be a rocket scientist to understand why (although economists would have us believe otherwise). The time has come to start debunking this myth, explaining to people far and wide that it's simply a con trick.

Free trade is a fashion that's had its day. We need to turn our backs on it and start designing new, fair and sustainable economies for the 21st century.

Ronnie Hall has been the Trade, Environment and Sustainability Programme Coordinator for Friends of the Earth International (FOEI) since 1992. She coordinated a team of 40 FOEI campaigners in Seattle.
ronnieh@foe.co.uk

Notes

1   UNEP, 1999, *Global Environment Outlook 2000* (United Nations Environment Programme, New York).
2   WorldWatch/UNEP, *Vital Signs 2001: The Trends That are Shaping Our Future.*
3   UNDP, *Human Development Report 1996* (United Nations Development Programme, New York).
4   UNEP, *Global Environment Outlook 2000* (United Nations Environment Programme, New York).
5   IUCN.
6   UNEP, 1999, as above.
7   Proposed by Morris Tabaksblat, ERT chairman at a 'business forum' in Switzerland in April 2001, quoted in *Inside US Trade*, 18 May 2001.

Texts

► HE Daly and J Cobb, *For the Common Good* (Greenprint, 1989).
► Friends of the Earth International, *The World Trade System: How it Works and What's Wrong With It* (Amsterdam, 1999).
► Friends of the Earth International, *The World Trade System: Winners and Losers: a Resource Book* (Amsterdam, 1999).
► UNDP, *Human Development Report 1996* (United Nations Development Programme, New York).
► UNEP, *Global Environment Outlook 2000* (United Nations Environment Programme, New York, 1999).
► WorldWatch/UNEP, *Vital Signs 2001: The Trends That are Shaping Our Future.*
► WTO, summary. *About the WTO: Basics* (World Trade Organisation, Geneva).

'In closing the ports the ILWU is demonstrating to the corporate CEOs and their agents here in Seattle that the global economy will not run without the consent of the workers. And we don't just mean the longshore workers, but workers everywhere in this country and around the world.

When the ILWU boycotted cargo from El Salvador and apartheid South Africa, when we would not work scab grapes from the California Valley, or cross picket lines in support of the fired Liverpool dockers, these were concrete expressions of our understanding that the interests of working people transcend national and local boundaries, and that labor solidarity truly means that when necessary we will engage in concrete action.

That is why the ILWU is here today, with all of you to tell the agents of global capital that we, the workers, those who care about social justice and protecting our rights and our planet, we will not sit quietly by while they meet behind closed doors to carve up our world.

We know what they have in mind for us is a race to the bottom, dismantling our protective laws wherever they find us weak, that they want to pit workers of one country against the workers of another, to erase our protections and standards in an international corporate feeding frenzy in which workers are not just on the menu—we are the main course.

We will not cooperate!

And let us be clear. Let's not allow the free traders to paint us as isolationist anti-traders. We are for trade. Don't ever forget it is the labor of working people that produces all the wealth. When we say we demand fair trade policies we mean we demand a world in which trade brings dignity and fair treatment to all workers, with its benefits shared fairly and equally, a world in which the interconnectedness of trade promotes peace and encourages healthy and environmentally sound and sustainable development, a world which promotes economic justice and social justice and environmental sanity. The free traders promote economic injustice, social injustice and environmental insanity.'

—Brian McWilliams, President of the Longshoreman's Union, Seattle 1999

A steel worker on the protest against the IMF and World Bank, Washington April 200...

Labour
Mark O'Brien

● ● ● ● ● ● ● ● ● ● ● ● ● ● ● ● ● ●

The presence of organised labour at Seattle opened up the possibility of new alliances and coalitions that had previously been unimaginable. A growing recognition had been emerging before Seattle of the common ground between workers and those fighting for a safer and more just world. Many of the issues that have brought so many people out onto the streets in protest in the last 18 months: privatisation, poverty and low pay, sweatshops, have been concerns of trade unionists for years. But it took the focus of attention on the events in Seattle to broadcast the message of solidarity between trade unionists and other activists around the world.

The commentators who tried to play down the role of labour unions in Seattle argued that the interest of the trade unions represented were restricted to a short list of issues that were chiefly to do with trade and labour standards. But for most of the union members present the questions being asked at Seattle went much further. There was much more to the workers' protest than 'protectionism'. They were linked arm in arm with environmentalists, students, feminists and Third World activists because the neoliberal onslaught to which all of us have been subject worldwide raises questions about every sphere of our lives and demands a united, internationalist response.

Yes, some of the trade union leaders were content to push an agenda of economic nationalism which concentrated on how free trade damaged US jobs. They oppose the entry of China into the World Trade Organisation (WTO) on the grounds that it would damage US jobs, wages and conditions not because of the devastation it would wreak on the lives of millions of Chinese workers. (These consequences are examined in more detail in Helen Shooter's piece on China in this volume, but are worth restating.) The import of American foodstuffs, for example, will destroy around 40 million jobs in Chinese agriculture over the next ten years, causing a massive migration into the cities in search of work. Jobs in manufacturing industries are also being shed at a frightening rate as competition on world markets intensifies. By the end of 1999 some 6.5 million Chinese workers who had been laid off by state industries were still without work. Entry into the WTO will lay off millions more. The failure to recognise that China's entry into the WTO is a lose-lose scenario for working people globally and to respond with a united strategy continues to be a weakness in the approach of some trade unions.

But others at Seattle, as the powerful speech by Brian McWilliams reprinted above shows, have a much broader, more comprehensive sense of what is at stake. Although McWilliams expressed anger and concern at the loss of American jobs, his language was that of internationalism. The 'race to the bottom' is seen as something which is a threat to workers in every part of the world and also as something which must be resisted with international solidarity. But, more than this, we see in his speech a concern for the environment and economic and social justice. The target here is unregulated trade which favours the major corporations at the expense of workers' rights, be they in Seattle, South Africa, El Salvador or Liverpool. His words chimed well with the miner representative of the South African Labour Network who won applause and cheering from the 25,000-strong crowd when he called out 'In the words of Karl Marx, "Workers of the world, unite!"'

Sweatshop labour and student activism

Sweatshop labour represents one of the extremes of capitalist exploitation. Working conditions that haven't been seen in Britain in over 100 years are commonplace to millions of workers in factories and textile plants in Indonesia, China and parts of Latin America.

The fact that fellow human beings are being forced to live and work in such degrading conditions in the 21st century has been a major impetus in the politicisation of many of the new generation of activists in the anti-capitalist movement. This anger has galvanised into a powerful movement of solidarity and protest which has brought together workers, students, young people, human rights campaigners and consumers in new and dynamic coalitions.

In the US United Students Against Sweatshops (USAS) was set up on many campuses in 1998 to campaign around the issue of the exploitative conditions of contract labour used by major brand name corporations. One example of this was the working conditions in the Formosa plant in El Salvador which produces a number of lines for Nike and Adidas.

Testimony from workers at the plant describe 12 hour days in hot, unventilated conditions. Workers are given backless wooden benches from which to work. Cushions are not allowed. Supervision is brutal, with constant verbal abuse against those who do not keep up the required pace, physical violence and sexual harassment. Permission is required to drink water or use the bathroom. The drinking water is not purified and comes from the cistern. Only one visit to the toilet is allowed each day. No toilet paper is available and the toilets are filthy. Male supervisors come into the women's toilets to harass the women back to work. Talking is not allowed. Workers leaving the plant are subjected to humiliating body searches. Workers are expected to work when they are sick. One or two days pay is deducted for a visit to the clinic. Women are made to undergo pregnancy tests which they have to pay for themselves. Pregnant workers are fired instantly. In some plants supervisors give depo-provera contraceptive injections to women who are told that they are getting anti-tetanus jabs.

> We are paid 42 colones a day, which is the minimum wage (which I am told is $4.80 per day).
>
> When I saw the price of this Nike shirt, $75, which would be more than 650 colones in El Salvador, I couldn't believe it. It is very unjust, because they pay us very cheaply to make a very expensive product.[1]

Many sweatshop workers are children. India alone has around 44 million child labourers. The International Textile, Garment and Leather Workers' Federation estimates that 250 million children are at work across the world, half of them under 14 years old. All these children could be put in school at a cost of $6 billion, or a mere 2 per-cent of the world's armaments expenditure.[2] High profile Western corporations found to be using child labour have been thrown on to the defensive. When a photograph appeared in the Western press showing a young boy in Pakistan stitching a Nike football, Nike had to promise to investigate the conditions of all its manufacturers.

USAS has campaigned around the issue of exploitative condi-tions, especially in the garment industry, in both the developing world and the US. Choosing an issue that was traditionally the pre-serve of organised labour, the mass involvement of students and other non-labour groups gave voice to the growing wave of oppo-sition to corporate capitalism. The success of the campaign in high-lighting the worst abuses of workers' rights by US corporations has been remarkable. Demanding that their universities sign up to the Worker Rights Consortium, which monitors labour standards acc-ording to the campaigns own charter, the USAS now has 125 college campus chapters across Canada and the US. Naomi Klein captures the historical novelty of the new relationships when she remarks:

> Times have changed. As William Cahn writes in his history of the Lawrence Mill sweatshop strike of 1912, 'Nearby Harvard University allowed students credit for their mid-term examinations if they agreed to serve in the militia against the strikers. "Insolent, well fed Harvard men" the *New York Call* reported, parade up and down, their rifles loaded, their bayonets glittering.' Today, students are squarely on the other side of sweatshop labour disputes: as the tar-get market for everything from Guess jeans to Nike soccer balls and Duke embossed baseball hats, young people are taking the sweat-shop issue personally.[3]

The historical irony alluded to by Klein continues with the recent victory by students at Harvard University in Boston. In April 2001 around 40 students stormed and occupied the university's

Massachusetts Hall protesting at the low wages received by janitors and catering workers. The occupation lasted for three weeks during which the students were supported by massive workers' rallies. A tent-city sprang up on the campus where student supporters and community members slept over to show solidarity. The occupation was supported directly by the Hotel and Restaurant Employees union (HERE Local 26) and the Service Employees International Union (SEIU Local 254). The students emerged from their occupation victorious as the Harvard authorities conceded pay rises, negotiations with the relevant unions, and student and worker representation on the body set up to review conditions for university workers.

The Living Wage Campaign is another initiative which has seen unions and students working together in the US. Anti-sweatshop sit-ins have occurred at the University of Michigan, the University of Iowa, SUNY-Albany, the University of Wisconsin, Wesleyan and the University of Kentucky. This new alliance is partly the result of the 'Union Summers' organised by the AFL-CIO federation and particularly by the Union of Needle Traders, Industrial and Textile Employees (UNITE). The Harvard Progressive Student Labour Movement (PSLM), for example, grew directly out of the Union Summer of 1997.

The environment

The issue of environmental degradation has been another of the themes around which the new coalitions between organised labour and other organisations have formed. Historically workers' interests have often been seen as at fundamental odds with those wishing to protect the environment. Economic development, expansion of production and increased employment has been seen as one of the major causes of pollution and environmental damage. But it has always been the case that much environmental damage, whether it is radiation leakage from nuclear power stations, asbestos poisoning or polluted water, has a disproportional affect on those people working in the industries themselves and their communities. So there has always been a case for unity. What is significant about today's protests and campaigns are the overt links being made between workers and other campaigners about the environmental effects of the rampant expansion of the market.

The Alliance for Sustainable Jobs and the Environment is a good example of this kind of solidarity. Formed only a few months before the Seattle anti-WTO events, it had grown out of a coalition between environmental groups such as the Earth Island Institute and members of the United Steel Workers of America (USWA). In May 1999 David Brower of Friends of the Earth and the Earth Island Institute, and David Foster, director of District 11 of the USWA, drew together their forces to oppose the Houston-based company Maxxam which was in the process of taking over two other companies, Pacific Lumber and Kaiser Aluminium. By simultaneously clear-cutting ancient redwoods in Northern California, and locking out striking steel workers in five cities, Maxaam had inadvertently set up a unity of interests that was recognised and valued by both sides. At Seattle trade unionists were not marching alongside environmentalists as strangers—many were already acquainted.[4]

Privatisation

Around the world privatisation, deregulation and public sector cutbacks have become a major focus of trade union and broader social struggles. The involvement of private companies in the provision of health, education, transport and other public sectors comes at a great cost to workers and all those who rely on these services. Private companies do not become involved in these areas of business without an expectation of considerable profit. Substantial profits can only be made by companies putting less into the service (eroding trade union rights, lowering wages, reducing safety standards, minimising training periods, etc) and/or by us getting less out of the service (higher treatment costs, fewer teachers, higher priced train tickets, fewer buses, etc). In reaction against such attacks, there have been, on every continent, strike waves against selling off state industries and utilities in recent years.

The most dramatic example is that of Bolivia in 1999 which has been mentioned in several of the pieces in this volume. The demonstrations and riots which followed the privatisation of the country's water supply took the company and government completely by surprise. The city of Cochabamba was shut down for four days by a general strike which shook the Bolivian establishment. They were forced into a humiliating retreat and had to take water back into public ownership.

In Britain, where the level of workers' struggle has not been as high as other parts of the globe in recent years, there have been some high profile campaigns and protests over privatisation. Workers on London Underground, for example, have taken strike action, even when it defied court injunctions, to protest about the threat to safety which would result from the privatisation of the tube. Another example is the hospital workers in Dudley who have fought a courageous campaign against the privatisation of their hospitals with wide support from the public and users of the National Health Service

These struggles, and others like them, have been inspired both by the direct threat to the livelihoods of workers and their families and also by a growing awareness of the deeper implications of basic social services being exposed to the profit system. The demand which trade unionists and other activist organisations can make through campaigns, strikes and occupations is for the renationalisation of these public services without compensation. Private companies who have taken over public services have made enough profit from us already in the form of government subsidies, higher user costs and lower standards. They don't need to be compensated—we do. Where union bureaucracies are unprepared to demand renationalisation, activists from all traditions must vocally and actively express their support for rank and file members who are willing to do so.

One example of an organisation making progress in this direction is Jobs with Justice, the social movement arm of the AFL-CIO. Its activists organise local teach-ins, rallies and direct actions bringing together labour, student and environmental organisations. In solidarity with the S26 protests in Prague, Jobs with Justice issued a call asking organisations to plan actions around local labour disputes. By the time of the mobilisation against the FTAA in Quebec, it had developed a national network of activists who helped organise over 80 local actions in cities across the US. This kind of conscious, coordinated intervention of a broad coalition of activists into the anti-privatisation struggles of rank and file trade unionists will be an effective strategy for reversing the growing poverty and insecurity which privatisation is causing worldwide.

Poverty

The time for optimism about the 'catching up' of the Third World with the West and real achievements in terms of national development for the poorest countries has now faded from memory. There are 2.2 billion people living in poverty according to the World Bank; in the Third World between one quarter and one third of children die before the age of five—in the poorest countries it is closer to half. These figures and others like them contrast cruelly with the mind-boggling figures which illustrate the wealth circulating in the world economy: the $1 trillion a day changing hands on the foreign exchange markets, the three wealthiest individuals who own and control more wealth than the 43 poorest countries, the combined wealth of the world's 225 richest people equalling the income of the poorer half of the world's population. The enormous poverty that we experience as the free market reaches into every corner of our lives is growing rapidly and is unprecedented in the history of human existence.

We all recognise that poverty is a problem, but it may seem paradoxical to consider it a labour issue. After all, employment seems for many people a way to gain greater financial security. But in fact, in modern society the kind of poverty we face globally as well as within our own countries can only be understood as the consequence of the relationship between business and labour. People are not born poor. Poverty is not a naturally occurring phenomenon in the modern world. It is wholly man-made. Each and every starving person around the world is socially created—every child that dies, every illness that goes untreated. We know that we have more than enough resources and human energy to clothe, feed, educate, medicate and provide artistic development for the world's population. The fact that we do not has nothing to do with human nature or the misanthropy of corporate interests. It has everything to do with the way in which our social relations are organised—otherwise known as capitalism.

So how is it that capitalism creates poverty? In exactly the same way as it creates profits—through the labour of human beings. Poverty and profits are two sides of exactly the same coin. Those defenders of the system who argue that capitalism creates enormous wealth are in fact acknowledging nothing more than that it extracts enormous wealth from the vast majority, in terms of human energy, thought and action, and distributes most of it to a minority in the form of financial profit.

Working people are, of course, compensated financially for their physical and mental labour, but if corporations were to buy raw materials at their real value, pay their workers for the real value of their work and sell the product at its new real value (the value of the original resources plus the full value of labour including administration and managerial work) they would make no profits at all, let alone the obscene rates of profit they do make. Under capitalism, businesses must give their employees less than the value of what they put in and/or must ask for more than the final product is worth in order to make any profit. In this way, capitalists relentlessly cream off for a small minority the value which the vast majority of people contribute in the process of their work. Then, through the pricing of products, people's access to the goods which they themselves, and others like them, have made is severely restricted.

The huge subsidies which governments administer to corporations are often referred to, quite accurately, as 'corporate welfare'. What we actually see from our understanding of the labour-capital relationship above is that capitalism itself is a system of corporate welfare. Capitalism involves the redistribution of wealth, not from the few rich to the labouring masses, not slowly, not through a trickle-down system, not if they work hard enough or long enough or are clever enough, but not at all. Capitalism does precisely the opposite, it directly redistributes the natural wealth of human productivity from the poor to the rich in the form of profits. These profits are our sweat and ingenuity signed, sealed and delivered to a minority whose wealth bears no relation to their ability or need. That is capitalism and that is why poverty is a labour issue.

Conclusion

Reactionary protectionism, environmental degradation, child labour, sweatshop labour, low wages and privatisation are all consequences of capitalism but, as I have argued above, wage labour is its basis. It isn't a coincidence, and shouldn't cause us to doubt our own judgement, that it is working people who recognise the nature of this relationship and not the corporate elites and their puppet governments. We have had the impetus to investigate the cause of our own immiseration to a degree they have not.

What this means, equally, is that we have a responsibility to do something about it. We can't wait for media moguls to report to the world that indeed all goods and services should be produced in a democratically accountable way, in the interests of human need—that won't happen. We need to shape world opinion ourselves by relentlessly articulating the fundamental nature of the problem at hand and more importantly we need to begin exercising *our* greatest power at the very point at which they derive *their* greatest power. We need to withhold our collective mental and physically productive abilities from those who profit from them and redirect them to serving those who need them. This is the promise and excitement that strikes, general

We need to withhold our collective productive abilities from those who profit from them and redirect them to serving those who need them

strikes and occupations can bring. We can take these actions at first to pressure for reform and ultimately to make the transition to better managing our productive abilities ourselves.

At the moment, the dynamism and radical consciousness of the anti-globalisers is coalescing with the organisation and power of workers the world over. Environmentalists, students, trade unionists, anarchists, socialists and activists of all backgrounds are recognising the height of the stakes and the potential of a much bigger drama to come.

Mark O'Brien is a lecturer in Politics and Public Policy at Liverpool University, researching labour internationalism. He stood as a Socialist Alliance candidate in the May 2001 general election.
markobrien@excitingtimes.freeserve.co.uk

Notes

1   Testimony of Julia Esmeralda Pleites,
     www.nicnet.org/nike/julia.htm
2   Susan George, *The Lugano Report*
     (Pluto, 1999) pp175-176.
3   Naomi Klein, *No Logo* (Flamingo,
     2000), p410.
4   Alexander Cockburn and Jeffrey St
     Clair, *Five Days That Shook the World*
     (Verso, 2000), pp8-9.

Sites

- **www.asje.org**
  Alliance for Sustainable Jobs and the
  Environment
- **www.jwj.org**
  Jobs with Justice (JwJ) is the social
  movement arm of the AFL-CIO.
- **www.labourstart.org**
  Labour Start is an excellent source of
  news on labour struggles worldwide.
- **www.nlcnet.org**
  The National Labour Committee
  (NLC) is one of the most important
  organisations investigating and
  exposing adverse labour conditions
  abroad.
- **www.nosweat.org.uk**
  A UK organisation campaigning
  against sweatshop labour.
- **www.usasnet.org.**
  United Students Against Sweatshops
  (USAS) has over 150 chapters on
  college and university campuses,
  principally in the US with a few in
  Canada.

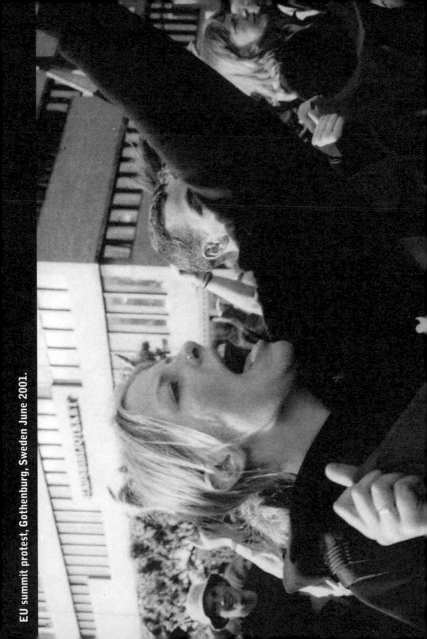

EU summit protest, Gothenburg, Sweden June 2001.

Women
Carolyn Egan and Michelle Robidoux
● ● ● ● ● ● ● ● ● ● ● ● ● ● ● ● ● ● ●

Women have enthusiastically involved themselves in the growing anti-capitalist movement. Theorists and leaders such as Vandana Shiva, Susan George, Naomi Klein, Medha Patkar and Maude Barlow have inspired people around the world. Women have been in the streets and organising at every level of the movement from Seattle to Prague to Porto Alegre to Quebec City. Young women are radical-ising in huge numbers and older women have taken up the challenge as well.

The ravages of global capitalism are pushing greater and greater numbers of women into action against the system, around issues such as the degradation of the environment, exploitation, human rights violations and war. But women are also responding to the way in which capitalism specifically impacts on women's lives, both North and South.

The World March of Women

In the year 2000 the World March of Women mobilised hundreds of thousands of women worldwide under the theme 'an end to poverty and an end to violence'. Local actions took place in many countries in October of that year, including in Mozambique, Chile, Mexico, Belgium, the US and Canada. Representatives from 6,000 women's organisations and trade unions in 161 nations worked together to raise issues that were critical to women's lives.

The threat of globalisation and its effects on women were integrated into the demands of the march. Women's groups called for an end to structural adjustment programmes, an end to cutbacks in social budgets and public services, and rejection of the Multilateral Agreement on Investment (MAI). They went on to call for the cancellation of the debt of all Third World countries:

> We demand the immediate cancellation of the debt of the 53 poorest countries on the planet, in support of the objectives of the Jubilee 2000 campaign. In the longer term, we demand cancellation of the debt of all Third World countries and the setting up of a mechanism to monitor debt write-off, ensuring that this money is employed to eliminate poverty and further the well-being of people most affected by structural adjustment programmes, the majority of whom are women and girls.

A year before the Seattle protests against the World Trade Organisation (WTO), a planning meeting for the World March took place; 145 women from 65 countries of the North, South, East and West, speaking many different languages and with different life experiences, met in Montreal. As they discussed the demands of the march it was clear that globalisation and the neo-liberal agenda were driving more and more women into poverty worldwide. The participants concluded that:

> ...any ratification of trade conventions and agreements should be subordinated to individual and collective fundamental human rights. Trade should be subordinated to human rights, not the other way around... the elimination of tax havens, the end of banking secrecy, redistribution of wealth by the seven richest countries.[1]

These activists understood the role of the International Monetary Fund (IMF), the WTO, the World Bank and trade deals. These institutions and agreements work in the interests of the multinationals, and the deals are not about trade but about increasing the profits of the most powerful. A pamphlet put out by the Canadian World March Committee prior to the Summit of the Americas in

Quebec City in April 2001 stated, 'Neo-liberal capitalism...maintains the vast majority of women in situations where we are culturally inferior, socially undervalued and economically marginalised, where our work is invisible and our bodies commercialised.'

Globalisation and the neo-liberal agenda were driving more and more women into poverty worldwide

Almost 5 million signed petitions supporting the demands of the World March. In October 2000 they delivered these demands to the United Nations, the World Bank and the IMF, joining hundreds of thousands of others in a growing movement.

Women's day to day lives

Capitalism is concentrating wealth and power in fewer and fewer hands as the majority becomes poorer. Living conditions worsen. There is a clear link between structural adjustment programmes, trade deals and women's day to day lives. In Latin America 84 percent of all jobs are in what is referred to as the 'informal' sector. Women and child workers make up the majority of those employed in this area. They sell food in the market places, do piece-work, produce crafts or are casual farm labourers. Many of these women are single mothers. The jobs are poorly paid and very insecure. They have no choice but to take the work that is there.

In many countries women, because of economic conditions, must move to the cities where they work seasonally in hotels or services, in sweatshops or in the sex trade. Employment is often unregulated and women must endure low pay and unsafe conditions. They are subject to incredible exploitation and harassment. Most live in shanty towns in deplorable situations, attempting to bring up their children without healthcare or social services.

The *maquiladoras* in Mexico typify what many women experience. The first free trade area was established in the 1960s in a region bordering southern Texas. Industry was unregulated and it has grown dramatically since that time. NAFTA, the North American Free Trade Agreement, was signed in 1995 by Mexico, the US and Canada. Workers were told it would make life better. In Mexico unemployment rose to over 3 million in 1996 from a high of 1.8 million in 1995. Companies from all over the world set up shop there because of reduced costs and lax environmental standards.

Young women were offered jobs in the manufacturing plants of the free trade zone, and because of unemployment they flocked there. Depending on the industry they make up 60-90 percent of the workforce. The hours are long and the wages low. Health and safety standards are weak, and union organising is very difficult. The women live in horrible conditions in the surrounding areas. Water, sewerage and electricity are not provided. Industrial waste pollutes the water and the soil.

Governments tell us that globalisation will end poverty and share the world's riches, but in truth the market has brought huge increases in the price of consumer goods and social polarisation

People speak of the stench. Birth defects have been linked to the workplace hazards that women are exposed to.

Violence exists both in the workplace and outside of it. Over 100 women in Ciudad Juarez have been murdered in the period of a year and the authorities have done little. Sexual harassment is rampant. Women are fired for becoming pregnant. The age range of these women workers is between 14 and 25 years old. Workers are let go because they are 'too old'.

The *maquiladoras* are not new to the economic scene. But competition is increasing and capitalists are seeking new markets and increased profits, and exploitation is proliferating. Any barriers that stand in the way of profit must be overcome, and that is the goal of deals such as the Free Trade Area of the Americas (FTAA).

The Zapatistas, with the active involvement of women, began their uprising on the day that NAFTA, the FTAA's forerunner, came into effect. The destruction that indigenous communities in the Mexican state of Chiapas were experiencing was directly linked to the trade deal.

Governments tell us that globalisation will end poverty and share the world's riches, but in truth the market has brought huge increases in the price of consumer goods, social polarisation and a rise in unemployment in the countries of the South. Multinational companies are allowed to make huge profits without adhering to labour standards or environmental protection. They are given tax havens, and a small elite benefits, while the vast majority live in poverty.

In the Philippines more than 70 percent of the population lives below the poverty line, although there is heavy foreign investment. As in other areas of the world there is a massive migration from the country to the cities. There have been many factory closures. In the Philippines, because of a lack of formal employment, women are forced into the informal sector just as in Mexico; 66 percent of the poor in the cities are employed in the underground economy. It is estimated that 90 percent of traders are women in some sectors, according to the World March of Women. For the most part they are offering goods and services in the streets. They have no job protection, no health benefits, and live a very precarious existence.

The same is true for women in South Africa. The numbers of people in the informal economy has grown dramatically. Working conditions are very dangerous. Many don't even have a home to return to at night and sleep on the street or in a hostel. This leads to the breakdown of family and social conditions. The high rates of HIV/AIDS infection are ravaging both women and men. As one woman, Emma Makhaza, said:

> I have seven children and no one to help me. I make bricks. When it rains, I cannot work. So I gather wood and cold drink cans to sell. When I have no food, I go to the neighbours. If they have nothing to give us, we go to sleep without eating.[2]

Traditional ways of life in rural communities are under attack by multinational agribusiness. Corporations promote one type of farming aimed at the export market. Family farms are destabilised. Women's lives are being disrupted, and traditional support structures are undermined without any services to replace them. It becomes very difficult for women to take care of their families.

They can no longer grow enough to feed their children, and have to leave the land for the cities.

This is happening in country after country to serve the needs of global capitalism. The Las Mercedes free trade zone in Nicaragua contains many textile factories, and again the vast majority of workers are young women, many from the country-side. They need the jobs, and take them, even though their wages cover only 40 percent of their expenses. Their conditions are deplorable, and because of the large pool of available workers, the multinationals have a lot of power. In many of these zones union organising is barred, and wages are below minimum national standards. In many cases women's wages have actually fallen.[3]

These are the fruits of capitalism's drive for profit worldwide, and they are the reason there is a growing anti-capitalist movement globally, in which women are taking their part.

Women in the industrialised countries

The majority of the poor in industrialised countries are also women. In recent years there has been an increase in the number of women in poorly paid, temporary, part-time employment. In the US 55 percent of those with temporary jobs are women; 70 percent of part-time jobs in the US are held by women.

A recent Canadian study, *'And We Still Ain't Satisfied': Gender Equality in Canada A Status Report for 2001*, commissioned by the National Action Committee on the Status of Women and the Centre for Social Justice, documents that:

> A sizable income gap between women and men persists... The income gap is accounted for in part by the over-representation of women in non-standard (part-time, temporary, self-employment) jobs, and partly through women's continuing economic inequality in low paid, undervalued female job ghettoes.[4]

Canada has been designated by the United Nations as the best country in the world to live in, and yet one in five Canadian women is defined as on low income. The study states that women are 'considerably poorer than is generally believed'. Aboriginal and racial minority women are in an even worse situation. The number of full-time, permanent jobs is declining. Layoffs and contracting out are daily occurrences.

The restructuring of the economy to meet the needs of capital has created a widening gap between rich and poor, and the majority of women's lives are getting harder. Globalisation is giving more and more power to the corporations and this is leading directly to job losses, privatisation, the weakening of labour standards, and cuts to health, social services and education. Deficit and debt-reduction have become the mantra of politicians as they give tax breaks to the rich and the corporations. More and more of the burden of caring for the elderly, the sick or the young, is falling to women as governments opt out of any responsibility.

In 1989 unemployment insurance was available to approximately 80 percent of Canada's unemployed workers. Because of restructuring the benefit system this fell to 34 percent by 1999. Only 29 percent of women were able to receive benefits. The federal government had increased the eligibility requirements, and many temporary and part-time workers—the majority of whom are women—could no longer qualify. It has also become harder to access maternity benefits.

In the US there was a direct attack on welfare recipients under the Clinton administration in 1996. Individual states could develop their own standards, and a five year limit on benefits for mothers on welfare was instituted. Women were being scapegoated and blamed for their own poverty.

Many women have seen their wages go down as their work has increased. Canada has over 5 million living in poverty out of a population of 28 million—70 percent are women and children; 57.2 percent of single mothers are poor.

One of the conclusions of the Canadian study is that women must 'fight to change the present economic system that maintains women's economic inequality'.

Women fighting back

The cycle of continuing poverty and exploitation that millions of women face worldwide is not going unchallenged.

According to Carmen Garcia of the Guatemalan Federation of Food and Allied Workers, quoted in a trade union publication:

> No matter where we live in this hemisphere, we, as women trade unionists, understand that we are facing the same challenges. The only thing that keeps us apart is language and borders.[5]

Women are in the front-lines all over the world in the fight against multinationals. On the island of Bougainville in the South Pacific gold and copper were discovered and Rio Tinto, one of the largest mining companies in the world, was allowed by the Papua New Guinea government to disregard the rights of indigenous people in its hunt for profits. Women were in the leadership of the fight against the company, forcing shutdowns of the mine and facing military repression.[6]

We have seen in the US women janitors organising and winning union rights and better conditions in California. Korean women are active in labour struggles against restructuring and lay-offs. Domestic workers are organising in the European Union. In Nicaragua there is a Working and Unemployed Women's movement mobilising. In the Philippines, Gabriela, a large coalition of women's groups, is organising street vendors in Manila. Every fight isn't being won, but there are inspiring victories.

In Cochabamba, Bolivian women were involved in the successful fight against the privatisation of the water system. As described in Barry Coates' piece in this volume, the World Bank and the IMF demanded private ownership as part of the country's 'economic modernisation plan'. The details of the sale were kept secret. Bechtel, a multinational, bought the system and acted quickly to increase its profit margin. It instituted a rate increase of 200 percent, way beyond what the majority could afford. People making $100 per month were expected to pay $20 for water.

Tanya Parede, a mother of five who supports her children by knitting clothing, was told to pay a $15 a month increase. She and thousands of others went into the streets for four days of demonstrations and a general strike. The police met them with teargas and bullets. In the end seven people died and hundreds were injured.

The protests had strong support. As a leader said, 'The blood spilled in Cochabamba carries the fingerprints of Bechtel.' A company executive issued a statement: 'We are dismayed by the fact that much of the blame is falsely centred on the government's plan to raise water rates in Cochabamba.' As a correspondent from Bolivia said, 'There are about 100,000 angry Bolivian mothers who would love nothing better than to steer him straight'.[7]

Those 100,000 mothers along with many others stood up to the IMF, the World Bank, the Bechtel Corporation and the Bolivian government. They stood up to global capitalism and they won what was called the 'War of the Water'.

This same anger with the system is bringing women around the world into the growing anti-capitalist movement. Women have been involved in direct action in Seattle, trade union marches in Nice, meetings in Porto Alegre, and the extraordinary coming together of workers and young activists in the demonstrations in Quebec City.

Women are not only active in the anti-capitalist struggles. They are also leaders. This movement is still at its beginnings. More and more women are coming to the conclusion that the only way to end the horrible conditions that so many endure is to take on capitalism itself, a system that perpetuates racism, sexism and homophobia, a system that sees profit as its only goal, and will stop at nothing to make the rich richer, as a majority of the world's people sink deeper into poverty. There is a radicalisation taking place that we have not seen for decades, and women are at the heart of it.

Carolyn Egan was an organiser for the Canadian World March of Women. She is President of United Steelworkers of America, Local 8300, in Toronto.
cegan@uswa.ca

Michelle Robidoux is an anti-globalisation activist, a socialist and a member of the Ontario Coalition for Abortion Clinics.
michelle_robidoux@hotmail.com

Notes

1   World March of Women, special edition of the newsletter of the International Preparatory Meeting of the World March of Women in the year 2000 (Montreal), pp6-7. www.canada.marchofwomen.org
2   Martine David, *Changing the World Step by Step* (Montreal, 2000), p18.
    Ibid, p27.
3   Ibid, p27.
4   Karen Hadley, '*And We Still Ain't Satisfied': Gender Inequality in Canada, A Status Report for 2001* (Toronto, 10 May 2001), p3.
5   *Women of Steel Go Global* (Toronto), p3.
6   Martine David, as above, p8.
7   Jim Shultz, 'Bolivia: Bechtel Corporation at the Root of Civil Unrest', Pacific News Service, 12 April 2000.

Sites

▶ www.nac-cca.ca
   National Action Committee on the Status of Women, Canada's main feminist organisation. Its website contains information on women and globalisation, as well as archives on the World March of Women.
▶ www.maquilasolidarity.org
   Maquila Solidarity Network. Find out how to organise your own 'sweatshop fashion show', get up-to-date information on the struggles of maquila workers.
▶ www.chiapas.indymedia.org
   Centro de Medios Independientes del Sureste Mexicano. The website for the Chiapas Indymedia, which includes transcriptions of speeches by Zapatista women and updates on the struggle of indigenous women and men in Mexico.

• ► www.geocities.com/
• migrante_australia
• Migrante Australia, a website about
• the struggle of Filipina migrant
• workers.

Protesters in South Africa successfully beat back drug companies which tried to bar
the production of cheap generic drugs for AIDS sufferers

Pharmaceutical patents
Kevin Watkins

● ● ● ● ● ● ● ● ● ● ● ● ● ● ● ● ●

Unless you happen to be a corporate patent lawyer, World Trade Organisation (WTO) rules dealing with intellectual property hardly make for scintillating reading. Yet the Trade Related Intellectual Property Rights (TRIPs) agreement is at the heart of one of the most intensive battles in the struggle to reform globalisation. It is a battle that pitches some of the world's most powerful corporations, currently backed by most Northern governments, against some of the world's most vulnerable people. The outcome will have a decisive bearing on our ability to replace current patterns of globalisation with a new order built on the foundations of social justice.

Nowhere is the intellectual property conflict being fought out more intensively than in the field of public health. The TRIPs agreement creates, for the first time, a system of global patent protection, enforceable through trade sanctions. It will have the effect of driving up prices for medicines vital for improving public health. In a world where over a billion people survive on less than $1 a day, and where 30,000 people die each day from poverty-related infectious diseases, many of them because they are too poor to afford basic medicines, it is not difficult to identify the losers.

It is even easier to identify the winners. The TRIPs agreement is the product of one of the most successful corporate lobbying campaigns in recent history, with the pharmaceuticals industry having provided much of the leadership and the finance. Why the effort? Briefly summarised, the WTO regime creates a legal monopoly for patent holders, enabling them to reap windfall profits on their products—and transnational companies account for over 90 percent of pharmaceutical patents. With sales in excess of $150 billion a year, the ten largest pharmaceutical companies will reap healthy dividends from the TRIPs agreement.

It is difficult to think of a more successful conspiracy to raise prices than the TRIPs agreement, or of a more abject failure on the part of Northern governments to defend public interest

Adam Smith, the selectively quoted ambassador of free market think tanks, once warned governments to be vigilant in protecting the public interests against the instincts of private traders. 'People of the same trade', he wrote, 'seldom meet together, even for merriment and diversion, but the conversation ends in a conspiracy against the public, or in some diversion to raise prices'.¹ It is difficult to think of a more successful conspiracy to raise prices than the TRIPs agreement, or of a more abject failure on the part of Northern governments to defend public interest.

Corporate influence has weighed heavily in the implementation of the TRIPs agreement. At the request of the Pharmaceuticals Research and Manufacturers of America (PhRMA), one of the world's most powerful industrial associations, the US government has used the threat of trade sanctions to enforce compliance. Countries such as India, Egypt, the Dominican Republic and Thailand have all recently felt the 'big stick' of US trade diplomacy. Brazil is now in the dock of a WTO dispute panel following complaints from the pharmaceuticals industry and the US. Its crime: passing a law allowing the government to waive the patent claims of pharmaceutical companies in order to control prices for vital drugs for the treatment of HIV/AIDS. Earlier this year 39 of the world's largest drugs companies abandoned a two-year case against the South Africa government, claiming that a law allowing government to promote access to cheap HIV/AIDS drugs violated the TRIPs agreement. This was in a country with over 4 million HIV/AIDS victims.

The South Africa case may go down in history as the pharmaceutical industry's Battle of Little Big Horn. Having dictated and driven the TRIPs agenda for over a decade, the public outrage generated by the trial in South Africa spawned a national and global campaign that, for the first time, brought the WTO agreement into the spotlight of public debate. Above all, the humiliating climbdown of the industry in the face of public pressure showed what could be achieved through public campaigning. The challenge now is to build on this momentum to achieve radical reforms of the TRIPs agreement.

The application of WTO rules to drugs raises at least three wider issues that go to the heart of public discontent about globalisation. The first concerns the credibility of global institutions. One of the key roles of public institutions in any industrialised countries is that of protecting the public interest, where necessary by regulating markets. Yet the WTO is being used to reinforce, rather than curtail, corporate power, despite the fact that vital public health interests are at stake.

The second issue concerns democracy. Protection of public health is one of the most important obligations facing any democratically elected government. Yet the TRIPs agreement, administered under the auspices of an unelected and unaccountable institution, effectively strips governments of the right to provide affordable medicines.

Finally, the application of WTO rules to medicines raises stark questions about human rights. The Universal Declaration of Human Rights establishes the right to adequate health provision as a basic human right, but the human right to health is being subordinated under the TRIPs agreement to the commercial rights of transnational companies.

Intellectual property rights and the WTO

In theory, patents are an attempt to strike a balance between the public interests of society in stimulating innovation, and the private interest of inventors in reaping the reward. Reduced to its essentials, a patent provides inventors with an exclusive marketing right, or a legal monopoly, for a fixed period. During this period the inventor can sell their product at whatever price they deem appropriate.

In practice, the history of patenting has been a history of struggle between private and public interest. In Europe absolutist monarchs distorted patenting into a system of royal reward designed to enrich the crown at the expense of the community. Under Elizabeth I and her successors the practice became so corrupt that parliament passed the Statute of Monopolies in 1623 to prevent abuses of the patent system.[2] Today the WTO is reviving the best traditions of the Tudor monarchy, placing the monopolists firmly in control.

Drugs and the WTO

Captains of global pharmaceutical coroporations like to describe patents as the lifeblood of their industry. They are certainly a source of profit. When Eli Lilly lost its battle to extend the patent life of Prozac in 2000, several billion dollars were promptly wiped of the company's share value.[3] Patents underpin profit rates in excess of 30 percent on sales—dwarfing the returns achieved in most sectors of industry.

Patent protection comes at a price to the consumer. Most drug prices bear no relation to their costs of manufacturing, which are frequently tiny. Reverse engineering means that drugs are also exceptionally easy to copy. Generic versions of patented drugs can be produced and marketed at a fraction of the price of their brand name equivalents. In theory, when consumers buy a patented drug they are paying for knowledge produced by investment in research and development. By restricting market entry for competitive products, patents enable companies to set prices at levels dwarfing marginal production costs safe in the knowledge that competition will be kept out of the market. This is why drugs companies invest so much in finding elaborate new ruses for extending the lifetime of patents.

Until recently, few developing countries granted patents for pharmaceutical products. This facilitated the early introduction of generic copies into the market, which in turn reduced prices. Countries with large generic drugs industries—such as India, Brazil and Egypt—were able to market drugs at a fraction of the price of the patented variety.[4]

The picture is now changing. Most developing countries are implementing legislation on the US patent model. Under the TRIPs agreement all countries are required to provide 20 year patent protection on products, or face the threat of trade sanctions.[5] This restricts the scope for developing cheap copies, with attendant implications for drugs prices.

Some safeguards have been built into the agreement. For example, governments can waive patent rights and authorise somebody other than the patent holder to produce a patented drug at a lower price (an arrangement known as compulsory licensing). But they can only do so if they are able to prove anti-competitive practices or a national emergency, and after they have compensated the patent holder.

Similarly, governments can import patented drugs from another country where they are marketed more cheaply (a practice known as parallel imports).[6] In practice, efforts to exploit these loopholes have been fiercely contested by the pharmaceuticals industry, often backed by the threat of US trade sanctions.

Corporate influence

Enforcement of the TRIPs agreement is the endgame in a protracted strategy developed by the global pharmaceuticals industry. That strategy has produced revolutionary changes in intellectual property rules without public debate, let alone public scrutiny of the implications.[7]

Until the Uruguay Round of world trade talks, the World Intellectual Property Organisation (WIPO) was the repository of global authority on patents, copyrights and other intellectual property issues. For pharmaceuticals companies anxious to project the patent protection they enjoyed in rich countries across the world, the problem with WIPO was twofold. First, it failed to provide a universal system of strong patent protection backed by enforcement mechanisms. The second problem could be summarised in a single word: democracy. One-country-one-vote rules restricted the scope for achieving change in WIPO through Northern government strong-arm tactics.

The solution was to shift authority to a body capable of imposing a global system. The obvious choice was the GATT, General Agreement on Tariffs and Trade (the WTO's predecessor). Unfortunately, the GATT's remit did not extend to intellectual property, and developing countries bitterly opposed any attempt to extend it in this area.

Pharmaceutical companies guided the Reagan administration's efforts to rewrite the rule book. By the mid-1980s the US was threatening trade sanctions against countries such as India, Brazil, Thailand and others deemed to be providing insufficient protection for the patents, or obstructing the transfer of power to the GATT. In 1988 trade sanctions were actually initiated against Brazil under the 'Special 301' provision, which was adopted to authorise unilateral trade sanctions. Meanwhile, companies such as Pfizer, Merck and Du Pont played a key role on the Intellectual Property Committee—a body set up to advise the Reagan administration on the Uruguay Round negotiations. This committee formulated US proposals for the TRIPs negotiations that were adopted in the WTO agreement.

The former chief executive of Pfizer, Edmund Pratt, in a moment of self-congratulatory reflection on the alliance between industry and the US government, said, 'Our combined strength enabled us to establish a global private sector/government network which laid the groundwork for what became TRIPs'.[8]

The implications of the drugs patents for developing countries

According to the global pharmaceuticals industry, patents are good not just for drugs companies but also for the poor. As Harvey Bale, director general of the International Federation of Pharmaceutical Manufacturers Association, puts it, 'The reality is that TRIPs will accelerate the introduction of new, patented medicines, including treatments for the infectious diseases that are the major killers of children and adults in developing countries.' It is difficult to imagine a less likely outcome.[9]

Health financing in a divided world: the price people pay for health

In contrast to rich countries, most health spending in developing countries is privatised. Poor people meet the cost of illness out of their own pockets, and spending on drugs is the single largest item of expenditure. This simple fact is central to any understanding of the threat posed by patenting. For the 1.4 billion people in the world living on or near the poverty line, even marginal changes in drugs prices can place effective treatment of life-threatening illnesses out of reach.

It goes without saying that far more is spent on public health in rich countries than in developing countries.[10] In the low-income countries of sub-Saharan Africa and South Asia public spending on health amounts to less than $10 per capita. In the middle-income countries of Latin America the figure rises to around $100. Governments in high-income countries spend in excess of $2,000 per person. The upshot is that global public spending on health is inversely related to need. Developing countries account for over 80 percent of the global burden of disease, but less than 20 percent of global health spending. Empty drugs shelves in public health facilities are one consequence of limited public health spending. While consumers in rich countries agonise over the choice of the best painkiller, over one third of people in developing countries lack access to vital medicines. Average per capita spending on drugs in America amounts to over $300, compared to $1-2 or less in much of Africa and South Asia.

Restricted public spending also reinforces financial pressures on households. In Britain less than 5 percent of total health spending is paid for directly by households. In countries such as India, Tanzania, Vietnam and Brazil the figure rises to over 50 percent. Drugs typically represent the single biggest item in household health spending, accounting for over 80 percent of the total in countries such as India.

In Zambia the cost of treating a single episode of pneumonia costs the equivalent of half the monthly income of a rural household living on the $1 a day poverty line, as over two thirds of households do.

Against this background it is not surprising that poor people themselves, as distinct from representatives of the global pharmaceuticals industry, consistently cite the unaffordability of medicine as a major concern. Evidence from a number of companies has linked the cost of medicines to household decisions not to seek medical help, or to prematurely end courses of treatment.

The impact of patents

The problem with the TRIPs agreement is that it will increase the cost of medicines to poor households and governments. This is not a future threat, though the full impact of the agreement will only become apparent with the next generation of patented drugs.

Comparisons between prices for generic drugs and patented versions highlight the problem.[11] Ciprofloxacin is one of the most effective anti-infective drugs used in the treatment of resistant shigella (or bloody diarrhoea in children). Within seven years of Bayer introducing its patented version in India, over 40 companies were producing a generic version at less than 10 percent of the price. Today prices in India are one eighth of those in neighbouring Pakistan, where there is no generic competition.

The impact of patents on drugs prices, and therefore affordability, is graphically illustrated by HIV/AIDS. There are currently over 36 million people infected with HIV, two thirds of them in Africa. In the developed world access to anti-retroviral drugs has dramatically cut death rates from the disease and improved the quality of life. Not so in developing countries, where patented 'triple cocktail' therapies costing between $15,000 and $20,000 in the US are far beyond the means of the poor. Yet generic companies such as the Indian firm CIPLA are able to market the same therapies at a price of $350 or less.

The price of these drugs is—quite literally—a life and death issue for millions of vulnerable people

Huge price variations are also apparent in the drugs used for the treatment of opportunistic infections. The drug Fluconazole, patented by the Pfizer corporation, is one of the most effective treatments for cryptococcal meningitis, a major source of mortality among HIV/AIDS sufferers. In Thailand, Pfizer was marketing the drug at a unit price of $7 until generic producers entered the market in 1998. Today, one of these producers markets the drug at a unit price of $0.30. Elsewhere in the developing world Pfizer continues to market the drug at prices of between 10-15 times those charged by generic firms in India and Thailand.

Looking to the future, the danger is that patents will inflate prices for the next generation of drugs. At a time of growing anti-microbial resistance to the current generation of drugs used to treat major killers such as respiratory tract infection, the price of these drugs is—quite literally—a life and death issue for millions of vulnerable people.

Enforcement by trial

Attempts by the pharmaceuticals industry to enforce patent protection on HIV/AIDS drugs have been at the heart of conflicts over TRIPs. They have also helped generate a mass global protest movement.

In 1997 the South African government passed a Medicines Act authorising the government to allow parallel importing of drugs. It was rewarded for its efforts with the threat of US trade sanctions following representations from PhRMA to the then vice-president, Al Gore. While the sanctions threat was eventually withdrawn, 39 drugs companies initiated a legal action against the 1997 act. Mass public campaigning in South Africa by the Treatment Action Campaign, and internationally by non-governmental organisations (NGOs) like Médicins Sans Frontières, Oxfam, and Act Up, eventually persuaded the companies to drop the case.[12]

The corporate debacle in South Africa was instructive. There are over 4 million HIV/AIDS victims in South Africa, and in excess of 120,000 deaths. Almost half a million children have been orphaned by the disease. By 2010 AIDS will have reduced life expectancy by 20 years. If this case did not constitute a 'national emergency' allowing for patent claims to be waived in the interests of providing cheap medicine, it is difficult to know what would. Yet the global pharmaceuticals industry used the TRIPs agreement to restrict the scope for government action, raising questions about existing safeguard provisions.

The same scenario is now being re-enacted, this time through a WTO dispute panel in Brazil. In March 2001 the Brazilian government announced that it would authorise local production of imported patented drugs, unless the patent holders agreed to reduce their prices. The move was prompted by concern over the fact that almost one third of the $300 million AIDS drugs budget was being absorbed by just two imported drugs, Nelfinavir, produced (under license from Pfizer) by Roche, and Efavirenz, which is manufactured by Merck. The US Pharmaceutical Research and Manufacturers Association (PhRMA) promptly protested to the US Trade Representative's Office, demanding that Brazil change its 1996 Industrial Property Law, under

> **There is a revolving door between the US Trade Representative's Office and the pharmaceuticals industry — Alan Holmer, the current president of PhRMA, is the former deputy US Trade Representative**

which the government can authorise local production in the event of a patent holder abusing their monopoly.[13]

Leaving aside the small question of democratic accountability, the US action represents an attack on a good example. Brazil's HIV/AIDS programme must rank as one of the few success stories in the struggle to contain the pandemic. Since the mid-1990s mortality rates have been halved, and there has been an 80 percent decline in hospitalisations related to opportunistic infection. The free distribution of anti-retroviral drugs has been a central element in this success story. By authorising generic production of patented drugs, Brazil has cut the price of triple therapy treatment to about one quarter of the level in the US. The policies behind this success are now under threat.

Corporate bullying and big-stick trade diplomacy

Having dictated the TRIPs agreement, the global pharmaceuticals industry is seeking to enforce it by bringing the full weight of US trade power to bear on recalcitrant developing countries. The influence of the PhRMA has been particularly significant, not least because it has reduced the US Trade Representative's Office to the status of an enforcement agency working on its behalf.

In September 2000 the PhRMA wrote to the then US Trade

Representative, Charlene Barshefsky, urging her to initiate WTO dispute procedures, along with bilateral trade sanctions, against Egypt, India, Brazil and Argentina. The list was carefully selected to include the countries with the strongest generic drugs industries, and hence the strongest source of potential competition for patented drugs. The aim was clearly stated in the PhRMA letter:

> By vigorously challenging the worst TRIPs offenders through early WTO dispute settlement proceedings, the US government will help facilitate the global implementation of adequate and effective intellectual property systems.[14]

The US government has been only too willing to oblige. India has been warned to amend legislation allowing for compulsory licensing, or face the prospect of action at the WTO. In Vietnam the PhRMA has complained of 'a pronounced trend towards protectionism in favour of locally produced pharmaceutical products'— and the country has been placed on the 'Special 301' hit-list. Following PhRMA complaints about a law allowing for flexible compulsory licensing, the Dominican Republic has been threatened with the withdrawal of trade preferences for its textile exports, placing an estimated 200,000 jobs under threat. Like Brazil, Argentina is facing the threat of action at the WTO for being, in the colourful language of PhRMA's representation to the US Trade Representative, 'the worst expropriator of US pharmaceuticals in the hemisphere'. The list could be extended.

The use of 'Special 301' as a battering ram for the pursuit of corporate self-interest reflects the symbiotic relationship between the industry and the administration. That relationship is built partly on financing. Between 1997 and 1999 PhRMA spent almost $300 million lobbying Congress and the administration, with two thirds directed towards the Republican Party. But the ties that bind are not just financial. There is a revolving door between the US Trade Representative's Office and other key posts in the administration on the one side, and the pharmaceuticals industry on the other. For example, Alan Holmer, the current president of PhRMA, is the former deputy US Trade Representative.

Research and development

What of the argument that stronger patent protection will boost research and development in diseases afflicting poor people? The research and development deficit in developing countries is certainly a serious problem. Only 13 percent of the 1,223 new compounds launched on the market in the 20 years up to 1997 were intended for tropical diseases. This reflects the bias of research and development towards diseases of rich countries that account for over 80 percent of global drugs sales. Pneumonia, diarrhoea, tuberculosis and malaria—a group of diseases that claim about five lives every minute of every day—account for less than 1 percent of the global health research budget.[15]

Will reinforced patent rules change this picture by creating new incentives? The answer to this question is no. To understand why, it is necessary to reflect on some simple market realities. Total spending on drugs in sub-Saharan Africa (excluding South Africa) is probably less than $1 billion a year. To put this figure in context, the Pfizer corporation has eight drugs with sales in excess of $1 billion, including Viagra. Bluntly stated, minor sexual problems in rich countries make serious money, while life threatening diseases among poor people do not. Patent protection will not significantly change the relative profitability of finding cures for diseases afflicting rich and poor countries for the simple reason that poor people lack purchasing power. That is why increased public investment in research and development holds the key to correcting the current imbalance in research and development.

The case for reform: beyond corporate philanthropy

Over the past year public protests and growing awareness of the public health threats posed by the WTO's intellectual property rules have generated a powerful momentum for reform. Belatedly, the TRIPs agreement and the principles that underpin it are now being debated in public.

The global pharmaceuticals industry has developed a twin-track response. The first track is based on an unremitting commitment to reinforced patent protection. The second track offers corporate philanthropy, mainly in the form of price discounts and drug donations, to provide affordable drugs to low-income populations.

Valuable as it may be in some contexts, corporate philanthropy is not enough. It is certainly not a substitute for government responsibility to provide vulnerable populations with affordable medicine. For this responsibility to be discharged, fundamental reforms to the TRIPs agreement are needed, including at least three new principles:

▶ *Scrap the universal 20-year rule.* Inventors need some protection but they are getting too much, especially in the developing world. We need to scrap the WTO's one-size-fits-all system, which is producing absurdities, and replace it with one that responds to real public health needs in poor countries, and to market realities.[16] Stringent application of current TRIPs rules in poor countries will raise prices for vital drugs, without creating incentives for research and development. Bluntly stated, the 20 years rule is as indefensible on economic grounds as it is on moral grounds. *Low-income countries should be exempt from TRIPs rules, and middle-income developing countries should retain the right to limit the scope and duration of patent protection.*

▶ *Reinforce public health safeguards.* It is now clear that the existing safeguards for public health built into the WTO agreement are insufficient. While the letter of the law allows for compulsory licensing and parallel importing, the spirit of implementation restricts the scope for action in these areas. Moreover, the burden of proof on national governments citing national health emergencies as grounds for waving patent claims is unrealistically high. *Any future TRIPs agreement should reduce the burden of proof on governments, and include a clear statement that governments retain the right to place public health priorities before the claims of patent holders.*

▶ *Outlaw the use or threatened use of trade sanctions.* The US in particular has used its economic power as a negotiating tool on behalf of pharmaceutical companies.

'Special 301', which allows for bilateral trade sanctions, represents a clear violation of the multilateral principles enshrined in the WTO. *As such, unilateral trade sanctions should be outlawed under WTO rules.*

It goes without saying that reforming TRIPs is not a magic bullet for improved access to medicine. There is an almost universal need across the developing world for increased investment in infrastructure, more equitable patterns of public spending, and the integration of health policies into poverty reduction strategies. Yet the fact remains that the TRIPs agreement will undermine national and international efforts to close the obscene health gap that separates the people of rich countries from those of poor countries. That is why it has to go.

Kevin Watkins is Senior Policy Advisor at Oxfam, where he works on social and economic policy issues. His publications include the Oxfam Education Report and *Patent Injustice: How World Trade Rules Threaten the Health of Poor People*, both published by Oxfam.

: Notes

1   A Smith, *Wealth of Nations* (Oxford Clarendon Press, 1976), vol 1, p457.

2   M Ryan, *Knowledge Diplomacy* (Brookings Institute, Washington, 1998), p24.

3   'Eli Lilly's Drug-Induced Depression', *The Economist,* 12 August 2000.

4   J Lanjouw and I Cockburn, 'New Pills for Poor People? Empirical evidence after the GATT', *World Development*, vol 29,2 (2001), pp265-289. On the efficiency with which generic producers were able to introduce copies of brand name drugs shortly after their arrival on the market, see K Maskus, *Intellectual Property Rights in the Global Economy* (Institute for International Economics, Washington, 2000), ch 7.

5   For a good overview of the TRIPS agreement and its application to developing countries, see C Correa, *Intellectual Property Rights, the WTO and Developing Countries* (Zed Books, 2000).

6   Oxfam, *Patent Injustice: How World Trade Rules Threaten the Health of Poor People* (Oxford, 2001).

7   The role of pharmaceutical corporations in influencing US policy and the Uruguay Round agreement on intellectual property rights is insufficiently explored. One of the best detailed accounts is R Weissman, 'A Long Strange TRIPs: the Pharmaceutical Industry Drive to Harmonise Global Intellectual Property Rules', *Journal of International Law* (University of Pennsylvania, Winter, 1996). See also P Drahos, 'Global Property Rights in Information: the Story of TRIPs at the GATT', *Prometheus,* vol 13 (1995), and P Drahos and J Braithwaite, *Information*

Feudalism (forthcoming 2002).

8   Cited in R Weissman, as above.

9   H Bale, *Patents and Public Health: a Good or Bad Mix?* Pfizer Forum, paid advertisement in *The Economist*, 2-8 May 2001.

10   The following section on health inequalities and health financing draws on the following documents: World Health Organisation, *Health Reform and Drugs Financing*, DAP series 6 (Geneva, 2000), D Filmer et al, *Health Policy in Poor Countries* (World Bank, 1997), R Davidson et al, *The Burden of Disease Among the Global Poor* (World Bank, 2000), OECD, *Health Data* series (Paris, 1998). On the threat posed by microbial resistance see World Health Organisation, *Infectious Diseases Report 2000* (Geneva, 2000).

11   On price differences between patented brand name drugs and generic copies see the various examples cited in Oxfam, *Patent Injustice: How World Trade Rules Threaten the Health of Poor People*. See also J Watal, *Access to Essential Medicines in Developing Countries: Does the WTO TRIPs Agreement Hinder it?* Science Technology and Innovation Discussion Paper No 8 (Centre for International Development, Harvard University, 2000).

12   On the South Africa case, see the various reports on the Oxfam Cut the Cost website: http://www.oxfam.org.uk

13   On the Brazil case, see Oxfam, *Drugs Companies Versus Brazil: the Threat to Public Health* (2001).

14   The best source of information on the activities of the Pharmaceutical Research and Manufacturers of America and its targeting of developing countries for the threat of trade sanctions is its own website. http://www.phrma.org

15 On the failure of the pharmaceutical companies to undertake research and development into 'diseases of the poor' see Oxfam's paper on Glaxo Smith Kline, *Dare to Lead: Public Health and Company Wealth* (Oxford, 2000).

16 Contrary to the received wisdom that stronger patent protection is inherently good for innovation, many economists—and, ironically, *The Economist*—argue that patents can have the opposite effect by 'locking out' competition and raising the cost of new technologies. See, for example, W Kingston, 'Innovation Needs Patent Reform', *Research Policy* 30 (2001), pp403-423. For *The Economist*'s criticism of current patenting practices see 'Who Owns the Knowledge Economy', 8 April 2000.

Sites

▶ **www.oxfam.org.uk**
The research and analysis underpinning Oxfam's Cut the Cost Campaign, along with detailed studies of the South Africa and Brazil cases.

▶ **www.phrma.org**
Information on the Pharmaceutical Research and Manufacturers of America and its targeting of developing countries for the threat of trade sanctions.

'The genetic manipulation of a plant or animal enables companies, by enforcing industrial patents, to become owners of all the modified plants and animals subsequently produced.

By buying up rival seeds and patents, or removing competitors from the market, a firm can become the owner of an entire species. It's the logic of industry, applied to life. Genetic manipulation is a way of being paid royalties for life itself.'

— José Bové, farmer activist who dismantled the McDonalds at Millau.

Monsanto-produced soya bean GM crops on trial.

GM foods
John Baxter

● ● ● ● ● ● ● ● ● ● ● ● ● ● ● ● ●

The politics of food is at once global and personal. Vast multinational companies like Monsanto, Cargill and DuPont/Pioneer dominate food production. American and European governments have fought trade wars over bananas and beef. In Britain one food scandal has followed another, from salmonella in eggs to BSE and foot-and-mouth disease in cattle. These scandals are linked by their origins in the intensification and industrialisation of food production. In its rush to maximise profits, global capitalism has reached into the heart of our everyday life, poisoning the food on our table.

In the last five years the issue of genetically modified (GM) food has become a focus of protests and campaigns. Farming communities have protested against nearby trials of GM crops, and environmental activists have destroyed experimental plantings. One of the many issues motivating protesters at Seattle was the fact that the World Trade Organisation (WTO) intended to set up an international body to facilitate the spread of GM crops by reducing the time taken for new crops to gain approval. One of the many successes of Seattle was that this body was never formed.

What is genetic modification?

Techniques developed over the last 25 years allow the insertion of genetic material directly from one species to another. Genes involved in the production of a natural insecticide found in snowdrops

can be transferred into potatoes, in the hope that the
crop will be more resistant
to insect damage. Tradi-
tional plant breeding allowed the transfer of pro-
perties between closely

related species, but genetic engineering allows transfer between any
organisms, and even from animals to plants.

What is genetic modification used for?

Despite promises from the biotechnology multinationals that GM
technology will feed the world (see below), the vast majority of
genetic modification has involved traits designed to maximise
commercial profits:

▶   Soybean, oilseed rape, maize and cotton have been
     modified to make them more resistant to weedkiller.
     Companies like Monsanto sell the seeds to farmers,
     forcing them to sign a legal agreement that they will
     only buy Monsanto's Roundup herbicide. The company
     then employs private detectives to ensure that the
     agreement is enforced.

▶   Maize, cotton and potatoes have had Bt toxin genes
     inserted. These produce an insecticide which occurs nat-
     urally in a type of bacteria. Companies hope to increase
     crop yields by minimising insect damage. There are fears
     that the insecticide, which is heat resistant and not bro-
     ken down in the human stomach, could cause allergic
     reactions.

▶   Tomatoes and other crops have been modified to delay
     ripening. This increases profit by allowing greater time
     to transport crops to point of sale, and increases their
     shelf-life.

▶   'Terminator technology' has been developed to prevent
     farmers sowing seeds kept back from the harvest. Crops
     have genes inserted which cause sterility in the next

generation. Farmers are forced to buy from seed merchants every year. Public outcry has forced some firms to retreat from the using this technology.

The case against GM crops and food

▶ Crops which have been genetically modified to resist insects kill not just the target insect but beneficial insects. They also threaten the habitats of other animals, such as birds.

▶ Crops which have been genetically modified to resist herbicides encourage the use of larger quantities of the herbicide, killing both weeds and beneficial plants indiscriminately. Increased use of herbicides like glyphosate (Roundup) and Bromoxynil threaten both human health and the environment.

▶ Crops which have been genetically modified to contain their own insecticide cause insects to develop insecticide resistance.

▶ GM plants may cross-breed with wild species to produce 'superweeds', which are not killed by normal herbicides. This is a particular risk with GM oilseed rape, which is particularly liable to pollinate wild species.

▶ GM plants contaminate conventionally grown and organic plants and honey. They may cross-pollinate with nearby crops to produce hybrids which contain genetically modified material. Currently the UK government has recommended distances of 200 metres from organic crops and 50 metres from conventional crops. Independent research has shown that rape seed pollen can be dispersed up to 4 kilometres.

▶ The use of GM seed encourages dependence by farmers on single seed suppliers, in the case of Monsanto, forcing farmers to buy seed and insecticides from the same supplier.

▶ The long-term effects of genetic modification are not well understood and the products are not properly tested before release (see below).

> ▶ Genetic material inserted into plants can be transferred into humans and animals across the intestinal wall, with unknown consequences.[1]

Haven't GM crops been tested?

Millions of dollars have been invested worldwide to research the development of GM food, but while governments in the US and UK both claim to have rigorous standards, in fact very little research has been conducted into the long-term risks. Some sources claim that Monsanto's Roundup Ready Soya beans were tested by feeding them to fish for ten weeks.

Governments in the UK and US have shown little interest in funding long-term research. This reflects the substantial influence wielded by biotechnology firms, particularly when it comes to funding research (see box). It was claimed that GM foods were 'substantially equivalent' to non-GM foods, and therefore that rigorous testing was largely unnecessary.

One government funded scientist, Dr Arpad Pustzai, was able to conduct research into GM potatoes. He found that potatoes modified to contain lectin , an insecticide found in snowdrops, damaged the immune system of rats. When his results were revealed by *World in Action* he was hounded out of his position at the Rowett Institute, and prevented from further discussing his work. When *The Lancet* later published his results the journal was condemned by establishment scientists. This was precisely the response to the first scientists who warned of the dangers of BSE, who were also driven from their jobs and condemned by government scientists.

Government influence

Tony Blair says one thing to the electorate, and another to the biotechnology industry:

> There is no doubt that there is potential for harm, both in terms of human safety and in the diversity of the environment, from GM food and crops... Nothing has puzzled me more than claims that this government is an unquestioning supporter of GM food. We are not

pro- or anti-GM food. We are pro-safety, pro-environment and pro-consumer choice.
—*Independent on Sunday*, 27 February 2000

This is an industry whose market in Europe alone is expected to be worth over $100 billion by 2005... The giants of British biotechnology, like Celltech, dominate the continent. I want to make it clear that we don't intend to let our leadership fall behind and we are prepared to back that commitment with investment.
—to the European Bioscience Conference, London, November 2000[2]

Political parties on both sides of the Atlantic receive substantial funding from the biotechnology giants. In the UK leading government figures and quango appointees have links with the industry. Here is a small selection:

Lord Sainsbury, minister in the Department of Trade and Industry responsible for the Biotechnology and Biological Sciences Research Council, is major backer of the biotechnology company Diatech; Jack Cunningham, former Minister of State for Agriculture and chair of the committee which coordinates government policy on the use of pesticide resistant crops, is a paid adviser to Albright and Wilson (UK) Ltd, a major agrochemicals firm and producer of pesticides; Paul Leinster, previously employed by the company which owns the biotechnology firm AgrEvo, is head of the Environmental Agency's Environmental Protection Directorate. In 1998 AgrEvo was condemned for its failure to comply with regulations for the testing of GM crops; Peter Doyle, chairman of the Biotechnology and Biological Sciences Research Council, responsible for funding government biotechnology research, is also executive director of the biotechnology firm AstraZeneca.[3]

Can GM food feed the Third World?

Worrying about starving future generations won't feed them. Food biotechnology will.
—Monsanto advertisement

The world's population is set to reach 8 billion by the year 2020 and 10-11 billion by 2050. The propagandists for GM food claim that only genetic engineering will allow us to feed our growing population without expanding the amount of land used for agriculture and therefore damaging the environment.

The major biotechnology companies are developing GM crops to maximise their profits—to tie farmers in to buying own brand herbicides, to lengthen the shelf-life of products, and to modify oil content to minimise further processing costs. There is no evidence of any major projects which would begin to tackle starvation.

But the reason that 19,000 children starve to death each day has nothing to do with the efficiency of agriculture and everything to do with a world capitalist system which condemns millions to live in dire poverty. The world currently produces enough food to provide a decent diet for every person on this planet, despite the fact that farmers in the West are paid not to cultivate their land. The problem is not that we don't produce enough food, but that we don't get it to the people who need it.

Patenting life

Biotechnology companies are engaged in a mad scramble to patent the genes of all living creatures, including humans. In the month of October 2000 the number of genes patented rose by 27 percent from 126,672 to 161,195. By the end of 2000 Monsanto alone held patents on 45 oilseed rape gene sequences, 78 wheat sequences, 30 rice sequences, 102 maize sequences, 62 potato sequences and 203 cotton sequences.

Despite opposition in a number of countries, the US has been able to use the WTO Agreement on Trade Related Intellectual Property Rights (TRIPs) to legitimise worldwide 20-year patents on gene sequences. This has tremendous implications in the field of human health, where patents on genes limit those who can do research and allow companies to make huge charges for the use of diagnostic kits.

In the field of GM crops the patents on gene sequences allow companies to own patents on modified seeds and prevent farmers from re-sowing crops, whether or not they have 'Terminator technology' inserted.

An industry in retreat

Countries like Britain and France have seen protesters ripping up fields of GM crops, but protest has not been confined to the West. In India thousands of farmers destroyed GM crops in the 'Cremate Monsanto' campaign, even sending union leaders to Europe to help destroy crops there. In November 2000 Filipino farmers held massive demonstrations at Monsanto's offices in Mindanao, joined by farmer's unions from Indonesia, Thailand, Japan and Korea. In January 2001 some 1,200 Brazilian farmers and members of the landless labourers movement, the MST, stormed a Monsanto research centre, destroying crops and occupying it.

The vast multinationals producing GM crops and food are on the defensive. Over the last three years the campaigns and protests have forced concession after concession from companies like Monsanto and Aventis. Supermarkets have ceased to stock GM food; restaurants have to issue disclaimers that their food is GM free. The big players in the field have rushed to change their names after the initial bad publicity.

The companies have been eager to publicise the development of a second generation of GM food. These so-called 'functional foods' will be modified to enhance their nutritional value. Foods will be altered to contain more vitamins, to lower sugar content, or to increase levels of protein.

The most widely publicised of these foods, all of which are still under development, is 'golden rice', which will contain increased levels of beta-carotene, which is converted into vitamin A in the body. Vitamin A deficiency (VAD) is an important cause of illness in developing countries, resulting in blindness and reduced resistance to infection. The propagandists of GM food claim that 'golden rice' could eliminate VAD. But apart from the possible risks involved in genetically modifying the rice, this kind of technological quick fix is not the way forward. If a fraction of the money spent on developing GM rice was spent on helping the poor develop a more mixed diet, VAD could be eliminated overnight. VAD is a disease of poverty; what is needed is programmes to eliminate poverty.

Conclusion

The calendar below only shows a fraction of the campaigning from the last few years, but it does show that protest works! The biotechnology industry is on the defensive, but it is not about to write off the billions it has invested in GM research.

In this country hundreds of test sowings of GM crops are still under way, with scant regard to the dangers to our environment or health. The fact that in a pre-election period the New Labour government was prepared to stop one crop trial in a marginal seat should give us no illusion that the new Blair government will stop being a friend to the biotechnology industry.

In the year 2000 some 44.2 million hectares were sown with GM crops, mostly in the US. Given the global nature of food production, and the US's campaign to remove barriers to food trade through the WTO, these pose a threat to the health of everyone on the planet. Under the Clinton administration the lax regulations allowed the contamination of hundreds of food products with potentially toxic GM Starlink corn. Things are hardly likely to get better under Bush.

We have to keep up the protest. Starlink corn is coming to a tortilla chip near you!

John Baxter is a lecturer in science at Stockport College, an activist in the Socialist Alliance and a member of the Socialist Workers Party. He has written on the politics of science and other issues in *Socialist Review* and *International Socialism* journal.

Notes

This article has been compiled largely from information available on the internet. Any data not referenced directly can be found in the Briefings supplied by Genewatch UK.

1 This section adapted from 'What's Wrong With Genetic Modification?' www.connectotel.com/gmfood/gmwrong
2 Quotes from *Genetic Engineering: A Review of Developments in 2000*, Genewatch Briefing 13, January 2001.
3 See George Monbiot, *Captive State* (London, 2000).

Sites

► **www.dmac.co.uk**
Site of the Genetic Engineering Network, a UK organisation campaigning against genetic engineering.

► **www.foe.co.uk**
Friends of the Earth website.

► **www.genewatch.org**
An excellent site with a number of useful briefings on issues related to GM foods and crops. Includes database on field trials of crops in UK.

► **www.geneticfoodalert.org.uk**
Site of Genetic Food Alert, a campaign of the wholefood industry against GM food.

► **www.grain.org**
Genetic Resources Action International

► **www.gn.apc.org**
Non-violent campaign to destroy GM crops.

► **www.greenpeace.org**

► **www.gm-info.org.uk**
The sites of GM crop trials in the UK (part of the Corporate Watch website)

► **www.purefood.com**
Site of the American Organic Consumers Association, with details of campaigns like those against Starlink and Starbucks.

March 1998► Iceland supermarket removes GM products from shelves.

August 1998► *World In Action* reveals Arpad Pusztai's research showing that GM potatoes damage the immune system of rats.

March 1999► Sainsbury's and Marks & Spencer remove GM ingredients from own-brand products.

April 1999► Tesco, Bird's Eye, Cadbury's and Nestlé all go GM-free.

June 1999► Northern Foods, McDonald's, Pizza Express and Domino's Pizza go GM-free.

EU passes legislation requiring labelling of food containing GM ingredients.

July 1999► Deutsche Bank produces report 'GMOs are Dead' that advises against investment in companies developing GM crops.

At a farm in Lyng, Norfolk, Greenpeace protesters cut down GM maize and seal it in bags—28 are charged with theft and criminal damage.

August 1999► Poll shows 62 percent of British are opposed to a GM trial in their area.

September 1999► UK legislation forces restaurants to inform customers if they use GM ingredients.

October 1999► Monsanto and AstraZeneca commit themselves not to use 'Termin technology' which makes second generation seeds sterile, and prev farmers from holding back seeds for re-sowing.

December 1999► At Seattle efforts to set up a WTO committee to assess GM foods as countries resist attempts to remove national decision-making.

Iceland and Tesco ban GM ingredients in animal feed.

March 2000► Monsanto merges with Pharmacia-Upjohn—the Monsanto name will only be used for the agrochemicals division.

April 2000► Jury acquits the 28 Greenpeace activists of theft after the protest in L in July 1999, but fails to reach a verdict over criminal damage charges. Crown Prosecution Service announces it will seek an immediate retrial

May 2000► UK government admits 4,700 hectares have been sown with GM-contaminated oilseed rape.

AstraZeneca buys rights to 'golden rice', with agreement that it can be used for fre poor farmers in developing countries. The company expects to make profits by selli the same technology in the West.

August 2000► Novartis, the top GM crop producer, announces it will no longer us ingredients in its foods, including Ovaltine and Gerber baby produc

September 2000► Taco Bell taco shells shown to contain Starlink corn, a GM containing potent allergens, only licensed for use in anima The shells and over 300 other products are recalled.

In the retrial, a second jury acquits the 28 Greenpeace activists of criminal damage after the protest in Lyng in July 1999.

► Sources
'GM Crops and Food: A Review of Developments in 1999', Genewatch UK Briefing Number 9, January 2000,
'GM Crops and Food: A Review of Developments in 2000', Genewatch UK Briefing Number 13, January 2001.
'Genetic Engineering: A Review of Developments in 2000', Genewatch UK Briefing Number 13, January 2001.
www.purefood.org, www.geneticfoodalert.supanet.com, and other resources on the web.
Lori Wallach and Michelle Sforza, The WTO, Five Years of Reasons to Resist Corporate Globalization (New York, 1999).

October 2000► Damaged by the Starlink debacle, Aventis announces it is selling off AgrEvo, its agrochemical and seeds section.

November 2000► Monsanto apologises for being arrogant and dismissive of public concerns, and pledges to be 'honourable, ethical and open' in the future.

nsanto's new contract for farmers using patented GM crops in the US is published.
mers must waive any rights to sue if the crops do not perform as advertised.

Filipino farmers hold demonstrations at Monsanto's offices in Mindanao, joined by farmers' unions from Indonesia, Thailand, Japan and Korea.

Novartis and AstraZeneca merge their agrochemical divisions to form Syngenta, now the world's largest GM crop developer.

ember 2000► Canteen at Monsanto's UK headquarters bans GM ingredients.

January 2001►1,200 Brazilian farmers storm and occupy a Monsanto research station.

The US is accused of buying up GM crops and sending it as food aid to Africa and elsewhere.

May 2001► Under pressure from New Labour, the GM crop trial which threatened Henry Doubleday Research Association Organic Garden, situated in the eighth most marginal seat, is abandoned in the election build-up.

A THREAD
TO KILL
MILLIONS
IS ILLEGAL
TRIDENT PLOUGHSHARES
2000
CND ☮ CND

Police arrest a protester blockading the Faslane nuclear submarine base in Scotland 2001.

War
Lindsey German

● ● ● ● ● ● ● ● ● ● ● ● ● ● ● ● ● ● ● ●

The bombs which dropped on Hiroshima and Nagasaki in 1945 marked the beginning of a nuclear age of mass destruction. It was now impossible to believe that war could be kept apart from civilian life. As the bombing of Guernica, Coventry, London, Hamburg and Dresden had already shown, aerial bombardment was central to war. The search was on for bigger and better weapons of death. But these actions also triggered a movement against the weapons and the governments that used them.

The Campaign for Nuclear Disarmament (CND) was launched in 1958 against a background of proposed H-bomb testing in Britain. Its first march at Aldermaston atomic research centre near Reading, an establishment connected to the manufacture of the bomb, took place that Easter and from then became a celebrated annual event. They were some of the best known protests and a prelude to the great movements for equality of the 1960s. One of the leading organisers, Peggy Duff, wrote of the protesters:

> They were just the sort of people who marched, most of them young, wearing anoraks and sandals, a few with bare feet, a few with funny hats... Yet it was...these people who marched, and planned the marches, who booked the halls for the meetings, flyposted the posters, gave out the leaflets, sold the pamphlets, wrote letters to the local press and every year organised the contingent to the Aldermaston

marches—these were the people who created a fever of opinion which for a time the orthodox political leaders could not stay. They were the ban-the-bombers.'

In May 2001 I spoke at a Globalise Resistance conference in Oxford on weapons and war. On the platform were women who had just come from protest at Aldermaston the previous weekend, where the police had arrested around 50.² The demonstration was organised by Trident Plough- shares, campaigners against Trident missiles and the Fas- lane nuclear submarine base in Scotland.

> **This new generation comes to the movement on the wave of post-Seattle anti-capitalism—it is part of a more general protest against capitalism itself**

These women were vet- eran peace campaigners, inv- olved in CND and the Green- ham Common women's peace camp in the early 1980s. They were enthused by the involvement of young people at Aldermaston and saw it as a sign of the revival of the movement. That revival is cer- tainly there: protests ranging from the Faslane blockades to the CND demonstration in Whitehall at Easter 2001 against US propos- als for National Missile Defence all feature young people wanting to stop militarism and war. Unlike the previous big movements against nuclear weapons, this new generation comes to the movement on the wave of post-Seattle anti-capitalism. So this movement has not only the potential to grow much bigger—it is part of a more general protest against capitalism itself.

Lost in space

There are many issues which have galvanised this new movement, but perhaps its greatest recruiter has been US president George Bush. There are many reasons to be scared of Bush: his escalation of the bombing of Iraq immediately after his inauguration, his intimate relationship with the big oil corporations, his hawkish attitude to the Palestinian question. But most scary are his plans for Ballistic Missile Defence (BMD), a revival of the Reagan 'Star Wars' plan of the 1980s. Reagan and his advisors wanted an anti ballistic missile (ABM) shield which would be partially based in space. Their plans were abandoned for a number of reasons, but have now led to BMD, a radar controlled ABM system which can shoot down long-range missiles. Bush's motivation is clear: the US is protecting itself against a series of 'rogue states' that threaten 'world peace'. In a recent speech he claimed that 'today's most urgent threat' stems from 'a small number of missiles' in the hands of 'some of the world's least responsible states' for whom 'terror and blackmail are a way of life'.[3]

Many could be forgiven for thinking that the greatest threat to world peace lies in the world's biggest military power and that the threat from these 'rogue states' is greatly exaggerated. Attack on the US by missiles armed with chemical, biological or nuclear weapons by a small country such as Iraq is closer to Hollywood fantasy than to reality. Two writers from the Brookings Institution, James Lindsay and Michael O'Hanlon, make this point: 'The image of the US amid a sea of hostile countries armed with missiles is alarming. But it is not one that describes the world we live in or are likely to live in during the next decade'.[4]

Few countries with missiles have the ability to attack the US. Apart from the big nuclear powers of the US, Britain, China, France and Russia, six others have missiles with ranges up to 3,420 miles. Of these, Israel and Saudi Arabia are described as 'close security partners', India and Pakistan are friendly to the US, so the only two remaining are Iran and North Korea.

BMD, far from making the world a safer place, is making it more dangerous and unstable

Although US embassies and troops have been attacked by hostile states in recent years, this has always been done by groups such as suicide bombers. No state has directly attacked the US and these states would find it very difficult to do so.

A Star Wars system would be banned under the present ABM treaty signed by the US and the Soviet Union in 1972. It is argued that if a state has an ABM shield as well as nuclear weapons then it can attack without fear of retaliation. The shield actually can make nuclear war more likely. Britain will be on the front-line, since any system will be partly sited here at Menwith Hill and Fylingdales. US intentions have not yet been fully spelt out. The shield is meant to be thin, to intercept 'rogue state' missiles, rather than thick, which would intercept a major missile attack from Russia. But once the system is in place it would be relatively simple to increase the number of interceptors to create a thick shield. It is hardly surprising that Russia and China see these developments as a threat and are considering responding by building more missiles in the case of China and by putting multiple warheads on single warheaded Topol-M intercontinental missiles. BMD, far from making the world a safer place, is making it more dangerous and unstable. As if it were not far too dangerous and unstable already.[5]

Double standards

Much of that instability has come from Western interventions over the past decade. It was commonly assumed that with the collapse of the Eastern bloc and the end of the Cold War swords really could be turned into ploughshares, and that the wealth of the world would no longer need to be poured into weapons spending.

The increased globalisation of capital has had the opposite effect. The US-led extension of the market to every part of the globe and the adoption of neo-liberal policies, often imposed by the International Monetary Fund (IMF) in the form of structural adjustment programmes, was accompanied by a greater desire to intervene in parts of the world which had previously been regarded as off-limits during the old superpower carve-up (as in the case of Yugoslavia) or in regimes which had been erstwhile allies (as in the case of Iraq.) The 'balance of terror'—a deadly equilibrium between the two major powers—was replaced by intervention on a limited regional basis in order to impose the West's political and economic agenda and to ensure that like-minded states elsewhere in the world thought twice before bucking the system in the New World Order. The buzzwords of the 1990s became 'humanitarian intervention', organised by the 'international community' against a series of 'rogue states' who had stepped out of line. Any combination of these phrases used by Western politicians, media and commentators should be enough to strike fear into the heart, because they signify the war without end which is now a feature of large parts of the

It would be hard to argue that the situation of the ordinary people of these regions has been helped by the 'humanitarian' wars which the Western powers have launched world. It is surely more than coincidental that the two areas of direct intervention by the Western powers have become unstable in the past decade and remain probably the two major flashpoints for further conflict.

Interventions in the Balkans and the Middle East have been justified in terms of concern to remove dictators and to protect those who are suffering at their hands. The Gulf War in 1991 was ostensibly in defence of the population of Kuwait, the desert state invaded by Saddam Hussein's Iraq in 1991. The successive Balkan wars, culminating in the bombing of Serbia in 1999, were supposedly to stop ethnic cleansing and defeat Slobodan Milosevic's dictatorship. Yet in both cases these same Western powers had worked with the leaders whom they now reviled. Hussein was a Western ally against Iran during the First Gulf War and was only turned against when he began to challenge Western interests.

As recently as 1995 Milosevic was drinking whisky with Western negotiators following the Dayton agreement, which left the whole question of Kosovo in Milosevic's hands. And there were double standards involved with the victims of aggression. The 'liberation of Kuwait' was billed in the Western press as a fight for democracy, but Kuwait is probably one of the least democratic states in the world, run as a one-family state by the al-Sabah family. While ethnic cleansing of Kosovan Albanians by Serbs was condemned, barely a word was said in condemnation of the ethnic cleansing of 200,000 Serbs from the Krajina region of Croatia following NATO bombing which gave Croatia a decisive advantage in the 1995 war.

Double standards were also in evidence elsewhere. Iraq was condemned for repressing groups within its borders, notably the Kurds and the Marsh Arabs. But NATO member and close Western ally Turkey has a terrible record of repressing Kurds within its borders. Milosevic is condemned as a war criminal but Israeli prime minister Ariel Sharon has a far worse record, having been directly responsible for atrocities such as massacres at the Sabra and Shatila refugee camps.

It would be hard to argue that the situation of the ordinary people of these regions has been helped by the 'humanitarian' wars which the Western powers have launched. In Iraq Western sanctions have resulted in the deaths of half a million children, the impoverishment of a whole population, and the shortage of basic medicines and educational materials including pencils which contain lead! Saddam Hussein remains intact, and indeed has a standing in other parts of the Middle East because he has been seen as an opponent of the West. His decision to send money to the families of those Palestinians killed by Israel in the intifada has only enhanced this view. Meanwhile bombing of Iraq continues on a regular basis, carried out by US and British bombers with little regard for the consequences.

> **'Capitalism, whatever its diverse national forms, cannot escape the principal responsibility for societies whose economies and cultures have engaged in armed conflicts throughout this century'**
> —Gabriel Kolko

The Balkans is now composed of a number of partitioned or ethnically-cleansed states. Two of them—Bosnia and Kosovo—are effective protectorates of the West, run by the Western powers. The other states are increasingly dependent on Western aid and grants in order to survive and are forced to accept Western political agendas if they are to do so. A list of the problems which still remain indicate the failure of intervention: ethnic cleansing and discrimination are rife; the region is a centre for arms and drugs dealing, and prostitution, especially in Kosovo; the refugee problem in the former Yugoslavia is the worst in Europe; Bosnia and Kosovo are full of foreign troops who seem incapable of dealing with ethnic cleansing (by ethnic Albanians against Serbs in Kosovo, for example); and as in Iraq, the land is poisoned by the weapons used in the bombing and the war against Serbia.

And war looms again. Macedonia is on the edge of civil war as a direct result of the settlement in Kosovo, which gave the Kosovo

Liberation Army hopes of territorial expansion to a 'Greater Albania', while at the same time solving none of the problems of the region. Such a war could involve Bulgaria, Greece and even Turkey in a grisly replay of the Balkan Wars at the beginning of the last century which led directly to the First World War.

Capitalism and war

We live in a dangerous world. There are more wars, the wars are more deadly in terms of the weapons deployed, and they are more likely to involve civilians as casualties, than at any time in human history. The shadow of war is inescapable: all the major countries devote a sizeable part of their revenues from tax to the maintenance of armies, navies and air forces, to the development of weapons of destruction, and to the sale and promotion of these 'military services' around the world.

It is stretching credulity to imagine that this increasing militarism is unconnected with an increasingly bloody capitalism itself. A global system which regards the whole world as its resource for both labour and raw materials, and which wants to protect existing markets and extend new ones into sometimes 'unstable' areas, has every need of sophisticated weapons and armies which can do its bidding. The idea that you can't have McDonald's without McDonnell Douglas is not just a cultural choice but reflects a relationship at the heart of US capitalism—trade and weapons travel hand in hand. This relationship is not new. The British Empire was built on this basis. The First World War was about economic and colonial rivalry between the great powers. Although its participants regarded the Second World War as primarily a war against fascism, it too had at its centre economic rivalry over control of the world's resources such as oil. Marshall Aid—US investment to rebuild Europe after the war—came at an economic, military and political price.

When you say capitalism you say war. 'Capitalism, whatever its diverse national forms, cannot escape the principal responsibility for societies whose economies and cultures have engaged in armed conflicts throughout this century', wrote Gabriel Kolko in *Century of War*. He went on to explain why this was so:

There is no inherent rationality in the whole panoply of capitalist doctrines but only a fiercely selfish devotion to the protection and growth of economic interests, which operates whether or not primitive, chauvinist concepts also help it to galvanise wars... The egotism and avarice its ideology sanctifies creates an ideal setting for the development of values and aspirations conducive to international expansion and, ultimately, conflict.[6]

The favoured status of the euphemistically named 'defence' industries and the ministries which protect them is instructive. In Britain, whereas ministers and civil servants in departments such as health or education see their jobs as cutting back resources and attacking 'vested interests' (the people who know most about running the industry), there are very different priorities where the military and weapons are concerned. 'Defence' costs the British public £22 billion a year and uses the skills of 400,000 in industry whose talents could be put to better use. The Ministry of Defence controlled the activities of 214,000 service personnel and 119,000 civilians in 1998. It is estimated that the Eurofighter will cost every man woman and child in Britain £350.[7]

The humanitarian motives with which our rulers now justify their actions hide the stark truth: economic interests are paramount

Public money does not just go to the armed forces but is used to sustain and underwrite private companies which deal in arms. Take the example of the Export Credit Guarantee Department (ECGD). This department, attached to the Department of Trade and Industry, was originally to allow extended credit to poor countries so that they could buy British goods. As Tim Webb reports, 'The share of its budget devoted to arms exports rose from less than 10 percent in 1980-81 to 48 percent in 1993-94.' Much of the guaranteed credit (if anything goes wrong with the arms exports the ECGD—ie public money—picks up the bill) goes to some of the most repressive regimes in the world. The Suharto dictatorship in Indonesia was a major recipient of publicly underwritten defence exports. Another was Saudi Arabia.[8] Most of these regimes wanted weapons at least in part to repress their indigenous populations rather than fight conventional wars. British governments and manufacturers have been only too happy to supply them. Instead of aid to avert famine, hunger or poverty in the poorest countries, their governments have been aided and abetted in arming themselves—often against the very people whose hunger or poverty causes them to rebel.

Protest for peace

Wars create protest and resistance. There is a long history of opposing war, initially by small groups of people but then by much larger numbers as the full horror of its effects becomes apparent. The connections between war and globalisation are stark. Despite the claim by then director general of the World Trade Organisation Renato Ruggiero in 1996 that the choices facing us are 'globalisation or war', the drive to competition on a world scale makes war more likely. Wars rage around the globe. There is no thought for the soldiers who fight in these wars or for the civilians increasingly on the receiving end. Soldiers from the Gulf War suffer as a result of the weapons used: 80,000 US veterans and 3,000 in Britain have Gulf War syndrome, believed to have been caused by the use of depleted uranium in weapons. Iraq has seen a sharp increase in cancers since the war in 1991, and up to a quarter of a million Iraqis have been affected. In Bosnia, bombed using depleted uranium weapons in 1995, cancer rates have also shot up, and a number of European soldiers who served there have died of cancer.[9]

The humanitarian motives with which our rulers now justify their actions hide the stark truth: economic interests are paramount. Imperialism remains a central feature of our world and one which is intimately connected with globalisation. Oil in the Middle East explains the Western presence there. The war in the Balkans involved the eastward expansion of NATO and crucially the development of oil pipelines from the Caspian Sea to the Mediterranean through the region. This theory was derided at the time, but there is now a projected pipeline running from Bulgaria to Albania through...Macedonia![10]

It is a straightforward case: if you are against global capitalism then you have to oppose the wars and militarism it creates. The direct action of the movement is in a long tradition of anti-war and peace protests. The demonstrations at Faslane, Aldermaston, Fylingdales and Menwith Hill can all point to a new movement. But if the movement is to be successful it has to link to the wider concerns of the anti-capitalist movement—about debt, the environment, privatisation and welfare. In this way it can become a genuinely mass movement able to confront the masters of war.

Lindsey German is the editor of *Socialist Review*, the author of *Sex, Class and Socialism*, and the editor of *The Balkans, Nationalism and Imperialism*. She was a member of the Committee For Peace in the Balkans.
sr@swp.org.uk

: Notes

1   Peggy Duff quoted in Jill Liddington,
     The Long Road to Greenham (London
     1989), p189.
2   See *Socialist Review* 253, June 2001.
3   *Financial Times*, 9 May 2001.
4   *Financial Times*, 9 May 2001.
5   Much of the information in this section
     comes from CND.
6   Gabriel Kolko, *Century of War* (New
     York, 1994), p474.
7   Figures from Tim Webb, *The Armour-
     Plated Ostrich* (1998), pp13-15.
8   Ibid, p107-108.
9   Dragan Plavsic, 'The Stuff of
     Nightmares', *Socialist Review* 249,
     February 2001.
10   For this debate see John Rees, 'Nato
     and the New Imperialism' in *The
     Balkans, Nationalism and Imperialism*
     (London, 1999), p173. See also
     Dragan Plavsic, 'Wars without End',
     Socialist Review 251, April 2001.

: Sites

▶ **www.gn.apc.org/tp2001**
  Trident Ploughshares is a non-violent,
  direct action organisation in the
  nuclear disarmament movement.
▶ **www.caat.org.uk**
  Campaign Against the Arms Trade.
▶ **www.cadu.org.uk**
  Campaign Against Depleted Uranium.
▶ **www.cnduk.org**
  Campaign for Nuclear Disarmament.
▶ **www.faslanepeacecamp.org**
  Faslane Peace Camp has been
  opposing nuclear weapons at this site
  in Scotland since 1982.
▶ **www.viwuk.freeserve.co.uk**
  Voices in the Wilderness breaks the
  economic sanctions on Iraq by hand
  delivering supplies.

A Kosovan refugee awaiting dispersal in Dover, England, holds photographs of his fam~~ily~~ who were killed in a grenade attack, and his brother who is in prison.

Immigration
Teresa Hayter

● ● ● ● ● ● ● ● ● ● ● ● ● ● ● ● ● ● ●

The governments of the rich industrialised countries and their agencies the World Bank, the International Monetary Fund (IMF) and the World Trade Organisation (WTO) are trying to open markets throughout the world, and especially in the Third World, so that multinational corporations and private banks can profit from taking over public services and industries and exploiting natural resources. They want to remove all restrictions on the movement of goods and capital, even when these exist to protect the interests of ordinary people.

At the same time they are imposing ever harsher and more brutal restrictions on the movement of people (unless they are white, or exceptionally rich). And also at the same time they are demanding policies which create unemployment and poverty and which are at least partly responsible for the wars and political repression from which people flee.

Imperialism and migration

People have migrated over thousands of years. The current theory is that humans originated in east Africa. If this is so then we, white racists and the rest of us, are all descended from east Africans.

When European imperialism later expanded into the rest of the world, the need for labour became a preoccupation for mine and plantation owners and then industrial capitalists. Migration became the object of large scale coercion: first to cause it to happen, and then to stop it. The imperialists obtained labour by force, first through transporting between 10 and 20 million African slaves to work in the mines and plantations of the Americas, then through various forms of indentured labour in which over 30 million Indians and Chinese were more or less coerced to migrate. Africans and Indians were also forced, through tax demands and sometimes physically, to work for European colonisers.

> **People need to migrate for two main reasons: first to improve their economic situation, and second to escape from wars and persecution—imperialism bears much responsibility for both needs**

In the 20th century colonial subjects fought and laboured for Europeans in Europe, especially during the European wars. After the Second World War some of them returned voluntarily to Europe to meet labour demand, after the countries they were living in (and sometimes had been forcibly transported to) had been blighted by imperialism. Others were recruited under various 'guest worker' schemes. This 'return migration', from colonies and former colonies to the metropolitan powers, amounted to about 35 million people, a little more than half the number of Europeans who migrated in the other direction.

So-called globalisation, or latter-day imperialism, has created or helped to create new pressures to migrate. But the situation has changed. The governments of the rich countries, rather than forcing people to migrate against their will, are now intent on stopping them migrating when they wish to. Since the beginning of the 1970s legal migration for work in Europe has virtually ceased, except for a few people whose skills are highly desired or who have a large amount of money. Even visiting relatives has become hard. Seeking asylum in theory remains a right, but governments try to stop people exercising this right.

People need to migrate for two main reasons: first to improve their economic situation, and second to escape from wars and persecution. Imperialism bears much responsibility for both needs. It has created extreme polarisation of wealth internationally. When European expansion began in the 16th century the levels of prosperity and technical development they encountered in what is now the Third World were often more advanced than what then existed in Europe. The Europeans plundered the Third World, destroyed industries, and reduced much of it to levels of poverty and malnutrition which had not previously existed.

The process continues. The major capitalist powers are now doing similar things to Eastern Europe and the former Soviet Union. Having established their industrial domination through centuries of force and protection, they try to stop Third World and other countries protecting their own industries and agriculture and demand free access to their markets and resources. Governments and private banks first pushed Third World and East European governments into borrowing from them in the 1970s, and then, when in response to their own capitalist crisis they raised interest rates to exhorbitant levels, they forced governments to make deep cuts in spending and sell off public services and industries at cut rates to multinationals so as to extract debt servicing at these new crippling rates.

The development of global capitalism has created both opportunities and needs. Multinationals which set up low cost industries in Third World countries recruit people from rural areas, many of them women. The intense exploitation of work in export processing industries wears people out, but they often cannot return to rural areas. For some the only alternative is to migrate further, to low-paid jobs in agriculture and in the service sectors of the rich countries. These are often abundant and shunned by the natives of those countries. Because the workers have no legal immigration status employers exploit them savagely. Families sometimes raise the money for their members to migrate; the migrants then save money from their low wages to support parents and siblings at home. These 'remittances' make a small dent in international inequality. They are bigger than official foreign aid, and superior to it because they do not have to be repaid and come without conditions.

The second main reason for migration is to escape from wars

and repression. The rich countries have some responsibility for these too. When they exploit the resources of Third World countries, the profits go abroad and to small elites within these countries. The discovery of new sources of oil or diamonds becomes a curse, leading to war.

The West also supports and sells arms to right wing repressive regimes. If these are overthrown by popular movements, it intervenes to crush them, directly or through financing and arming surrogates. It sells arms to participants in wars and conflicts, often financing these sales through official loans.

The impoverishment of Third World countries, especially through the extraction of debt servicing, may exacerbate divisions and the pressures of nationalism. Most of the recent increase in refugees coming to Europe, for example, is from Yugoslavia. The West's hostility to Communism gave rise to offers of loans by its agencies the World Bank and the IMF on condition the government embarked on privatisation. When the debt crisis began, they demanded more privatisation and cuts to enable debt servicing, causing severe poverty and unemployment. They also forced the federal government to cut transfers to the regions, and so contributed to anti-federal nationalism, the break-up of Yugoslavia and war.

Immigration controls are a 20th century phenomenon

Immigration controls were first introduced in Europe at the beginning of the 20th century. In Britain their introduction followed agitation against Jewish refugees by Tory MPs with links to the far right, including Major Evans-Gordon MP, one of the founders of the British Brothers League. Like others before and after him, he accused immigrants of importing disease, crime, overcrowding, 'sweating' and threatening 'a storm'—slurs which have been used against Jews, Flemish, Lombards, Huguenots, Irish, Caribbeans, Asians, Roma and most new immigrants. In 1905 the first Aliens Act was passed, allowing the new Immigration Service to refuse entry. The right of asylum remained, but did not stop the refusal of many thousands of Jewish refugees in the 1930s, who were driven back to the concentration camps.

Commonwealth citizens had free entry until the first Commonwealth Immigrants Act in 1962. Throughout the 1950s and early 1960s mainstream politicians of all parties denounced any notion of controls on Commonwealth citizens. But openly racist organisations such as the Birmingham Immigration Control Association and the Southall Residents Association agitated for controls. In private the Conservatives were trying to devise ways of excluding black Commonwealth citizens while admitting white ones. Official reports found no reason for excluding black Commonwealth citizens apart from their supposed 'non-assimilability'; immigrants were needed for the expansion of the economy, and were not prone to either disease or crime.

Far from appeasing the racists, immigration controls feed and legitimate racism

Eventually the 1962 act made admission conditional on the possession of job vouchers. These did discriminate, but between skilled and unskilled workers; the government hoped the former would be white. The Irish, whose labour was needed, were exempted from controls. The pretence that immigration did not discriminate on the grounds of race was later abandoned. Job vouchers were granted in diminishing numbers and abolished in 1971. They were replaced by temporary work permits for certain categories of skills, and free admission for 'patrials' (mainly white Commonweath citizens with a British parent or grandparent) and European Union citizens.

The right of refugees to seek asylum is currently embodied in the 1951 United Nations Geneva Convention. But governments retain the sole right to decide whether or not to grant it. Rates of acceptance of asylum claims in Europe declined from nearly half in 1984 to less than 10 percent in the 1990s. Some 76,000 people applied for asylum in Britain in 2000, mainly from Yugoslavia, Iraq, Iran, Afghanistan, Somalia, Sri Lanka, the former USSR, China and Turkey. The numbers claiming asylum are roughly similar to the numbers of European Union citizens and patrials entering Britain to work.

The British government now proposes that European

governments should finance reception camps in countries neighbouring the refugees', from whom governments would select a favoured few for asylum in Europe. Under his proposals, the Geneva Convention would be revised so that any refugees who still attempted to exercise their right to enter Europe to apply for asylum could be 'promptly' returned to these camps.

Immigration controls are explicable only by racism

Immigration controls were introduced as a result of racist agitation by the far right. Far from appeasing the racists, they led to demands for more. They feed and legitimate racism. Much the same applies to the current attempts to stop refugees coming here, and in particular the outrageously false claims that most of them are 'bogus', only here to scrounge off the state.

In Britain the Labour government is currently engaged in a shameful competition with the Tories to prove who is 'toughest' on asylum seekers and other migrants. When the Tories attack Labour for not doing enough to deter asylum seekers, Labour's response is to say it has done a lot and will do more. In the process it has done as much as, or more than, the Tories and the media to incite racism. It has stigmatised, pauperised and criminalised refugees and other migrants. Even the police report that each time politicians make speeches about 'bogus' or 'abusive' asylum seekers, there is a significant increase in racist attacks on people who look or sound foreign.

Immigration controls, suffering and human rights abuses

By far the strongest reason for opposing immigration controls is that they impose harsh suffering on migrants and refugees in the hope of deterring others. They undermine a long list of human rights: the right not to be subjected to inhuman and degrading treatment, the right not to be tortured, the right not to be arbitrarily arrested and imprisoned, the right to a fair trial by a properly constituted court, the right to family life, the right to seek work where it is available. Oddly and illogically, they do not contravene the 1948 Universal Declaration of Human Rights. This states that people should have free movement within the borders of their own countries and should be allowed to leave any country, including their own. It says nothing about the right to enter another one, unless it is to claim (but not necessarily obtain) asylum from persecution.

To deter people from coming to Britain for refuge or perhaps for work, the state currently locks up over 1,500 asylum seekers at any one time, including many who claim asylum at ports and airports and later get refugee status. It does this on the say-so of junior immigration officials, with no trial, no time limits and no discernible criteria, apart from filling spaces in detention centres and prisons. These have more than doubled since Labour took office. Labour plans to increase them to 4,000 by 2002. Other asylum seekers are freed and given 'temporary admission' but not allowed to work for at least six months. They must survive on less than the minimum considered necessary for the natives. This means food vouchers spendable only at certain supermarkets, and dispersal often to substandard accommodation in areas of high unemployment, where they become targets for racist attack, at a cost to the government 50 percent greater than the cost of ordinary benefits, let alone allowing asylum seekers to work.

Governments impose visa requirements on 'refugee producing' countries and so make it possible to escape only on false documents or clandestinely, and then, by setting up checks at airports abroad, make even travel on false documents increasingly hard, so that people suffer and die in lorry containers, the holds of ships and even the undercarriages of aeroplanes. They then have the gall to lament this suffering, and the £7 billion profits made by 'criminal networks' they have themselves created. They build razor wire fences on frontiers and multiply their surveillance and detection techniques. They extend surveillance to the interior of countries, where they give powers of search and arrest to immigration officials.

In Britain all this costs at least £800 million a year, and possibly much more. The democratic and human rights of the rest of us are threatened too, in what some have called a creeping fascisisation of society.

Immigration is in the self-interest of the current inhabitants of the rich countries

If immigration controls preserved the privileges of a rich white minority they would still be indefensible, much as apartheid in South Africa, with which they have many parallels, was. But, as it happens, controls are probably not in the economic self-interest of either capitalists or the working class in the rich countries. Migrants' work was needed in the post Second World War expansion, and will be so again as West European populations decline and age. Without migrants some industries would close or be relocated abroad, with a knock-on effect on other jobs. Contrary to prejudice, the effect of immigrants on the jobs and conditions of the natives is, if anything, positive. After the Second World War there was net emigration from Britain, and net immigration to France and Germany; wages are higher in the latter.

> The democratic and human rights of the rest of us are threatened too, in what some have called a creeping fascisisation of society

A United Nations Population Division report published in 2000 estimates that in Western Europe alone 13.5 million net immigrants per year would be needed over the next 50 years merely to counter the effects of ageing and declining populations. European governments' response is to 'cherry-pick' refugees and migrants whose skills they desire (even though economists point out that there is a need for unskilled as well as skilled labour), but to crack down ever more harshly on refugees and migrants who try to enter Europe without work permits. This is a blatantly cynical manifestation of national self-interest, which also exposes migrants to extreme exploitation.

Similarly with the effects of migration on public expenditure. Because migrants are self-selected as young fit adults, rich countries obtain their labour without paying education and health costs. If, eventually, migrants settle with their families, their cost to welfare services is no more than other workers'. A Home Office report published in January 2001 estimated that the 'foreign-born population' made a net contribution to public finances in 1998-99 of £2.6

billion. The supposed 'burden' imposed by asylum seekers derives almost entirely from the fact that they are not allowed to work.

Free movement and its possible consequences

Immigration controls have a smaller effect on the number of people migrating and settling than is usually supposed. Sooner or later, they will probably be abandoned as unworkable. The escalating repression involved in the attempt to keep foreigners out has not led to a decline in the numbers claiming asylum. And, after months or years of suffering and cruel uncertainty, the great majority of those whose asylum claims governments reject are not deported.

Until the threat of immigration controls, migration to Britain correlated with job vacancies. Most immigrants came in the 18 month period before the 1962 act. The act ended the possibility for young men to come for short periods, return, and be replaced by younger family members, and forced them to settle in Britain with their families. In a survey of Sri Lankan refugees, the vast majority said they would like to go home if they could be sure of being able to return if the situation in Sri Lanka worsened again. Government-created 'people traffickers' sometimes actively recruit migrants. People are then trapped in the countries they have migrated to. If they were free to come and go, they would probably do so.

People who are reduced to extreme poverty by imperialism cannot migrate. It is a myth to say that free migration would lead to the rich countries being overwhelmed by the impoverished masses of the world. Most people do not wish to uproot themselves from their families, friends and culture. Those who migrate are, and always will be, exceptionally enterprising, probably skilled, and with access to money. They come because there are jobs or because they have a desperate need to flee.

If governments object to migration they should recognise their own part in causing it. They should stop using the World Bank and the IMF to enforce privatisation and to extract payments on an unjust debt. They should stop propping up right wing repressive regimes. They should not supply arms to them or to anyone else.

In an ideal world the current situation would be reversed. Hospitals, schools, industries, natural resources, and the land would be owned by ordinary people and planned and democratically controlled by them so that they meet needs, end poverty and pollution, and create more equality, rather than profits for unaccountable big business. In such a world no one would be forced to migrate, but everyone would be free to do so if they wished.

Opening borders could make the world a more harmonious and peaceful and less racist place, and make possible greater democracy and greater cooperation between people to build a better society.

Teresa Hayter is the author of *Open Borders: The Case Against Immigration Controls* (Pluto Press, 2000).

: Sites

- ► **www.anl.org.uk**
  The Anti Nazi League is a broad based, mass organisation with the single aim of stopping the BNP, the NF and other Nazi organisations from growing.

- ► **www.asylumaid.org.uk**
  Asylum Aid is a charity which provides free legal advice and representation to refugees and asylum seekers and campaigns for their fair treatment.

- ► **www.barbedwirebritain.org.uk**
  Barbed Wire Britain's Network to End Refugee and Migrant Detention links up active campaigns against detention sites throughout the country.

- ► **www.carf.demon.co.uk**
  The Campaign Against Racism and Fascism has a magazine and webzine which covers the criminalisation and mistreatment of asylum seekers.

- ► **www.defend-asylum.org**
  The Committee to Defend Asylum seekers campaigns against government scapegoating of asylum seekers.

- ► **www.ncadc.org.uk**
  The National Coalition of Anti-Deportation Campaigns has a site with useful facts, figures and campaign information.

- ► **www.refugeecouncil.org.uk**
  The Refugee Council is the largest organisation in the UK working with asylum seekers and refugees, giving advice, campaigning, lobbying and researching.

- ► **www.statewatch.org**
  Statewatch encourages critical investigation into the role of the state and civil liberties.

- ► **www.unhcr.ch**
  The United Nations High Commission for Refugees is a good source of statistics.

REGIONS

'Because I want peace
and not war
because I don't want to see
hungry children
squalid women
men whose tongues
are silenced
I have to keep on fighting
Because there are clandestine
cemeteries
and Squadrons of Death
drug-crazed killers
who torture
who maim
who assassinate
I want to keep on fighting

Because there are liberated
territories
where people
learn how to read
and the sick are cured
and the fruits of the soil
belong to all
I have to keep on fighting.
Because I want peace
and not war.'

Salvadorean-born poet,
Claribel Alegria,
quoted in Duncan Green's
'Faces of Latin America'

Holding a Molotov Cocktail made from a Pepsi-Cola bottle, a lone protester
makes a stand against riot police. Water privatisation struggle, Bolivia 2000.

Latin America
Mike Gonzalez

● ● ● ● ● ● ● ● ● ● ● ● ● ● ● ● ● ● ●

Two dates and two sets of initials define the period in this part of the world: NAFTA 1994 and FTAA 2001. Declared on 1 January 1994, the North American Free Trade Area (NAFTA) was the first step in the incorporation of the region into the global economy. The presidents of the US, Canada and Mexico announced on that day the elimination of all barriers to the free movement of capital (but not, of course, of workers). The final stage of the process, the creation of the Free Trade Area of the Americas (FTAA), was announced in April 2001 in Quebec City.

Preparing the ground

The ground in Latin America had been prepared long before; the structural adjustment programmes, imposed in the 1980s by the International Monetary Fund (IMF) and the World Bank as a condition of their loans, concealed behind the euphemism a strategy of wholesale privatisation of publicly owned assets, the removal of all subsidies (because they inhibited the free market) and the opening of both capital and property markets to external involvement. The consequence (fully intended) was a generalised collapse in living standards, structural unemployment and the concentration of power and wealth. The victims of the process were workers in industry and services, agricultural labourers, peasant farmers and small business, as well as students, the urban poor and the unemployed who might previously have been eligible for some form of state support.

Chiapas: first shoots of resistance

If the representatives of global capital anticipated a free run, they were proved dramatically wrong on the very day that NAFTA's launch was announced. In Chiapas, in southern Mexico, the armed occupation of the state capital, San Cristóbal de las Casas, by the Ejército Zapatista de Liberación Nacional (EZLN—Zapatista National Liberation Army), announced that there would be resistance to globalisation.

Its first communication with the world, the First Declaration of the Lacandón Forest, announced the rising of the oppressed, and provided the anti-capitalist movement with a symbolic focus and a core slogan: Ya Basta! (Enough is enough). The Zapatistas represented the joint struggle of over 30 indigenous communities of southern Mexico whose first declaration listed their repeated expulsion from communal lands as agribusiness relentlessly expanded its operations together with a history of ethnic and cultural oppression.

If the representatives of global capital anticipated a free run, they were proved dramatically wrong on the very day that NAFTA's launch was announced

Their spokesperson Subcomandante Marcos, a ski-masked revolutionary of non-indigenous origin, entered into a permanent dialogue with the world through the internet, while at the same time the Mexican army initiated a double process of prolonged peace negotiation combined with a tightening military encirclement which put the Zapatista communities under a permanent siege involving up to 60,000 Mexican military personnel.

The armed rising lasted some 12 days; thereafter the EZLN continued its dialogue with the world from an enforced physical isolation.

In March 2001 the Zapatistas marched to the capital, Mexico City, with three demands for new president Vicente Fox—an end to the military presence in Chiapas, the release of Zapatista prisoners, and the implementation of the San Andres Accords concerning rights for indigenous communities. It is not yet clear whether agreement to all three demands will in fact materialise.

A struggle grows and spreads

While Chiapas has come to symbolise the growing anti-capitalist resistance in the region, the level of struggle and resistance has developed further and combined far larger forces elsewhere in Latin America. The object of their protest and resistance, however, has been the same enemy, albeit one that works through different agencies—the capitalist economy, seeking to impose its own general laws on the whole region, whatever the social cost.

In Bolivia, for example, the Banzer government was a willing servant of global imperatives, which included the privatisation of public resources. The struggle against the attempt to privatise water brought together a range of affected sectors in an extraordinary 400-mile protest march from Cochabamba to La Paz in April 2001. It included farm workers, small traders, small farmers, and indigenous organisations, as well as trade unionists. And despite ferocious police repression the coalition convened a Popular Assembly to organise continuing and escalating protests for May and beyond. (For more on this issue see Barry Coates's discussion of GATS and Bolivia earlier in this volume.)

Ecuador has been at the forefront of the struggle against globalisation—expressed as the 'dollarisation'—which is increasingly emerging as the key instrument of regional capitalist integration. In early 1999 the attempt by the government of Jamil Mahuad to impose the policy, with its accompanying massive price rises, rationalisation of production and elimination of subsidies, provoked a massive response led by the indigenous organisation CONAIE (Confederación Nacional Indígena del Ecuador) jointly with the United Workers Front and a number of other organisations. Agitation and protest continued through the year until, despite his last minute reversals of policy on fuel price rises, Mahuad was forced out of power by a mass insurrection in January 2000. For a brief period, power clearly lay with the mass movement that had brought the economy to a standstill and held power in the streets of Quito and expressed in a National Popular Assembly. In the end, however, vice-president Guillermo Noboa in conjunction with the military took power; despite the inclusion of a leader of CONAIE in the new government, it was clear that Noboa's priorities differed little from his predecessors.

Noboa's attempt to reimpose dollarisation met once again with a mass response culminating in a national strike called for 7 February 2001. The government of Ecuador signed an agreement with the mass organisations, releasing Antonio Vargas, the detained leader of CONAIE, undertaking not to implement the policies imposed by the IMF and establishing Ecuador's refusal to become involved in the Plan Colombia (see below). The pressures are mounting, however, and it can be assumed that new struggles will erupt before 2001 reaches its end. It is worth noting that El Salvador accepted dollarisation in January 2001, and that advisors to President Bush are advocating accelerated dollarisation as the favoured economic instrument of US economic policy in the area.

Where the arrow points

Perhaps the shape of things to come is already visible in Argentina, where structural adjustment programmes implemented by the De La Rua government have produced runaway inflation and unemployment at levels unknown in the country for many years. In March 2001 the announcement of ferocious austerity measures, including education cuts and the abolition of subsidies on gas and electricity, produced an unprecedented strike wave accompanied by highway blockades, street occupations and public demonstrations throughout the country by students and pensioners as well as organised workers. In April confrontations between police and demonstrators produced 30 seriously wounded people and 50 arrests.

Brazil has produced some extraordinary examples of mass organisation in the last 20 years. In the late 1970s it was the mass strikes in industry that prepared the way for an end to military rule and laid the foundation for the establishment of the PT, the Workers Party. In the 1990s the Landless Peoples Movement (MST) mobilised hundreds of thousands of the poorest and most oppressed sectors of

Brazilian society in an extraordinary struggle for land and the right to housing. The PT meanwhile has become a major political actor in the country, holding key positions in a number of states; yet it frequently finds itself caught between a mass movement with which it does have organic connections, and the demands of national government and a global economy pressing in on it relentlessly. In the early 1990s it initiated extraordinary measures for the creation of a popular economy through mass consultations and assemblies. As pressure mounts on the Brazilian economy from the FTAA, the defence of measures that favour the majority of society will have to move beyond the institutions of government.

The counter-measures that the rising movement against global capitalism in Latin America will have to confront are perhaps on display in Colombia today. Some $1.3 billion of US military support for the Plan Colombia has already found its way south; but the aid has taken the form of military equipment and personnel on the one hand, and chemical agents designed to burn out coca production on the other. But what is ostensibly a war against drug trafficking appears to have very different concerns underpinning it.

Colombia is a country separated into virtually autonomous regions, some of them under the control of the guerrilla armies of the Fuerzas Armadas Revolucionarias de Colombia (FARC) and the Ejército de Liberación Nacional (ELN). The Colombian state has a history of providing only a space for negotiation between different regional interests, a function subverted systematically since the early 1980s by the sheer volume of drug money. In the early 1990s the attempt to draw the guerrilla organisations into the political process collapsed in the face of multiple assassinations by paramilitaries closely tied to the armed forces and/or the drug barons.

The Plan Colombia, despite its name, was actually presented to the US government by Colombian president Andrés Pastrana in English before it was offered to the Colombian parliament. In effect it is a programme for hemispheric security and economic discipline. The extermination of the coca crop affects mainly small and middle farmers with no obvious alternative products to turn to. It has to be seen in the context of mounting economic crisis throughout the society, strikes and workers' resistance to the impact of economic austerity over the last five years, and to a generalised resistance throughout the continent.

The effect of the Plan Colombia has been to militarise the Colombian state, but also to give it a wider role; a military base near the Colombian border in Ecuador has already fallen under the effective control of US military personnel, and it is quite clear that the temptation for the US will be to regionalise the conflict. The 'war against drugs' can be used to justify interventions in Peru, Ecuador or Bolivia, for example, where coca is widely grown. And since the process of globalisation is already producing both crisis and resistance, that eventuality seems less remote with every day that passes.

> **What Latin America has shown with blinding clarity is that no state committed to the imposition of the imperatives of global capitalism can or will act as advocate for those who suffer as a result**

In Peru the ignominious collapse of the Fujimori government and the exposure of the repressive apparatus headed by the sinister Vladimiro Montesinos have produced a new president. Both candidates in the final run-off, ex-president Alan García (accused of embezzlement on a massive scale and now perhaps back for more), and Alejandro Toledo, now the new president, expressed a prior commitment to the programmes of the global capitalist economy. And despite his Socialist Party background, so too did Ricardo Lagos, Chile's current president.

The overall picture, then, is becoming very clear. The process that began with the so-called 'transition to democracy' of the late 1980s is coming to completion. The priority then was to establish civilian governments which could carry through a programme of 'structural adjustment' and 'liberalisation' of Latin America's economies. Many of these new governments embraced ex-leaders of the guerrilla organisations (in Guatemala, El Salvador and Colombia, for example) or former members of the political opposition (as in Chile). Resistance, where it emerged, seemed increasingly associated with what came to be called 'social movements' or 'civic organisations' ranging from groups fighting for land or housing through to indigenous peoples' movements. What characterised those movements, however, was that they no longer posed an alternative model for society as a whole but instead mounted resistance, and often heroic resistance, against the impacts of mounting globalisation—ecological, social, economic, human rights etc. Theirs was a discourse, often, of rights rather than revolution.

Yet what Latin America has shown with blinding clarity in the period after Seattle, as well as before, is that no state committed to the imposition of the imperatives of global capitalism can or will act as advocate for those who suffer as a result of those laws of motion.

If Vicente Fox in Mexico is willing to make some concessions to the Zapatistas over indigenous land rights, this will not in any sense mean that he will go on to restore free higher education as demanded by the students who occupied the National University for 14 months in 1999-2000, or protect the labour rights of *maquiladora* workers on the US-Mexican border, or protect the wages or conditions of those who work in the factories of the City and Valley of Mexico. On the contrary, the concessions are almost certainly a prelude to new privations throughout Mexican society.

The arrival in power of the populist president Hugo Chávez in Venezuela may have led some to believe in the return of the national project, the creation of a strong nation-state based on oil revenues; yet the history of his own country serves as a salutary reminder of how the world market controls its dissidents, however much oil revenue they may be enjoying. In any event, Chávez need only glance across the Caribbean Sea at Cuba to see how limited are the prospects for an island of socialism adrift in a capitalist ocean. In the end it will survive by appropriating its economic imperatives, and its values—by obeying the remorseless laws of the market, which in any event have little or no respect for the boundary markers between nation-states!

The alternative is to be found in the Bolivian experience or in Ecuador, where those who have experienced globalisation at its most ruthless—as peasants, as indigenous peoples, as people of colour, as women, as the urban poor, as students, as people without land or homes—link their anger to the power of those who produce that wealth directly, to the workers without whom capitalism cannot function.

Mike Gonzalez is a senior lecturer in Hispanic Studies at Glasgow University. He was co-author of *The Gathering of Voices: The Twentieth Century Poetry of Latin America* and recently edited the *Routledge Encyclopedia of Latin American Culture*. He is an active member of the Scottish Socialist Party, writes a regular column for *Socialist Review* and is a regular contributor to *International Socialism*.
m.gonzalez@hispanic.art.gla.ac.uk

: Sites

► www.nacla.org
  Website of the North American Congress on Latin America.

► www.pulsar.org.ec
  A free subscription news site based in Ecuador that provides daily news from across Latin America.

► www.utlanic.texas.edu
  Latin American centre at the University of Texas which gives access to the wide range of Latin America related sites.

► fzln-l@nopal.laneta.apc.org
  A site giving direct daily news from Chiapas and the Zapatistas.

A woman throws stones at the police during protests against water privatisation in Latin America.

Demonstrators at the IMF/World Bank meeting, Washington, April 2000.

North America
Roger Burbach

● ● ● ● ● ● ● ● ● ● ● ● ● ● ● ● ● ● ●

In the Pacific Northwest in the waning days of the old millennium, a new type of militancy and protest politics captured the world's attention. There, during a wet and rainy week with winter approaching, tens of thousands of demonstrators gathered in the streets of Seattle to protest the meetings of the World Trade Organisation. The established political parties were largely absent, and no singular coalition spoke for the demonstrators. Organisations as diverse as the Sierra Club, the Direct Action Network, the National Family Farm Coalition, the Humane Society, the AFL-CIO, Earth First, and the Council of Canadians helped mobilise environmentalists, human rights lobbyists, church groups, AIDS activists, trade unionists, farmers and many others.

The politics of protest had become 'decentered'. If there was a thread of unity among these disparate groups, it was the belief that something had gone terribly wrong in a world dominated by multinational corporations and the logic of free trade and neo-liberalism. Action needed to be taken, and it could be expressed through any one of a potpourri of groups and organisations that descended on Seattle.[1]

If there is one organisation that serves as an example of the new politics at work in the 'Battle of Seattle', it is perhaps the Direct Action Network (DAN). A loose coalition of individuals and organisations set up in the months leading up to the confrontation, DAN called for a 'festival of resistance' in Seattle. In one of its invitations DAN listed 13 issues that demanded attention: 'War, low wages, deforestation, gentrification, gridlocked cities, genetic engineering, the rich getting richer, cuts in social services, increasing poverty, meaningless jobs, global warming, more prisons, and sweatshops.' In preparation for Seattle, DAN trained hundreds of people in civil disobedience tactics at sites throughout the Northwest.[2] Since Seattle the Direct Action Network has become a loose continental network with locals in at least a dozen cities.

While the protests against globalisation in Seattle by DAN and its sister organisations and networks caught the world by surprise, the genesis of this new continental movement actually began half a decade earlier in the jungles of southern Mexico.

The Zapatistas' first communique denounced the North American Free Trade Agreement, or NAFTA, which took effect on the same day as the uprising. They were calling NAFTA 'the death knell' of indigenous peoples everywhere. Facilitated by the web, Zapatista support organisations sprang up around the continent, in Mexico, the US and Canada. Then after the 'Intercontinental Encuentro', attended by delegations from around the world in the jungles of Chiapas in the summer of 1996, these organisations became more directly linked together via the Intercontinental Network of Alternative Communication against Neoliberalism and for Humanity.

The challenge to neo-liberalism and the use of the internet by Zapatistas and the solidarity organisations helped lay the groundwork for the new politics that took hold in the US and Canada in the months leading up to the Battle of Seattle. It's not that groups like DAN mimicked the approach of the Zapatistas. Rather the Zapatistas were at the cutting edge of a new politics whose time had come. (For more on the Zapatistas, see Mike Gonzalez's article on Latin America in this volume.)

After the Battle of Seattle this new politics of protest took hold at a number of events in the US and Canada. The demonstrations against the World Bank/International Monetary Fund (IMF) meetings in Washington DC in April 2000, the protests in Windsor, Canada, in June at the meeting of the Organisation of American States, the summer 2000 protests at the Republican and Democratic party conventions in Philadelphia and Los Angeles respectively, the demonstrations at George W Bush's installation as US president in January 2001, and most recently the massive demonstrations in Quebec City against the establishment of the Free Trade Area of the Americas (FTAA)—these events and others brought out a plethora of groups and organisations determined to confront corporate-led globalisation in all its forms.

It is difficult to categorise the different groups and organisations that participate in these events. Virtually all of them are opposed to globalisation, viewing it as a process that serves the multinational corporations. Some go even further, putting forth an anti-capitalist agenda. Both currents direct their attacks against free trade agreements and the institutions that sustain the globalisation process, particularly the IMF and the World Bank. The formal movement against these two institutions actually began at the time of the Zapatista rebellion with the Fifty Years is Enough campaign in 1994, the year that marked the 50th anniversary of the World Bank and the IMF. Most of the organisations that backed this campaign were later active in the preparations for Seattle, and continue to be pivotal in the drive against globalisation. Among them are: the Environmental Defence Fund, Food First, Friends of the Earth, Global Exchange, Greenpeace International, the Institute for Agriculture and Trade Policy, the Institute for Policy Studies, the International Rivers Network, Oxfam America, Oxfam Canada, Probe International, and Witness for Peace.[3]

In 1999 many religious organisations around the world launched the Jubilee 2000 campaign. Drawing on the biblical tradition in which slaves are set free and debts cancelled in a jubilee year, the campaign called for the abolition of the debt of the poorest Third World countries along with the redistribution of wealth and an end to the ravishing of the earth's environment. Jubilee 2000/USA and the Canadian Ecumenical Jubilee Initiative launched campaigns aimed at getting their respective national governments, along with the IMF and the World Bank, to forgive debts and to abandon structural adjustment programmes that had decimated social services and impoverished millions of people in the Third World. Given their base in virtually all the major churches in the

Americas, the Jubilee 2000 campaign was particularly effective in taking many of the issues raised by the Fifty Years is Enough campaign into ordinary households and the mainstream press.

Labour and the politics of globalisation

Trade unions in the US and Canada clearly represent the more established organisations active in the campaigns around globalisation issues. The two largest labour confederations, the AFL-CIO and the Canadian Labour Congress, have endorsed the major protests against globalisation that relate to free trade agreements. Among the more militant unions in the US are the International Longshore and Warehouse Union, the Service Employees International Union, and the United Steelworkers of America.

In Canada, Lawrence McBrearty, national director of the United Steelworkers, is one of the more vociferous opponents of the process of globalisation. The Canadian Union of Public Employees, the Canadian Auto Workers, and the Canadian Union of Postal Workers are also very active in the campaign to stop corporate dominated free trade agreements. In the French-speaking province of Quebec the Centrale Syndicale National and the Federacion des Travailleurs du Quebec have been particularly fervid in denouncing globalisation and the impact of free trade on their workers.

One of the most common critiques leveled at the trade unions, particularly in the US, is that they are protectionist, that they oppose free trade agreements simply because US workers want to hold on to their own jobs to the detriment of workers in Third World countries. This critique is probably true of the International Brotherhood of Teamsters under Jimmy Hoffa, which supports many of the pro-corporate policies of the Bush administration while largely limiting its opposition to free trade agreements to trying to stop Mexican truckers from driving their rigs into the US. However, other US trade unions have a broader perspective on the globalisation process and have moved away from the national chauvinist policies they held in the past.

In February 2000, for example, the executive council of the AFL-CIO abandoned its long-standing policy of calling for employer sanctions against undocumented workers. Instead the AFL-CIO advocated a new amnesty for the undocumented and endorsed a broad new programme to educate immigrant workers about their rights. Since NAFTA the AFL-CIO has also sent delegations to Mexico and initiated a dialogue with some Mexican trade unions about how to advance labour rights on both sides of the border. In general, the AFL-CIO under John Sweeney has moved labour in the direction of collaborating with other social movements, particularly the environmental and social justice movements.

One of most important movements advocating basic labour rights has emerged on university campuses in the US and Canada. The Canadian Federation of Students, with over 400,000 members on university campuses, has endorsed campaigns against sweatshops and mobilised students around globalisation issues. The United Students Against Sweatshops has over 150 chapters on college and university campuses, principally in the US with a few in Canada. Recognising that universities profit from global sweatshop practices through the collegiate licensing industry, students have come together to raise awareness on campuses concerning the horrid working conditions of sweatshops around the world. They lobby their school administrators, demanding that codes of conduct are established for sweatshop plants, including the right to collective bargaining, living wages, freedom from forced labour or forced overtime, and adequate sanitary and health conditions in the workplace.

The National Labor Committee (NLC) is one of the most important organisations investigating and exposing adverse labour conditions abroad, providing information to groups like the United Students Against Sweatshops. The committee works with a network of local and international groups to build coalitions that promote labour rights and pressure multinational corporations to adhere to existing labour codes and human rights standards. Among NLC's more important campaigns have been those in Central America, particularly in El Salvador where none of that country's 229 apparel sweatshops, or *maquiladoras*, are unionised. NLC has also filed reports on labour conditions in China, Nicaragua, Burma and Bangladesh and Haiti.

Beyond labour issues, other groups like TransFair Canada and TransFair USA are working to improve the income that small producers and peasants receive for their exported commodities. The TransFair organisations label and certify commodities that are produced under their fair trade guidelines. They tend to work in particular with producer cooperatives that use democratic principles to ensure that working conditions are safe and dignified, and that the producers have a say in how their products are sold. Focusing its principal campaign around coffee, TransFair USA achieved a major breakthrough when the Starbucks Coffee Company agreed to market Fair Trade Certified coffee in over 2,000 retail locations.

Alternative spectacles and the media

The new protest movement is proving especially adept at inventing new media forms and activities that capture public attention. The Independent Media Center, commonly referred to as Indymedia, is the largest and most innovative of the alternative media groups. Originally, established by various independent and alternative media organisations and activists for the purpose of providing grassroots coverage of the World Trade Organisation protests in Seattle, Indymedia served as a clearing house for journalists, providing up-to-the-minute reports, photos, audio and video footage through its website. Since Seattle, Indymedia has become a global network with 26 collectives in the US and eight in Canada alone. Indymedia activists are found at all the major protests and demonstrations, and its website is a rich source of camera footage and reporting, aimed at bypassing the 'corporate media's distortions'.[4]

Although not strictly defined as media organisations, there are a number of groups and organisations that recognise the importance and usefulness of the 'spectacle' is this media-driven age. Art and Revolution, for example, is a collective founded in the Bay Area of California that 'brings dance, music, theatre and giant puppets to the streets to bring attention to the critical issues of our times'. Art and Revolution is particularly known for instigating and helping construct many of the giant puppets that grace the various demonstrations against globalisation. Apparently viewed as a 'threat' by the authorities, the police in the Washington DC and Quebec City demonstrations raided puppet construction facilities, arresting people and carting away the puppets as 'evidence'.

In Canada, during the days leading up to the FTAA meetings in April 2001, a number of groups announced their intention of combining theatre with protest politics. More explicitly anti-capitalist than many organisations in the US, they proclaimed a 'Carnival Against Capitalism'. One group, known as the 'Bikeshevik Revolutionaries', stated:

> We are a biker gang of the best kind: non-motorised, unarmed, ideologically progressive, and counter-criminal. Our goal is to take on the criminal gangs, motorised, armed and ideologically reactionary that are leading the way to the Free Trade Area of the Americas.

Another group issued a call for model airplanes and their pilots to join the 'League of Radical Toy Airplane Pilots' in Quebec. Their proclamation reads:

> Imagine: A squadron of black model airplanes. When the planes reach the 3 metre fence, they perform tricks [and] one by one, the planes peel away and head towards the meeting site. One is hit by a plastic bullet. Another falls victim to a Patriot missile. One makes it halfway to the site, before running out of fuel and crashing through the window of a local McDonald's.

The 'Kite Brigade' had a specific scenario for the big labour-led demonstration in Quebec City:

> Imagine on 21 April countless colourful kites flying in the skies above Quebec City besieged. They will fly high over the heads of protesters protecting them from getting filmed by cameras in police helicopters.

The Kite Brigade also suggests:

> These kites could carry small balloons of smelly perfume or other stinky liquids that might be released every time they fly above the cops who protect [Canadian prime minister] Chretien or Bush and their friends at the FTAA Summit. They stink too!

The array of Canadian organisations active in the movement against globalisation were represented in the People's Summit, which took place at the same time as the gathering of the 34 heads of state in Quebec City. Common Frontiers was one of the main coalitions convening the People's Summit. It defines itself as 'a multi-sectoral working group which confronts and proposes an alternative to the social, environmental and economic effects of economic integration in the Americas'. Among the groups active in Common Frontiers are: the Americas Policy Group of the Canadian Council for International Cooperation (APG), the Canadian Auto Workers (CAW), the Canadian Consortium for International Social Development, the Canadian Environmental Law Association (CELA), the Canadian Federation of Students (CFS), the Canadian Labour Congress (CLC), the Communications, Energy and Paperworkers Union of Canada (CEP), the Council of Canadians, the Ecumenical Coalition for Economic Justice (ExCEJ), the Inter-Church Committee on Human Rights in Latin America (ICCHRLA), Low Income Families Together (LIFT), the Maquila Solidarity Network, Oxfam Canada, the Sierra Club of Canada, the Steelworkers Humanity Fund (SHF), and the United Church of Canada's Latin American and Caribbean Division.[5]

Anarchists and the toxic society

The anarchists constitute the most controversial group that has emerged in the new era of anti-globalisation protests. Making their first appearance at the Battle of Seattle, 50 or so youthful anarchists led an assault on storefronts like Nike and Starbucks. Immediately denounced by other protest groups for their use of violent tactics and for provoking a brutal police crackdown, the anarchists responded that the property of corporations that inflict so much damage and suffering on humanity should not be exempt from attack.

By the time of the demonstrations in Washington DC in April 2000, the anarchist movement had burgeoned, attracting to its ranks large numbers of discontented and alienated youth. About 300 anarchists assembled in Washington, calling themselves the 'Black Bloc', referring to their black garb and flags as well as their official name, the Revolutionary Anti-Capitalist Bloc. They were the more militant contingent of the protest movement, but their tactics had shifted since Seattle.

While they paraded through Washington chanting, 'Whose streets? Our streets,' virtually no violence was directed at storefronts, even against big names like Nike.[6] And unlike Seattle, there were few if any divisions between the anarchists and the rest of the movement over tactics. The anarchists focused their more strident actions on trying to breach the metal and armed police barriers preventing access to the World Bank and the IMF. They also threw up their own barriers comprised of newspaper boxes, chain-link fencing and whatever else they could scavenge from the streets to block the police from attacking them and other demonstrators.

> **Not since the 1960s has there been such a sweeping rebellion against the established order—it is 'back to the future', and this new future is profoundly internationalist and diverse**

In Quebec City the Black Bloc was once again present. What was notable this time, however, was that on the first day of the assaults on the 2.5 mile chain-link fence that surrounded the 34 hemispheric presidents, the Black Bloc was actually outnumbered by other youthful militants. Even more striking was the fact that the Black Bloc and other demonstrators were overwhelmingly home grown, speaking French, the dominant language of the people who reside in Quebec City and the province of Quebec.

The next day, as tens of thousands gathered to march en masse to protest the free trade agenda of the Summit of the Americas, Maude Barlow of the Council of Canadians responded to the controversy around the aggressive tactics of some activists. While making it clear that she adhered to the Gandhian principles of non-violence, she pointed out that the actions of many of the youth were the product of:

> ...a toxic economy, a society that deliberately sorts winners from losers and measures its success by the bottom line of its corporations, not by

the well-being of its young. These youth are the result of years of poisonous economic and trade policies that have created an entrenched underclass with no access to the halls of power except by putting their bodies on the line. Their anger is our collective societal responsibility.

The question should be put to Prime Minister Jean Chrétien and President George Bush and all the other leaders here to promote the extension of this toxic economy: What are you going to do with them? It is your market economy, with its emphasis on ruthless competition and the wanton destruction of the natural world, that has created such deep wellsprings of anger in such large sections of today's youth, and it is you, the political leaders, so beholden to the private interests who put you in power, who must be held accountable.[7]

Most importantly, the anarchists and the anti-globalisation protests provide an outlet for the pent-up frustrations and the sense of alienation of a new generation. In the 1990s many youth joined the ranks of racist skinhead groups or even right wing militias. These reactionary tendencies still exist, but with the new politics of protest young people in ever increasing numbers are joining with other generations and an array of organisations to denounce and reject the unjust and violent world espoused by the advocates of corporate globalisation.

Not since the 1960s has there been such a sweeping rebellion against the established order. It is 'back to the future', and this new future is profoundly internationalist and diverse, linking up environmentalists and trade unionists, university students in the North and sweatshop workers in the South, mainline churches and destitute Third World governments, indigenous groups and human rights activists. It is a embryonic movement that will go through many unforeseen twists and turns as we agitate, organise, and construct new alternatives to globalisation from the bottom up.

Certainly there will be debates and discussions among these diverse groups and organisations as we construct a new future. But the tone has changed dramatically in the new millennium with the maturing of a decentered politics. We are already moving beyond the narrow sectarianism and the internecine debates that decimated the Communist parties of the 20th century and undermined the radical movement of the 1960s.

If we call for a carnival of life and a movement that allows for many shades of diversity and the participation of an infinite number of groups and organisations, we just might be able to create a global village that is able to prevail over the opulent and grotesque world that has been foisted on us by the new corporate robber-barons.

Roger Burbach is Director of the Center for the Study of the Americas (CENSA) based in Berkeley, California. He has written extensively on Latin America, globalisation, and the politics of protest and solidarity.
censa@igc.org

Notes

1 Roger Burbach, *Globalisation and Postmodern Politics: From Zapatistas to High Tech Robber Barons* (Pluto Press, 2001).
2 Janet Thomas, *The Battle In Seattle: The Story Behind and Beyond the WTO Demonstrations* (Fulcrum Publishing, 2000), p83.
3 Kevin Danaher (ed), *Fifty Years Is Enough: The Case against the World Bank and the International Monetary Fund* (South End Press, 1994).
4 www.indymedia.org
5 www.web.net/comxfront/cf_about.htm
6 R Burbach, as above, p146.
7 'The Fight for the Americas', *The Nation*, 8 May 2001.

Texts

▶ Roger Burbach, *Globalisation and Postmodern Politics: From Zapatistas to High Tech Robber Barons* (Pluto Press, 2001).
▶ Kevin Danaher (ed), *Fifty Years Is Enough: The Case against the World Bank and the International Monetary Fund* (South End Press, 1994).
▶ Janet Thomas, *The Battle In Seattle: The Story Behind and Beyond the WTO Demonstrations* (Fulcrum Publishing, 2000).

Sites

▶ **www.artandrevolution.org**
▶ **www.web.net/comxfront/cf_about.htm**
  Common Frontiers
▶ **www.canadians.org**
  Council of Canadians
▶ **www.cdan.org**
  Continental Direct Action Network
▶ **www.censa.org**
  Centre for the Study of the Americas

- ► **www.citizen.org**
  Public Citizen online is a research and campaigning organisation established by Ralph Nader.
- ► **www.earthfirst.org**
- ► **www.foodfirst.org**
  Food First of Oakland, California, conducts high quality research work on hunger and food issues, while also participating in a number of public action campaigns. Anuradha Mittal, co-director of Food First, is currently heading up a drive publicising the fact that in the era of globalisation hunger remains a critical issue in the United States, affecting one fifth of US children.
- ► **www.globalexchange.org**
- ► **www.J2000usa.org**
  Jubilee 2000 (US)
- ► **www.probeinternational.org**
  Probe International is a Canadian founding organisation of Fifty Years Is Enough, active in trying to stop the World Bank and the Canadian government from funding hydroelectric and oil drilling projects in China, India, Brazil and elsewhere.
- ► **www.quebec2001.net**
- ► **www.ruckus.org**
  Ruckus is a direct action training centre teaching how to climb trees, block roads, eat in extreme situations, scale buildings, deal with cops, show solidarity in custody, survive in jail, etc.
- ► **www.transfair.ca**
- ► **www.transfairusa.org**

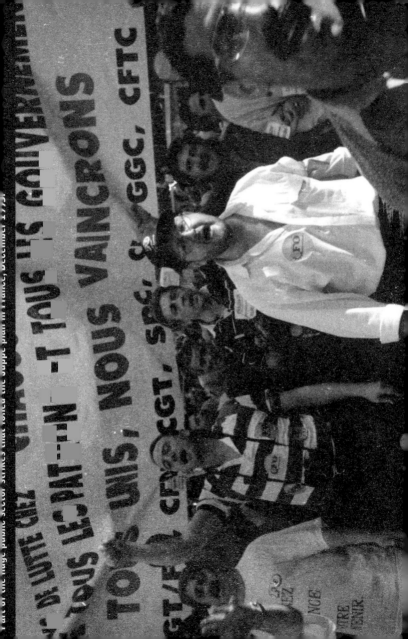

Part of the huge public sector strikes that rolled the public plan in France, December 1995.

Western Europe
Adrian Budd

● ● ● ● ● ● ● ● ● ● ● ● ● ● ● ● ● ●

A contradiction is haunting West European capitalism. On the one hand, mainstream politicians and business leaders are committed to neo-liberalism, the erosion of post-war class compromises, and the freeing of capital from, albeit inadequate, measures of state regulation and social control. On the other hand, amongst those at the base of society there is widespread disillusionment with mainstream politics, a rising curve of class struggle and, for the first time in a generation, a significant and growing activist opposition that has begun to question both neo-liberalism and the underlying processes and structures of capitalism upon which it rests.

Boosted by the November 1999 Seattle demonstrations against the World Trade Organisation (WTO), European demonstrators in Prague, Millau, Nice and elsewhere have maintained the momentum of a global anti-capitalist movement. The energy and creativity that had long been focused upon apparently separate single issues was now turned against a common enemy. For the intensification of global neo-liberalism under the auspices of world capitalism's ruling bodies, including the WTO, had produced a developing realisation that the different and partial aspects of capitalism—such as environmental degradation, sweated labour, rising inequality, etc—are mutually interdependent and components of an interconnected whole.

While variations between national capitalist models persist, capitalist globalisation drives them all towards greater integration with the world market, forcing activists to lift their gaze from national reform to global change.[1] Thus where Western Europe witnessed mass movements over specific national issues in the early 1990s (the poll tax in Britain, pensions reform in Italy, France, Germany and elsewhere), and the mid-1990s saw pan-European strikes that took up the slogan 'No to a neo-liberal Europe', today an important minority has identified capitalism as the problem.

A ruling class offensive

After the Second World War the world economy experienced an unprecedented three decades of boom and high rates of profit. But when the boom ended in the mid-1970s, and a cycle of booms and slumps returned, West European capital launched a process of restructuring aimed at restoring profit levels. Britain, Europe's weakest economy, blazed a neo-liberal trail under the Tories in the 1980s and 1990s that is now littered with relics of the post-war class compromise and which others are now following. Across Western Europe states have pursued business-friendly policies of deregulation, marketisation and privatisation in their efforts to play the role of junior partner in what Peter Gowan has called the US's 'global gamble'.[2]

The regulatory structures of weaker national economies in the Third World were broken open, with catastrophic impacts on living standards and all the other indices of social well-being, by the combined efforts of capitalism's global institutions such as the International Monetary Fund (IMF), the World Bank, and the WTO, backed where necessary by the West's military might. In Western Europe the European Union states deepened the process of integration after the end of the Cold War and German reunification in an attempt to forge a regional economy as both a launch-pad into and defence against global competition. This entailed a rigid discipline over social spending via the Maastricht convergence criteria and, later, the shifting of elements of macro-economic management to unaccountable institutions like the European Central Bank. Future reforming governments committed to increased welfare spending would thus encounter a set of structural constraints that would severely test their resolve.

Not surprisingly, ruling class self-confidence, and wealth, increased throughout the 1980s and into the 1990s, reinforced by the collapse of the Stalinist states. Thatcher's message that 'there is no alternative' to neo-liberal capitalism was echoed across Europe. France's rulers adopted a *pensée unique* that would tolerate no alternatives. Spanish socialist prime minister Gonzalez discovered that capitalism was 'the least worst' economic system, while imposing labour market flexibility in the form of temporary contracts (soon called 'rubbish contracts') for new workers. By 1987 only 5 percent of new jobs were permanent and by 1993 one third of all jobs were temporary, three quarters among under-25s in Catalonia, Spain's most advanced region. In Germany, Chancellor Kohl warned workers that they had been living for too long in a giant leisure park.

Yet ruling class triumphalism was short-lived, for while Europe's working classes, variously defeated in major class confrontations, disoriented by the betrayals and compromises of their social democratic, trade union and Communist leaders, and demoralised in the face of persistent high unemployment, had often acquiesced in the imposition of cuts and restructuring, their patience was not inexhaustible. Anti neo-liberal campaigner and sociologist Pierre Bourdieu argues that the 'left hand of the state' (reflecting previous struggles and embodied in the welfare state) has been rolled back, but the right hand (treasuries and finance ministries acting to secure the conditions for capitalist reproduction) has been strengthened.[3] The consequent widening of social inequality, the greater insecurity, longer hours and huge productivity increases of those in work, unemployment, poverty, homelessness, and deteriorating conditions in schools, hospitals and social services, all contributed to a new mood of resistance across Western Europe.

The revival of resistance

When Thatcher's government attempted to impose the poll tax in 1989 it discovered that such a generalised attack on workers' living standards could unite millions in opposition. Yet when the collapse of the Stalinist states, German reunification, and economic crisis came together in the early 1990s, Western Europe's rulers launched themselves along a Thatcherite path. Under the dictates of the Maastricht criteria that they themselves had negotiated, they began to impose deep cuts in state spending, notably on the pensions that workers' action had won in the long boom. Resentment towards growing inequality and corruption at the top of society, and alienation from mainstream politics – summed up in Germany under the notion of *Politikverdrossenheit* (being fed up with politicians) – quickly turned into mass resistance and a developing crisis of legitimacy for established political structures.

In Italy the Christian Democrats who had dominated postwar politics collapsed, dragging some of their allies with them, and the first Berlusconi government was brought down in 1994 by opposition to pensions 'reform', including a demonstration of 1.5 million, the largest since 1945. In Germany, while the ruling class debated the future of

Politikverdrossenheit: German for 'being fed up with politicians'

Germany as an investment location (Standort Deutschland) and imposed across the board tax increases to pay for reunification, the unions engaged in the highest level of class struggle since the late-1940s.[4]

In France the Gaullist Balladur government, despite a landslide victory in 1993 as voters punished the Socialist Party (PS) for mass unemployment and corruption, rapidly became a lame-duck in the face of opposition to attempts to cut state spending. Such was the government's unpopularity that would-be Gaullist president Chirac distanced himself from it and argued against social exclusion in the run-up to the 1995 presidential elections. The 6 million people in France solely dependent on social security payments had seen the value of their income fall to between 20 and 40 percent of average income between 1982 and 1995. Yet such was the pressure from capital to cut and restructure state spending that within a few months of victory his government too launched a major assault on social security—the Juppé plan. The response, public sector strikes of some 2 million in December 1995, often involving rank and file *coordinations* of strike activity, represented a turning-point in the combativity of European workers and contributed to the later development of the anti-capitalist movement in Western Europe. Daniel Bensaïd captured the significance of the strikes:

> ...political pundits and sociologists have been announcing, somewhat carelessly, that conflict had given way to consensus and the classes had dissolved in the grey mass of untrammelled individualism. The clocks have now been set right: class struggle continues and collective action is not a thing of the past.[5]

For all but a tiny minority, mass collective action was directed at neo-liberalism rather than capitalism. But, reminiscent of the process described by Rosa Luxemburg in *The Mass Strike*, the renewed confidence of French workers began to develop in mutual interaction and reinforcement with more overtly political campaigns, such as those of the unemployed, in support of immigrants (*les sans papiers*) and against the fascist Front National, which began to meet direct opposition at its meetings, culminating in a 70,000-strong demonstration at its congress in February 1997.[6] Protest movements which had oriented on the Socialist Party and government in the 1980s were increasingly independent and prepared to engage in direct action.

Although on a smaller scale, a similar process was unfolding elsewhere in Europe. In Germany, when the Kohl government attempted its own version of the Juppé plan in 1996, Bonn witnessed the biggest protests since the Second World War. The following year miners took to Bonn's streets and won a reprieve for the industry, and Germany's largest ever student movement won support from the trade union congress for its campaign against under-funding, cuts and overcrowding. And, just as the separations between issues were beginning to break down, so the Europe-wide strikes in support of Belgian Renault workers in early 1997 showed how workers' solidarity could breach national divisions.

Some of those involved in the Renault struggles raised slogans such as 'For a workers' Europe, not a bosses' Europe' and 'No to a neo-liberal Europe, yes to a social Europe'. The revival of struggle was clearly encouraging the opposition to specific attacks to address wider political questions, even if for the most part within the limits set by capitalism. This generalisation represented a shift to the left across Western Europe and resulted in the return to government of West European social democracy: the ex-Communist Democratic Party of the Left (PDS) dominated the Olive Tree Alliance elected in Italy in 1996, Blair's New Labour swept the Tories out in Britain in 1997, the PS returned to office the same month in France, and in 1998 the German social democrats (SPD) formed a government with the Greens.[7]

A developing movement

A developing radicalisation and shift to the left in social attitudes not only clashed with the requirements of the capitalist system but also with the aspirations and programmes of its new managers. For West European social democracy has shifted, sometimes quite dramatically, to the right and any residual commitment to change is largely symbolic and rhetorical.

New Labour has led the charge, combining an uncritical attachment to the market and big business with hollow sounding commitments to fairness and social justice. Thus its Fairness at Work legislation, far from reversing the erosion of workers' rights suffered under the Tories, would, boasted Tony Blair, leave Britain with 'the most lightly regulated labour market of any leading economy in the world'.[8] Meanwhile, the trend of the last two decades towards increasing inequality continues under New Labour—as the income of the richest 10 percent of the population has grown by 82 percent in real terms in that period, that of the poorest 10 percent grew by just 6 percent.

In Germany the SPD-Green coalition has sacrificed the Keynesian Oskar Lafontaine under pressure from big business, embraced the Blairite 'Third Way' of labour market flexibility, shareholder value, and welfare 'reform', and bowed to the energy industry to renege on its commitment to decommission nuclear power stations. A sense of the pressures on the lives of ordinary people is provided by the evidence from one of Western Europe's most advanced industrial sectors: productivity has increased at DaimlerChrysler Aerospace (Dasa) where workers on the Eurofighter work six hour shifts with just a 2.5 minute 'comfort break'! In Italy the Olive Tree Alliance continued the privatisation and spending cuts of its predecessors.

In France the Socialist/Communist/Green coalition has been more constrained by radicalisation, has not formally embraced the Third Way, but operates according to prime minister Jospin's contradictory formula in favour of a market economy but not a market society. Yet to fund such a society has meant increased privatisation and tight control over social spending. The flagship social democratic policy of a 35-hour working week has faced a counter-offensive from the bosses' organisations and, in any case, the law has provided an opportunity to increase productivity and to restructure production. Meanwhile, nearly 20 percent of workers are on part-time contracts and, as Bertrand Tavernier's film, *It All Starts Today*,

Nowhere has West European social democracy reversed widening inequality, deepening environmental crisis and welfare retrenchment

powerfully depicts, even superhuman effort on the part of teachers cannot prevent the disastrous social consequences of neo-liberal budgetary rigour.

Nowhere has West European social democracy reversed widening inequality, deepening environmental crisis, welfare retrenchment, the blight of unemployment and the intensification of the social pathologies of capitalism such as drug abuse and crime. Protest has continued and, over the last two years, the fallout from Seattle has settled everywhere across Western Europe, such that the ideas and language of anti-capitalism are now commonplace. France again provides the clearest picture of a developing movement.

Pierre Bourdieu was instrumental in establishing *Raisons d'Agir* (*Reasons to Act*) at the time of the public sector strikes in December 1995. Campaigning against neo-liberalism, it has issued a call for a united European social movement, as part of an international movement against global capital, supported by the Greek and German unions. The *Confederation Paysanne*, representing small farmers, has protested against global agri-business, and the trial of one of its leading members, José Bové, for attacking a McDonald's restaurant attracted 60,000 to the small town of Millau in July 2000. The best known grouping is ATTAC (Association for the Taxation of Financial Transactions for the Aid of Citizens), established in 1998 to campaign for the imposition of the Tobin Tax on financial speculation and the distribution of the proceeds for development of the poorest parts of the world. It has committees across France and associations in some 20 other countries.

None of these are unequivocally anti-capitalist organisations, and combine moderate reformers, those seeking a more stable capitalism, anti neo-liberals, as well as more radical elements. But while the ravages of international capitalism intensify, supported by key social forces and governments in the major capitalist powers, these groupings have been compelled to address wider systemic questions such as the nature of capitalism, the interests behind the dominant institutions of the world system, and the impact and interests of transnational corporations. As radicalisation deepens, these groupings, whose publications can sell in the tens of thousands, have become crucibles for important discussions of the best way forward for the movement – for example, over the relative merits of lobbying parliament and direct action.

Elsewhere in Western Europe the imperatives of global capitalism have similarly forced people to move to the left of mainstream parties and engage in direct action, thereby creating conditions for the deepening of an anti-capitalist mood that unites people around common interests and breaks down sectionalism. In Germany, for example, the issues of nuclear power, waste and reprocessing have been taken up by thousands of demonstrators who might once have placed their faith in the parliamentary actions of the Greens. In Britain Globalise Resistance has been successful at uniting various sections of the anti-capitalist left and staging actions and speaking tours. In Spain anarchists, young people, students, ecologists, feminists, and young rank and file workers, have begun to work together over both local issues such as housing and wider issues like militarism and rights for immigrant workers. In Italy a far left autonomist tradition has brought the anti-capitalism of the Mexican Zapatistas to a wide audience of young people, outside the stultifying embrace of social democracy and Stalinism. The potential of the movement was illustrated by the 200 May Day demonstrations across Italy this year.

Now, the dynamism and creativity that many have displayed in single issue campaigns is potentially at the service of a global movement for liberation

In May's general election Berlusconi's *Forza Italia*, promising mutually contradictory tax cuts, pensions increases and a huge public works programme, benefited from a backlash against five years of austerity and privatisation under the Blairite Olive Tree Alliance. But Berlusconi's populism wilted in the face of capital's demands in 1994, provoking massive demonstrations that precipitated his fall from office. Today his room for manoeuvre is just as limited, and within a fortnight of victory he suffered humiliating defeats in local elections in Italy's major cities. In the context of a developing anti-capitalist movement, whose next port of call is the G8 meeting in Genoa in July, the stage is set for another, and possibly more intense, round of conflicts.

A world to win

The institutions of global capitalism and the shady business organisations that operate alongside them have a totalising mission — to subordinate everyone and everything to the dictates of the market and the interests of the biggest firms and their states. That mission has often gone undetected and uncontested, but today millions have begun to resist. To do so they have had to begin to look at the system as a whole and to surmount the apparent boundaries between separate causes and movements, to emphasise the common interests of all who suffer the necessarily negative consequences of a system in which more and more production is for profit, whatever the social and environmental costs. For even where their starting point appears to be a single issue, these are today so large and so mutually interdependent with other aspects of the system that the overall processes and structures of capitalism cannot be evaded. Even before the emergence of the anti-capitalist movement, the demoralisation that afflicted the West European left in the 1980s and 1990s—when defeat, incorporation or passivity imposed by labour and union bureaucracies often drove people towards a sectional concern with individual oppressions—was beginning to be broken down. Now the dynamism and creativity that many have displayed in single issue campaigns is potentially at the service of a global movement for liberation.

The Prague demonstration against the World Bank, the protests at Millau, the Nice European Union summit, and Davos were all magnificent mobilisations of tens of thousands of activists. Preparation for them brought together activists from different movements, with different traditions, in dozens of towns and cities across Western Europe. Returning activists reported on the protests and enthused the next wave of protesters. The anti-capitalist movement has rapidly become a forum for debate in a spirit of solidarity, and anti-capitalist protests provide a beacon of hope for others who want to fight back. But the capitalist plunder machine that is the root cause of the problems that anti-capitalists seek to resolve continues. It can most successfully be resisted, and ultimately broken, where workers are exploited and produce the profits that drive the system's destructive logic. Only by connecting anti-capitalist activism with the workers' movement can we ultimately ensure that our world will not be for sale.

Adrian Budd teaches politics at South Bank University, London, where he is an active member of the lecturers' union NATFHE. He has recently written articles and chapters on globalisation, sport under capitalism, and 'stakeholder' capitalism. He is a member of the Socialist Workers Party.
buddam@sbu.ac.uk

Notes

1   See D Coates, *Models of Capitalism:
    Growth and Stagnation in the Modern
    Era* (Cambridge, 2000).

2   P Gowan, *The Global Gamble.
    Washington's Faustian Bid for World
    Dominance* (London, 1999). On
    international business restructuring see
    W Ruigrok and R van Tulder, *The Logic
    of International Restructuring*
    (London, 1995). On the deepening
    interconnections between the British
    state and big business see G Monbiot,
    *Captive State: The Corporate
    Takeover of Britain* (London, 2000).

3   P Bourdieu, 'The Left Hand and the
    Right Hand of the State', in *Acts of
    Resistance: Against the New Myths of
    our Time* (Cambridge, 1998).

4   A Callinicos, 'Crisis and Class Struggle
    in Europe Today', *International
    Socialism* 63 (summer 1994). On
    Germany, particularly the illusions of
    stakeholder theorists like Will Hutton,
    see A Budd, 'The Contradictions and
    Crisis of Stakeholder Capitalism',
    Contemporary Politics vol 3, no 2
    (1997), and A Budd, 'Stakeholding', in
    V Bryson and G Blakeley (eds),
    Apologies for Capitalism? (Pluto,
    forthcoming 2001).

5   D Bensaid, 'Neo-Liberal Reform and
    Popular Rebellion', *New Left Review*
    215 (1996), p109. See also C
    Harman, 'France's Hot December',
    International Socialism 70 (spring
    1996).

6   See R Luxemburg, *The Mass Strike*
    (London, 1986).

7   For details see K Hudson, *European
    Communism Since 1989: Towards a
    New European Left?* (Basingstoke,
    2000).

8   T Blair, 'Foreword' to *Fairness at
    Work*, Cm 3968 (London, 1998).

An Israeli soldier takes aim at a Palestinian youth whose only weapons are stones

Middle East
Anne Alexander and John Rose
● ● ● ● ● ● ● ● ● ● ● ● ● ● ● ● ● ● ●

Edward Said's words will have rung true for many when he commented in December 2000:

> A turning point has been reached...and for this the Palestinian intifada is a significant marker. For not only is it an anti-colonial rebellion of the kind that has been seen periodically in Setif, Sharpeville, Soweto and elsewhere, it is another example of the general discontent with the post Cold War order (economic and political) displayed in the events of Seattle and Prague... What must be clear to every ruler, including Clinton and Barak, is that the period of stability guaranteed by the tripartite dominance of Israel, the US and local Arab regimes is now threatened by popular forces of uncertain magnitude, unknown direction, unclear vision. Whatever shape they eventually take, theirs will be an unofficial culture of the dispossessed, the silenced and the scorned.[1]

The Middle East, like every other region of the world, has been transformed by globalisation and imperialism. The fate of the Palestinians is intimately connected with the needs of multinational capital and the national state to control access to the precious oil supplies of the region. In addition, Palestine resistance has pushed thousands of people across the Middle East into confrontation with their own governments. Ever since the first uprising in 1987 the issue of Palestine has acted as a detonator for the anger and frustration of millions of people whose lives are being wrecked by capitalism. And because they run into the repressive power of the state, solidarity demonstrations quickly begin to raise slogans demanding political freedoms. Just as in Seattle and Quebec, protesters in Cairo, Damascus and Algiers have found that the first line of defence for the interests of the global elite is manned by their own national police force and army.

Oil and imperialism

Oil companies are the original multinationals, and petroleum the original branded product. Long before Nike and Adidas realised that in order to sell identical running shoes they needed to create a recognisable brand, Shell, Standard and Gulf were stamping their logos on oil cans, tankers and filling stations. These giant corporations were among the first to create integrated chains of production and distribution, operating across continents and time zones to keep the oil flowing. Modern capitalist society was transformed by cheap, plentiful oil in the early part of the 20th century; 100 years later the addiction is just as powerful, and despite dwindling reserves oil consumption is rising steadily. The bulk of remaining oil supplies lies in the Middle East.

The oil pipeline makes a good metaphor for the operation of multinational capital. It sucks out profit by the gallon and channels it straight into the pockets of the rich and powerful. For ordinary people there is no 'trickle-down' effect. They are simply bypassed by the wealth they helped to create. Although they live in a region producing one of the most valuable commodities on Earth, the majority of people of the Middle East live in poverty. Oil makes up 80 percent of Yemeni exports, yet falling prices meant a 30 percent cut in the budget in 1998, followed by a 25 percent cut the year after. Yemeni tribesmen have taken to demanding schools and clinics as ransom for kidnapped foreigners. During 1999 the main oil pipeline was sabotaged 20 times and the government had to use helicopter gunships to put down protests over austerity measures.[2]

These oil companies have never been content to rely on the free market alone to guarantee access to the precious deposits of oil. The history of the Middle East shows clearly the intimate connection between globalisation and imperialism. Ever since gunboats arrived at Alexandria in 1882 to guarantee the profits of British speculators, the interests of capital and the practice of imperialism have gone hand-in-hand. The US, which is currently the dominant power in the region, follows two strategies to ensure that oil supplies remain ultimately under American control. Firstly, through the usual methods of International Monetary Fund (IMF) bullying, arms dealing and occasional direct military intervention to remind local rulers where their loyalties should lie. But secondly and more importantly through support for Israel. This tiny state is the largest recipient of US aid in the world, much of it in the form of sophisticated military hardware. Israel is a much more reliable ally than the rickety monarchies and ailing juntas in the rest of the Middle East. As the Israeli newspaper *Ha'aretz* explained in 1951:

> If for any reasons the Western powers should sometimes prefer to close their eyes, Israel could be relied upon to punish one or several neighbouring states whose discourtesy to the West went beyond the bounds of the permissible.[3]

Israel was created on the promise of 'a land without people for a people without land'. The problem is that the empty land was a myth. At least half a million Palestinians were driven from their homes by the creation of the new Jewish state. There are now nearly 4 million Palestinian refugees registered by the UN in the Occupied Territories, Lebanon, Syria and Jordan.[4] In 1987 their frustration exploded into an uprising against the occupation. The first intifada resulted in the Oslo peace process of the 1990s—symbolised by the famous handshake of Palestinian leader Arafat with Israeli leader Rabin on the White House lawn in Washington. It seems that Israel had finally recognised that Palestinians had national rights. But few people realised at the time, especially in the West, just how much the Palestinians had sacrificed.

There were high expectations of a genuine peace—with justice. No one believed this more than one of Israel's most famous radical historians, Avi Shlaim. Yet today Shlaim is one of Oslo's most bitter critics. He argues that Oslo cheated the Palestinians by 'repackaging rather than ending the military occupation'. He is particularly scathing about the continuous expansion of the settlements, accelerated under Barak and, he insists, 'contrary to the spirit of Oslo'. A second intifada was inevitable. Avi Shlaim's book *The Iron Wall* is essential reading for all supporters of the Palestinians. Shlaim shows how the 'iron wall', the name for the overwhelming military force to break the will of the Palestinian people, has been policy for successive Israeli leaders, including 'peacemakers' Rabin and Barak.

> **The issue of Palestine has acted as a detonator for the anger and frustration of millions of people whose lives are being wrecked by capitalism**

Palestinian patience finally ran out following the visit of extreme right winger Ariel Sharon to the Haram al-Sharif around the Al-Aqsa mosque in Jerusalem at the end of September 2000. Israeli troops shot dead a large number of demonstrators and thus sparked a new uprising. Many Western commentators have tried to distort the second intifada. They claim that the armed militias which have dominated the clashes with Israeli troops do not truly represent the Palestinian people.

In fact the main militia, the Tanzim, according to a recent analysis, have their roots amongst the unarmed street fighters and stone-throwers of the first intifada. Some of the Tanzim are also elected deputies to the new Palestinian Legislative Council where they have led the crusade against the corruption and mismanagement of the Palestinian Authority. These militias are part of a long and honourable tradition of popular armed guerrilla resistance to Western colonial occupations.[5]

As an extract from the address by Palestinian poet Mahmoud Darwish on his recent commemoration on the 53rd anniversary of Nakba ('Catastrophe'—the name Palestinians give to the events in the year of Israel's foundation in 1948) puts it:

> The intifada, yesterday, today and tomorrow, is a natural and legitimate expression of resistance to slavery brought on by an occupation

practising the worst forms of racial discrimination—an occupation which strives under the guise of a fraudulent peace process to strip Palestinians of their lands and livelihoods, and to isolate them in demographically unconnected Bantustans surrounded by settlements and bypass roads, whilst they are offered the luscious carrot—in return for agreeing to 'put an end to claims and struggles'—of putting the name of their own state to the spacious prisons in which they have been well and truly caged.

Across the Arab world huge protests brought thousands onto the streets in solidarity with the Palestinians. University students in Egypt led demonstrations which fought pitched battles with the police and army, setting cars alight and demolishing a Kentucky Fried Chicken restaurant. High school students led pickets of shops selling Israeli goods and organised their own demonstrations. In Morocco half a million people marched in a demonstration which was led by government officials alongside leading opposition figures.[6] The Jordanian government banned all demonstrations, but repression did not stop thousands of students from taking to the streets.[7] Similar battles between the police and protesters took place in Syria and the Gulf states.[8]

Resistance to globalisation: 'IMF get out—this country is ours'

The sparks of the Palestinian intifada fall into a political climate which is as dry as tinder. The process of globalisation has been just as devastating in the Middle East as elsewhere. Ordinary people have seen their living standards forced down by cuts in state subsidies and unemployment has rocketed. Most governments now owe more in debts to international financial institutions than they did 20 years ago, despite intensive progammes of 'structural adjustment'. A thin layer of the elite have been the only beneficiaries. In Cairo they call them 'the whales', the fat cats who have gorged themselves on state industries and reaped the benefits of property speculation. In down-town Beirut a cluster of Starbucks outlets are starting to kill off the traditional coffee houses. The meagre water supplies of the Gaza Strip have now been privatised.

The impetus towards privatisation has always come from the

In the occupied territories

- Over 450 Palestinians have been killed, a quarter of whom are children, since the start of the new intifada.
- There are nearly half a million armed Israeli settlers on 200 settlements. Nearly a third of these settlements have been built since Oslo.
- Gross national product has fallen by a third since Oslo. Unemployment is over 50 percent in many parts. The average income of Palestinians is one tenth that of Israelis.
- Despite worldwide condemnation, Israel regularly assassinates intifada leaders and supporters.
- In addition Israel receives $3 billion every year from the US, making it the most heavily funded client-state of the US anywhere in the world.
- Israel ignores international law, with US support—in particular vital United Nations resolutions: Resolution 242, which calls for Israel to withdraw from the West Bank, Gaza and East Jerusalem; Resolution 194 which calls for the right of return of the 5 million Palestinian refugees excluded from Israel.

centre. In fact Egypt's president, Anwar al-Sadat, launched an experiment in economic liberalisation in the 1970s in an attempt to win the approval of the US and the IMF. The IMF proposed a massive programme of cuts in state subsidies for basic goods which sparked a popular uprising the length and breadth of Egypt. In every city tens of thousands of people poured into the streets to attack symbols of wealth and power.

Sadat only regained control of the situation by quickly reversing the subsidy cuts and sending tanks onto the streets. Egypt's urban uprising in 1977 was only the first of many similar battles across the region. Algeria exploded into massive protests in 1988 after the government attempted to bring in an IMF-backed austerity programme. Thousands of young people battled with the police and army.[9] Jordan was rocked by huge riots and demonstrations the same year in protest at subsidy cuts. Young workers and students fought the police to a standstill chanting, 'The intifada has come to the

East Bank'.[10]

Similar protests took place in 1994 when the government abolished fuel subsidies.

Poor living conditions in Iran have provoked massive demonstrations over the last few years. In June 2000 more than 3,000 Iranian women burned tyres and blocked a main road in protest at a lack of basic amenities including water, gas and electricity, while rises in bus fares sparked off demonstrations in the suburbs of Tehran.[11]

Privatisation programmes have also fuelled workers' resistance. For the multinationals eyeing up the spoils, Middle Eastern factories are burdened with 'inefficient' bonus schemes and fringe benefits. Yet for many workers these 'fringe benefits' are crucial to their families' survival. High unemployment is a disaster which pushes millions to the edge of starvation. Fierce workers' resistance has actually slowed down the privatisation programme in a number of countries, particularly Egypt. Thousands of workers in the mill town of Kafr al-Dawwar occupied their factories in September 1994 in protest at job cuts

How globalisation helps rather than hinders solidarity with the intifada throughout the Arab world

'Cheap and readily available, locally produced satellite dishes have become a ubiquitous part of the landscape. Qatar's Al-Jazeera channel, Beirut's al-Mustaqbal and LBC, MBC from London and ANN from Spain have all become household names, and almost all channels boast well-known local correspondents and crews. Arab satellite TV...provides a steady diet of commentary from Palestinian and Arab analysts, political thinkers and leaders, which has helped define the meaning and goals of the intifada for the local population.

'By providing a type and degree of coverage far beyond what is allowed on state-run television, they have mobilised much more popular Arab protest and solidarity than was possible in the first uprising. At the same time, this powerful image of Arab solidarity is projected back into the West Bank and Gaza via satellite. Not since the heyday of Nasserism have Palestinians felt that the entire Arab world (if not the regimes) is behind them.'

—from 'Beyond Oslo: The New Uprising' by Rema Hammi and Salim Tamari, *Middle East Report* 217 (Winter 2000), www.merip.org

and loss of benefits. The strike only ended after the army occupied the town following three days of rioting.[12]

In Morocco privatised industries such as the SAMIR oil refineries have seen a war of attrition between workers and management over job losses which boiled over into strikes in summer 2000.[13]

Over the past 20 years Turkey has been through 17 economic restructuring programmes. The IMF's repeat prescription for the country's economic ills has pushed ordinary people to fight back. In December 2000 the IMF offered a $7 billion loan on the condition that the Turkish government speeds up privatisation of Turk Telecom and Turkish Airlines. Tens of thousands of public sector workers joined strikes against job cuts and austerity measures. Demonstrators filled the streets carrying banners saying, 'IMF get out—this country is ours'.[14]

Why economic liberalisation means political repression

The scale of resistance gives some idea why economic liberalisation has not been matched with political openness. Even liberal critics of the Middle Eastern regimes find themselves victimised and imprisoned. In May 2001 Egyptian courts sentenced the respected sociologist Sa'ad Ed-Din Ibrahim to seven years in prison for accepting funding from the European Union for a voter education project.[15] Amnesty International notes hundreds of cases of 'disappearances', extra-judicial execution, torture and harassment from around the region every year.[16] RAID, the Tunisian equivalent of ATTAC, has been refused permission to register with the Ministry of Social Affairs and its members have been harassed and imprisoned on trumped-up charges.[17]

Lack of respect for human rights is common to every country in the region, not just those which are labelled 'dictatorships' by the Western media. Saudi Arabia and Turkey are key allies of the US in the Middle East. Turkey, a NATO member, receives huge amounts of military aid from the USA and is applying for membership of the European Union. This is despite well-documented human rights abuses connected to Turkey's campaign against the Kurds. According to the Federation of American Scientists:

The Turkish regime has spent over $120 billion on its military campaign against the rebel Kurdistan Workers Party (PKK), siphoning off scarce resources from investment in infrastructure and contributing to the overall fragility of the economy, a Congressionally mandated State Department report, along with independent reports from Amnesty International and Human Rights Watch, all documented the use of US-supplied weapons in the commission of human rights abuses.[18]

Saudi Arabia is another favourite client of the US and the UK. Since 1989 US government foreign military sales to the kingdom have topped $40.6 billion. Executions are common in Saudi Arabia, and an increasing number of crimes now carry the death penalty, including apostasy, drug dealing, sodomy and 'witchcraft'.

Iraq is another country which has been armed by the West despite an appalling human rights record. Four British arms deals in 1988 and 1989 transferred $28 million of military equipment to Saddam Hussein's regime. This was despite the Iraqi regime's long running campaign against the Kurds which included bombing villages with poison gas and executing around 180,000 people.[19]

Repression serves a simple purpose, to guarantee stability for the multinational investors. The

Iraq in figures

Since the end of the Gulf War the Iraqi people have lived under the most severe sanctions regime ever imposed by the United Nations.

The current population of Iraq is 21 million. Since 1990 around 1 million people have died as a result of sanctions including at least 5,000 children a month. One in four children in Iraq are malnourished, an increase of 73 percent since 1991. Radiation levels in some areas in southern Iraq are 84 times higher than the World Health Organisation's safe limit. Rates of cancer have risen by 500 percent in Mosul, northern Iraq, probably as a result of radioactive pollution from depleted uranium weapons used by US and allied forces during the war.

—'Iraq: What United Nations Sanctions Have Done', New Internationalist, September 1999 power of the state is a vital safety net for global capital, not a remnant of old-fashioned military dictatorship. The state has also had to bail out the economy when promised foreign investment has failed to appear. According to opposition parties, direct foreign investment in Egypt dropped by 60 percent between 2000 and 2001. Meanwhile central government spending over the same period increased by 30 percent.[20]

> **Repression serves a simple purpose, to guarantee stability for the multinational investors—the power of the state is a vital safety net for global capital**

Dreamland: living in the mirage

For those who can afford it, the future of the Middle East looks bright enough. Luxury flats around Cairo promise to blot out the untidy reality of globalisation:

> 'Dreamland', the TV commercials for the most ambitious of the new developments promise, 'is the world's first electronic city.' Buyers can sign up now for luxury fibreoptic-wired villas, as shopping malls, theme parks, golf courses and polo grounds rise out of the desert west of the Giza pyramids—but only minutes from central Cairo via newly built bridges and ring roads.[21]

For the millions scraping out an existence elsewhere in the city and around the Middle East globalisation has not brought prosperity. Instead it has increased pressures on ordinary people as welfare services and secure jobs evaporate. Environmental degradation, in particular water shortages, is adding further burdens on the poorest, and storing up conflict for the future. Meanwhile, the concentration of the world's remaining oil reserves in the region guarantees the continued interest of the imperialist powers and their local henchmen. In short, more wars, fewer jobs, less water, collapsing services and public transport, and rising levels of pollution.

At the beginning of the Oslo peace process Shimon Peres

mapped out a vision of a future demilitarized Middle East where 'the only generals are General Motors and General Electric'.[22] So long as the interests of profit come before the people of the Middle East, General Electric and General Motors will continue to do business in the very heavy shadow of their military counterparts.

John Rose is a Palestinian rights activist and a founding member of the Campaign for Palestinian Rights.

Ann Alexander works as an interpreter with refugees in Liverpool. She is a member of the Socialist Workers Party.
r_annealex@hotmail.com

Notes

1   Edward Said, *London Review of Books*, 14 December 2000.
2   *The Economist*, 6-12 Feb 1999.
3   *Ha'aretz*, 30 September 1951.
4   UNRWA in figures, UNRWA, Gaza, December 2000, also at www.un.org/unrwa
5   Graham Usher, 'Fatah's Tanzim, Origins and Politics', *Middle East Report* 217, (Winter 2000), www.merip.org
6   Hussein Khamis, 'Al-anthima al-arabiyya bayna al-ghadab al-sha'abiyya wa amrika', *Al-Sabar* 123.
7   'Al-quwa al-sha'abiyya al-urduniyya tarfud mawqif al-hukuma al-mana'l'l-muthahiraat', from ArabicNews.com, 10 October 2000.
8   'Al-talaba al-souriyyoun yatathahiyyoun did al-mathabah al-israiliyya', from ArabicNews.com, 4 October 2000.
9   Akhbar al-yawm, 8 October 1988.
10 Phil Marshall, *Intifada: Zionism, Imperialism and Palestinian Resistance* (Bookmarks), p188.
11 AFP report, available from iran-news@lists.payk.net
12 Joe Stork, 'Egypt's Factory Privatization Campaign Turns Deadly', *Middle East Report* (January-February 1995).
13 'Conflit social chez la SAMIR', *Liberation* (Maroc), 30 August 2000.
14 Chris Morris, 'IMF puts Turkey on $7 Billion Trial', *The Guardian*, 7 December 2000.
15 *Al-Ahram Weekly*, 24-30 May 2001, www.ahram.org.eg/weekly
16 www.amnesty.org
17 RAID website available at www.attac.org/tunisie
18 Client Profiles—Turkey, www.fas.org
19 'The Kurds: an Ancient Tragedy', *The Economist*, 20-26 February 1999.
20 *Al-Wafd*, 27 May 2001, www.alwafd.org

21 Timothy Mitchell, 'Dreamland: the
    Neo-Liberalism of Your Desires',
    Middle East Report 210, from
    www.merip.org
22 'Ploughed back into Swords: Peace
    Deals Will Not Stop Military Spending
    in the Middle East', *Financial Times*,
    9 September, 1994.

Sites

► **www.al-awda.org.uk**
Palestine Right to Return Coalition UK

► **www.alternativenews.org**
The Alternative Information is a
Palestinian-Israeli organisation which
disseminates information and research
of the Israeli-Palestinian conflict.

► **www.attac.org/maroc**
ATTAC Morocco

► **www.attac.org/tunisie**
ATTAC Tunisia, known as RAID
(Rassemblement pour une Alternative
Internationale de Developpement).

► **www.btselem.org**
B'tselem: Independent Israeli human
rights group covering the Occupied
Territories.

► **www.khrp.org**
Kurdish Human Rights Project

► **www.kurdishmedia.com**
Kurdish Media. Voices the Turkish
regime would like to silence.

► **www.indymedia.org.il**
Indymedia Israel

► **www.odaction.org/alsabar**
Al-Sabar: Socialist and internationalist
magazine published in Arabic by the
Organisation for Democratic Action.

► **www.palestinecampaign.org**
Palestine Solidarity Campaign

► **www.Palestinian-rights.com**
Campaign for Palestinian Rights

► **www.odaction.org/challenge**
English-language version of Al-Sabar.

LIFE
BEFORE
PROFIT

There are 25.3 million men, women and children infected with **HIV/AIDS** in Africa. It is estimated that a minimum of $3 billion per year is required to arrest the trend — the World

Africa
John Fisher

● ● ● ● ● ● ● ● ● ● ● ● ● ● ● ● ● ●

Sub-Saharan Africa, so rich in human and natural resources, remains the economically poorest region of the world. Half of its people live in poverty, and in many countries economic conditions have been getting worse for the last 20 years or more.

Poverty and debt

▶ Debt amounts to $230 billion and has increased 400 percent since 1980 when the International Monetary Fund (IMF) and World Bank started imposing structural adjustment programmes.

▶ Ten times more is spent on debt repayment than on healthcare and represents 300 percent of the value of its exports. The equivalent of 1 percent of the arms trade in Africa is spent on health.

▶ Poverty among the 630 million population of sub-Saharan Africa has increased with 48.5 percent living on less than $1 a day (47.7 percent in 1990). In Nigeria over 80 million (70 percent of the population) live on less than $1 a day. Ghana, quoted as a success by the IMF/World Bank, has 38 percent living at this level, with 20 percent of the population sharing less than 6 percent of the national income.

▶ Due to user fees introduced in Tanzania in the 1990s enrolment rates in schools have fallen from 93 percent in 1980 to 66 percent now.

▶ The World Bank admits that unless there is sustained, year on year economic growth of 5 percent, poverty will continue to rise. Economic growth in the 1990s did not reach 5 percent in any year.[1]

Health

▶ Currently there are 25.3 million men, women and children infected with HIV/AIDS; 55 percent are women. An estimated 3.8 million adults and children became infected during the year 2000, whilst 2.4 million died of HIV-related illnesses; 10 million children have been orphaned as a direct result of such deaths. Over 25 percent of the populations of Botswana, Zimbabwe and South Africa are infected, with the majority being in the age group 15 to 49.

▶ It is estimated that a minimum of $3 billion per year is required to arrest the trend, but this estimate seems low when it is forecast that, even with the victory against the 39 pharmaceutical companies in South Africa in April 2001, the bill for South Africa would be $1.5 billion. The World Bank has allocated a one-off payment of $500 million.

▶ It is reckoned that the effect of HIV/AIDS will cost an average of 0.5 percent of gross domestic product (GDP) and in the case of South Africa this will mean a loss of $22 billion in the next decade, not taking into account the cost of treatment.

▶ Over a million people die from malaria each year, mainly affecting pregnant women and children. Tuberculosis and severe respiratory diseases are at epidemic proportions.

▶ Half the world's 515,000 pregnancy-related deaths occur in this region—every two minutes an African woman dies either from pregnancy, childbirth or unsafe abortions. President Bush has, as part of his anti-abortion campaign, barred funds to the International Planned Parent Federation (IPPF) and other family planning organisations effectively preventing millions of women gaining access to contraceptives.

▶ Infant mortality which fell from 101 to 92 per 1,000 between 1990 and 1999, is said to be on the increase, and over a similar period the deaths of under-fives have increased from 155 to 161 per 1,000. In Sierra Leone in 1990, before the civil war, the rate of death was 323 per 1,000 and must now be higher.

Industry and economy

▶ Unemployment in South Africa has increased by over 500,000 in the last five years and officially is around 35 percent, but other estimates put it as high as 50 percent. Statistics for the rest of the region are very sketchy, but in most countries the number working in the informal sector—ie non-waged, relying on petty trading and subsistence farming—is over 50 percent. In Sierra Leone less than 20 percent of the population is in waged employment and often teachers and health service workers are owed salaries several months in arrears.

▶ Over half of the forests of Africa have been lost in the last 30 years. It is estimated that over 50 percent of this is due to an increasing population clearing forests to create arable land to grow food. Some 25 percent is due to logging companies that, deprived of hardwood in the more tightly regulated forests of the Northern world, have sought to satisfy demand through the export of African rainforest timber. The remaining losses are accounted for by the fact that in Africa the major source of domestic fuel is wood. African forests are believed to contain 45 percent of all global biodiversity.

▶ Some 20 percent of the regions population is affected by civil or interstate conflict. Most of these conflicts are connected with seizing resources—for example, diamonds in Sierra Leone, Liberia and Angola; diamonds and other minerals in the Republic of Congo.

▶ Privatisation of most public services is a major requirement of all IMF/World Bank loans. This has meant selling off electricity generating and supply, telecommunications, docks, railways, water and many other industries formerly owned by the state. Often this has been preceded by the state securing loans on the basis of improving the efficiency of these entities together with an insistence on full cost recovery—ie higher prices for users, and saving the privatising (usually a multinational) company investment costs.

▶ Agriculture accounts for 33 percent of Africa's GDP, 66 percent of its labour force and 40 percent of its exports, with mining taking up a large percentage of the remainder. This is the pattern laid down over a century ago following the carve-up of Africa by the imperial nations of Europe. In the last 20 years the terms of trade—ie the price of commodities compared with the price of manufactured goods—have adversely declined by a factor of at least 20 percent and subjected to unpredictable shifts.

International trade

▶ The top fifth of the world's richest countries enjoyed 82 percent of the expanding export trade and 68 percent of foreign direct investment; the bottom fifth, which includes most of sub-Saharan Africa (excluding South Africa), gets barely more than 1 percent.

▶ Import tariffs have reduced in the developed world by about 3 percent since the Uruguay Round of the General Agreement on Tariffs and Trade (GATT) in 1994, but in parts of the developing world, including sub-Saharan Africa, they have reduced by as much as 40 percent. In terms of quotas affecting textiles these have not yet been implemented. The region has also suffered from the import of second hand clothes, often destroying the small units of tailoring and cloth-making. Anti-dumping measures have been used by the US and the European Union (EU) on products from Africa, whilst maintaining high tariffs against agricultural products such as 244 percent on sugar and 174 percent on peanuts (US) and 213 percent on beef (EU).

- ► The TRIMS (Trade Related Investment Measures) agreement means that a 'local content' requirements will be prohibited, thereby allowing foreign multinationals to invest without any consideration of the effect on local industry.
- ► TRIPS (Trade-Related Intellectual Property Rights) means that the countries of Africa, along with others, will not be able to produce agricultural, medical and other essential products and processes, unless specifically exempted. The danger of Monsanto's patent on genetically modified (GM) seeds was an indication of the devastating effect of this, together with the more recent example of the drug companies seeking to enforce this right on South Africa in respect of HIV/AIDS drugs. Needless to say, the multinationals have an almost 100 percent control of the over 6,000 patents, thereby ensuring that no African country will be able to improve its technology and therefore its industry without the agreement of the multinationals.

The anti-capitalist movement

The economic problems of sub-Saharan Africa from the earliest times of capitalism have been caused by firstly the expropriation of labour in the form of the Atlantic trade in slaves and subsequently by the extraction of minerals and agricultural commodities aided by the exploitation of cheap labour. The latest stage of capitalism, termed neo-liberalism, is both a continuation and intensification of that system.

In the never-ending search for profits the only check has been the resistance of those who produce the wealth. Pressure has been exerted on both governments and employers to concede a basic standard of living and improved systems of welfare.

With the partial exception of South Africa, with its unique system of apartheid and valuable supplies of gold and diamonds, the rest of sub-Saharan Africa has remained without significant industrialisation. This has meant that the major force capable of challenging capitalism and the continued immiseration of its people has been underdeveloped—namely the working class.

There have nevertheless been heroic struggles, from the wars against the imperial powers in the 19th century to the resistance to paying taxes in colonial times, and the strikes by railway workers, miners and others. The courage of many who fought to liberate their countries knew no bounds. This spirit of resistance culminated in the magnificent overthrow, by the workers and the township people, of South Africa's pernicious system of apartheid.

Today, with their failure to achieve economic liberation, the struggle continues. The workers, both informal and formal, rural and urban, are forced to fight against their IMF/World Bank driven governments' neo-liberal agendas whether they are implemented by former ANC fighters in South Africa or reformed military dictators in West Africa. In this way every strike, every demonstration and every protest is a part of the anti-capitalist movement.

Many of the current problems relating to debt were caused in the 1970s when much of Africa was ruled by military or civilian dictators who received and borrowed huge amounts of money from the Cold War superpowers, neither of which had any regard for the indigenous people. In addition large amounts were lent by Western banks and spent on failed infrastructure projects, corruption and unwise investments. In the case of South Africa $25 billion is still owed from the apartheid era.

Resistance

The countries of South Africa and Nigeria represent over a quarter of sub-Saharan Africa's population of 640 million. The Nigerian Labour Congress (NLC) has over 4 million members. The Confederation of South African Trade Unions (COSATU) has 1.9 million and with the other two national centres, The National Council of Trade Unions (NACTU) and the Federation of Unions of South Africa (FEDUSA), there are probably over 2.5 million members in total. From this base they have represented the biggest challenge to their respective governments' neo-liberal policies.

In South Africa COSATU led a general strike of three days in June 2000 calling for a reversal of the government's economic policy and an end to job losses. It was estimated that 4 million stopped work. In September there were widespread demonstrations in support of the anti-capitalist protests in Prague. The South African Municipal Workers Union has also been conducting a militant campaign supported by non-governmental organisations (NGOs) against the privatisation proposals of both Johannesburg and Capetown municipal councils.

In Nigeria, when the government increased the price of petroleum products last June from N20 to N30 per litre, Adams Oshimolo, the charismatic president of the NLC led a general strike which drew an immediate reduction to N25, but Adams insisted on it being reduced to the former price. After six days, when virtually the whole country stopped work, a price of N22 was agreed. In March 2001, at the specific behest of the IMF representative, President Obasanjo announced plans to deregulate petroleum supplies with the express intention of raising prices. Again the NLC called mass rallies and stoppages of work from 20 to 31 March, with thousands taking part.

Strikes in March took place in Mali and Cote d'Ivoire against the plans to privatise Air Afrique, an airline jointly owned by 11 West African governments, on the insistence of the World Bank. Striking workers carried banners that read, 'The World Bank reinforces poverty.'

The Manual Workers Union in Botswana in January threatened mass action against 'premature implementation of privatisation' but appears to have settled for a wage increase.

The Ghana TUC is threatening action against water privatisation under the provision of debt relief under the Highly Indebted Poor Countries Initiative provided by the World Bank. Ten buckets of water will cost a family up to 3,500 cedis per day. The minimum wage has been increased from 4,200 cedis (58 cents) to 5,500 cedis (76 cents) per day with effect from 1 May. Fuel prices have increased by 64 percent, electricity tariffs by 103 percent and water tariffs by 96 percent.

In Ethiopia a 38-day strike by 2,000 construction workers at Midroc has secured an agreement to talks, but union leaders remain sacked.

The Angola Confederation of Unions (UNTA-CS) won a minimum wage of $50 per month, after an initial offer of $30 following strikes in December and January this year. The state controlled media did not even report the strikes.

In Benin the unions have taken strike action calling for a return of the privatised National Petroleum Company to state ownership and a reduction in petrol prices.

Workers in Cameroon laying pipelines for the Chad/Cameroon oil project struck and secured a 27 percent wage increase and job guarantees for the duration of the contract.

In the Central African Republic 72 protesters against the government's policies were arrested but couldn't be tried because the judiciary, including judges, were also on strike.

Lorry drivers in Congo-Brazzaville went on strike in January to protest about police and military roadblocks used to gain bribes.

In the Republic of Congo public sector workers have recently taken action over arrears of up to ten months salary payments.

Teachers went on strike for three days in Cote d'Ivoire and secured improved wages and better conditions Port workers in Abidjan went on strike for three days in February and five days in March to secure the implementation of an agreement on bonus payments.

In Djibouti the government has undertaken a regime of torture and arrest of trade unionists, together with election rigging in trade unions, since a general strike against the IMF structural adjustment programme in 1995. The International Confederation of Free Trade Unions (ICFTU) has called for international solidarity action against the government.

In Gambia striking bus drivers, journalists and sympathetic onlookers were beaten up and arrested by the military and national intelligence agents for protesting about fuel increases.

In Guinea-Bissau teachers, supported by students, have been taking strike action over non-payment of wages.

In Kenya there is widespread discontent with the government and the leadership of the Central Organisation of Trade Unions (COTI), whose general secretary is appointed by President Moi. Last year at the May Day rally workers walked away en masse in protest at the $6 increase in the minimum wage—and this year's increase of 7.5 percent coinciding with 1 May will not be received well, given an inflation rate in excess of 10 percent.

The three national university unions are uniting to challenge the Lesotho government's anti-union legislation, which is a crude means of smashing union recognition. The Lesotho Clothing and Allied Workers Union (LECAWU) is linking with Dutch unions to identify European clothing manufacturers that do not recognise the union and offer poor wages and conditions, with a view to a boycott campaign.

In February a strike at the Billiton Mozal newly commissioned $1.3 billion aluminium smelter in Maputo, Mozambique, has secured wage increases.

In Namibia there have been a number of walkouts of miners over such issues as tea breaks and non-payment of wages. There has also been a call for the public sector union NAPWU and the teachers' union NANTU to disaffiliate from the ruling party, SWAPO, because of their compromising positions with the government which have not been in the interests of their members.

Health workers in Niger took three days of strike action in April, following three days in February to demand better wages and conditions.

Dock workers in Sierra Leone struck in April to contest the transfer of their provident fund to the government.

Six leaders of the trade union movement in Swaziland, including the secretary-general of the Swaziland Federation of Trade Unions (SFTU), are facing charges in court arising from 'illegal' general strikes last November. This is a continuation of the government's campaign against trade unions which last year included expelling trade union leaders from South Africa.

The Zambia Trade Union Congress has threatened strike action within two months unless the wages and conditions of public sector workers are not increased.

The 7,000 demonstrators at the May Day rally called by the Zimbabwe Congress of Trade Unions (ZCTU) drove a 200-strong mob of ZANU-PF party supporters away in the latest example of the ruling party's campaign of terror against trade unionists.

At May Day rallies held in many African countries, with the participation of many thousands of workers, the common theme was opposition to government policies enforced by the World Bank and IMF, and the resultant privatisation and job losses.[2]

Links with civil society

The trade union movement throughout Africa is seen by many as the key force to unite civil society against the neo-liberal agenda of their governments, which without exception are implementing anti-people policies. There are a number of examples of broad coalitions of civil society and trade union organisations campaigning against IMF/World Bank measures, particularly in the case of the privatisation of the water supply. In South Africa the South African Municipal Workers' Union (SAMWU), Jubilee South, the Anti-Privatisation Forum, the Campaign Against Neo-liberalism in South Africa, human rights organisations and religious organisations have called strikes and demonstrations. In Ghana the Ghana National Coalition Against the Privatisation of Water comprises the Ghana Trades Union Congress together with a wide range of civil society organisations and some international NGOs such as Globalisation Challenge, which met in June 2001 for a four day conference to draw up plans for resisting the takeover of the water industry by foreign multinationals.

In Nigeria there has been a tradition of working with civil society movements, especially human rights organisations, forged over many years of resistance to military regimes. In Sierra Leone it was the Sierra Leone Labour Congress (SLLC) together with the Campaign for Good Governance which led massive demonstrations and strikes to bring about the restoration of democracy, and it was the SLLC which led the stayaway from work following the military coup in May 1997.

Of particular significance was the 'Dakar 2000: From Resistance to Alternatives' conference held in December. Leaders of NGOs and social movements, including some trade unionists, from all over Africa analysed the debt crisis and the impacts of IMF/World Bank structural adjustment programmes on Africa. Participants also considered strategies for resistance to the neo-liberal model and highlighted alternatives. The conference was an important turning point in the global Jubilee movement, and at the instigation of Jubilee South in conjunction with Global South networks it was resolved that:

The Third World debt is illegitimate and must be cancelled without conditions; structural adjustment programmes of the IMF and World Bank, under whatever name, including the new Poverty

Reduction Strategy Papers, must be rejected; that no conditionalities should be placed on the debt cancellation process by Northern governments or creditors; and that we must more consciously take account of the ecological impacts of the debt. New strategies for achieving 'life without debt' were proposed and Jubilee South, which has organisers in most African countries, would build social movements to get their governments to refuse to pay their illegitimate debts. The declaration then goes on, in some detail, to indicate how this will be achieved.[3]

This year alone there have been a great number of demonstrations in African capitals led by women's organisations and other bodies, particularly during a visit by the heads of the IMF and World Bank earlier in the year. In Tanzania and Malawi the demonstrators were met with severe police violence.

The key issues

The central demands of the many trade unions and progressive social organisations in Africa who are fighting back against corporate globalisation include:

- ► The fight to force their governments to oppose the neo-liberal policies of the Washington Consensus.
- ► Complete opposition to the intervention of the IMF and World Bank conditions, particularly privatisation and job losses.
- ► The establishment of full trade union rights, including those exempted in Export Processing Zones, and end to governments' anti-trade union activities.
- ► Opposition to the rule of the multinational corporations through international workers' solidarity.
- ► The funding of adequate free education and healthcare, especially in the fight against HIV/AIDS.
- ► A cessation of environmental degradation, particularly that caused by the multinational oil and logging companies.
- ► Unconditional cancellation of debt.
- ► The abolition of child labour.
- ► An end to corruption fuelled by the practices of Northern

governments in securing contracts for the multinationals.
- ► Fair elections, free of state repression, and transparent and accountable governments.
- ► An end to civil and interstate wars, including arms deals.
- ► Freedom of the press.

The future

The future under capitalism holds out no opportunity for the masses of sub-Saharan Africa to relieve themselves of the enormous daily burdens they are forced to suffer. However, the example of the tremendous struggle of the South African workers, students and townships in overthrowing apartheid shows what is possible. It now requires an even greater struggle to remove economic apartheid throughout Africa. This can only be achieved by bringing together on an international scale what as yet is an embryonic anti-capitalist movement, to create a force which will end the oppressive tyranny that subjects the majority of Africans and the rest of us to a life of servitude. We have nothing to lose but our chains.

John Fisher was a Manufacturing, Science and Finance union regional official and is now a trade union educator working with the Commonwealth Trades Union Congress. jmb_fisher@hotmail.com

Notes

1. For more information see the IMF and World Bank websites.
2. The LabourStart website is excellent and up to date. The COSATU website is also good.
3. For the full statement see the Jubilee South website, http://jubileesouth.net

Sites

▶ www.aidc.org.za
▶ www.allAfrica.com
  Provides a good newspaper cutting service.
▶ www.focusweb.org
▶ www.jubileesouth.net
▶ www.labourstart.org
  A good source of news on struggle worldwide on a daily basis.

On a day when all protests had been declared illegal by the Czech government, riot police block the main bridge to the conference centre, where IMF and World Bank delegates are meeting, Prague 26 September 2000.

Russia and Eastern Europe
Mike Haynes

● ● ● ● ● ● ● ● ● ● ● ● ● ● ● ● ● ● ● ●

If globalisation works as its propagandists tell us then nowhere should the benefits be more obvious than in the former Soviet bloc. When the Stalinist states collapsed in 1989-91 the promise was that access to the global market would transform these societies and improve everyone's lot. But it didn't work. In the first instance the explanation was that the new market was being held back by old structures and old mentalities. But as the past recedes, the present remains a monumental mess, leaving people scratching their heads and saying that 'it wasn't supposed to be like this'.

'A human crisis of monumental proportions is emerging in the former Soviet Union,' the United Nations Development Programme reported in 1999.[1] It was not one, however, that those who advised the Russian government had been much concerned with. Between 1989 and 1995 real output in Russia fell by some 50 percent and agricultural output by 20 percent. Male life expectancy was reduced by some six years which represented some 1.5 million excess deaths, and the birthrate plummeted. But for Professor Richard Layard of the London School of Economics and one of the Yeltsin advisers and for John Parker of *The Economist* in their 1996 book *The Coming Russian Boom* there was an upside—in Russia 'life continues with dignity in most cases, and the average young woman is more attractively dressed than in Britain or America (and more beautiful)'.[2]

In 1998 the Russian economy crashed, the boom never came and, six years on, the number of premature deaths has doubled again. Boris Yeltsin, on the other hand, was treated by the finest doctors in the world and left office with immunity from criminal prosecution, and Professor Layard, ex Eton College, Kings College and Yeltsin advisor and co-deviser of the 'crumpet index of economic improvement', had been promoted by Tony Blair to a life peerage as baron.

The real story of human crisis is the same in other parts of the former USSR, and in much of Eastern Europe it is not much better. In the Balkans, for example, after the end of the Kosovan war, the UN Commission on Europe, one of the more insightful sources of information, tried to stress how much there was to do. For these countries to catch up with where the central Europe transition countries were in the year 2000 would need as big

> **Regimes which in the name of the people had ruled over the people and then often failed to deliver even an adequate supply of toilet paper crumbled within weeks**

a leap forward as the central European countries are themselves trying to make to the European Union level. 'The time required for such a catching-up to occur is somewhat alarming: unless the current trends in economic performance are decisively broken, it will take decades, even on the more optimistic scenarios, for these poorest European countries to reach only the mediocre level of per capita income enjoyed by the more advanced central European transition economies'.[3]

The latter phrase is important, for in the ocean of failure that is the post-Soviet transition, countries like Hungary and Poland are held out as beacons of success. And it is true that Poland, the most successful, did indeed mange to recover much of the lost output of the early 1990s, but it remains marked by gross inequalities and overall 'a mediocre level of per capita output'. In 2001 unemployment returned to 16 percent and the prime minister, Kwasniewski (an ex-Communist) 'said he supported an increase in the political clout of business people, who complain that stringent labour rules—supported by Poland's powerful unions—are hampering their ability to create new jobs.' In fact the International Labour Organisation recently quoted one Western diplomat as saying that in Poland 'current legislation in support of trade union bargaining power is quite weak, and all power lies with the employers'.[4]

It was not supposed to be like this. The market, liberalisation and globalisation were supposed to bring success where the old state-controlled order had failed. The autumn of 1989 seemed a good time to be alive in Eastern Europe. Regimes which in the name of the people had ruled over the people and then often failed to deliver even an adequate supply of toilet paper crumbled within weeks. And in the USSR the top-down process of reform inaugurated by Gorbachev began to get out of hand as hundreds of thousands of miners struck. More than any other group they perhaps knew the shallowness of the claims that the Soviet Union was in any sense a workers' state. In some instances 'their' state had not even increased their soap allowance since the 1920s, and every year it sat back while hundreds died in accidents and roof-falls while thousands more began to show the first symptoms of lung diseases that would mark and finally end their days.

Now a new mood was in the air in which everything seemed possible. The Cold War was ending and the walls were coming down. Miklos Vasarhelyi (who had been imprisoned as Imre Nagy's press secretary after the suppression of the Hungarian uprising in 1956) told a *New York Times* reporter in 1989:

> First of all there will really be a Europe again. The countries of central and Eastern Europe will finally get an opportunity to unite with the West. We will begin to live under the same conditions. It will take time, but socially, politically and economically we will achieve what the Western countries have already achieved. The door is now open.[5]

But ideas like this were also mixed with a sense that those who had run these societies should now be held to account. 'Yes we have a two-party system. The *nomenklatura* [officials and privileged elite] with their nice apartments and special stores, and the rest of us with nothing,' said one worker in Siberia to a Western journalist.[6]

Ideas like this were commonplace and they were supported by the beginnings of a collective tradition. At the lowest point in its history the Stalinist regime in Russia, and those it imposed in Eastern Europe after 1945, had largely suppressed and atomised workers' resistance. But unevenly, and often haltingly, it had begun to return. The Solidarity Movement in Poland which sprang out of shipyards like those of Gdansk was its greatest achievement, at one stage containing more than half the national workforce, making Solidarity still the biggest trade union that has ever existed. The movement deep in the mines of Russia was another example of the beginnings of a collective potential.

Workers knew that they were against the old system but they were not sure how their hopes could be expressed, for the language of socialism had been stolen and abused by the regimes that ruled over them

The trouble was that few of those involved saw through the confusion of the slogans of the market which promised a solution to the ills of the society which exploited them. Workers knew that they were against the old system but they were not sure how their hopes could be realised or even how to express them, for the language of socialism had been stolen and abused by the regimes that ruled over them.

It was this confusion that allowed the revolution to be stolen from the ordinary people of the former Soviet bloc. Today most of the Gdansk shipyard is empty, rusting and decaying. It went bankrupt in 1996, declared inefficient. Now it stands as a monument not only to the heroism of the past but as a monument to the lost transition. Ironically in August 2000 leaders gathered there to remember the birth of Solidarity two decades before. But for Tadeusz Korzinski, a 45 year old welder who took part in the 1980 strikes and still works at the shipyard, the event left a bitter taste: 'There are no workers at this feast, just men in coats and ties. Nothing remains of Solidarity except its name. It has lost its essence. They have betrayed and forgotten us.'

The same is true elsewhere. In Russia the coal mines are

The 'transition' in the former Soviet bloc is a euphemistic term for what in reality has been a Great Depression

closing, the miners' often unpaid and the future bleak. In Vorkuta in the far north, for example, half the mines have been closed since 1991, including one of the newest and most productive. 'Many directors have come in and stolen money from the mine. Now there is nothing left to steal,' a miner told a visiting journalist in the Spring of 2001. But alongside the mine directors and the corrupt government was another enemy—the World Bank, which had constantly advised the closing of mines and especially the newest one. 'The World Bank said, "You don't need so much coal," so we never opened it in the end. They are the enemy of the people,' said a local union leader.[7]

What the former Soviet bloc needed was globalisation but of a very different kind from that on offer. By the 1980s the region had a huge industrial base but it was failing. It could have been renovated to supply the needs not only of the local population but those lacking basic necessities across the world. There was even the potential of what was called a 'peace dividend' to help as the Cold War ended. Perhaps this could even have been the beginning of a more generous politics of global redistribution that could have brought East and West together to address the abject poverty of the mass of the rest of the world.

But this is not what 'their' globalisation is about and this is not what figured in the calculations of the G7, the World Bank and the International Monetary Fund (IMF). The result has been disaster.

> The 'transition' in most of the countries in the former Soviet bloc in central and Eastern Europe and the CIS is a euphemistic term for what in reality has been a Great Depression. The extent of the collapse in output and the skyrocketing nature of inflation have been historically unprecedented. The consequences for human security have been calamitous. By conservative estimates, over 100 million people have been thrown into poverty and considerably more hover precariously just above subsistence.[8]

So said the United Nations Development Programme in its survey of a decade of transition. Perhaps in the transition region as a whole the excess mortality is as high as 10 million over the decade.

A social transformation to a world built on genuine cooperation did not figure in the thinking of crucial three groups. One of these was made of those who controlled the levers of power in the Soviet bloc. What they were interested in was saving their positions of power and influence and converting them to what they hoped would be a more stable market basis. In the process those who controlled the economy and the key institutions were happy to ditch the old Communist Party leaderships and the secret police so long as they could perpetuate the class power that they held before 1989.

Here their interests coincided with those who controlled the global economy in the West. Politically this group saw the retreat of Soviet power as a victory for 'their' system, ignoring the extent to which capitalism in the West was failing to deliver its promises for the larger part of the population of the world.

Economically global corporations too looked to the Eastern bloc as a region which would have little choice but to accept integration into the world economy on whatever meagre terms they set. Eastern Europe would be a market, it would be a source of raw materials, and it would be a production site for some limited manufacturing production and integrated financially. But in other respects it would be held at arms length as much as possible in the same condition as similar zones around the world.

What linked the perspectives of these two groups together was the role of a third group. The great institutions of global capital, the IMF, the World Bank and the newly created European Bank for Reconstruction and Development presided over the planned increase in the role of the market, drawing in Western academics and opinion-makers in these societies. How deeply they believed in their own myths is not clear, but they provided the ideology that helped disarm opposition. This was the belief that the global market would supply all that was needed to transform these societies. Instead it brought chaos and collapse. But their arguments achieved the wider objective of allowing opportunities for broader change to be squandered. They also allowed the more insightful members of the old order to complete their change of clothes so as to be able to run the new system and capitalise on and expand the wealth and position they had developed under the old system.

Some of the guilty men (for they were usually men) were prominent Western academics—Jeffrey Sachs, Joseph Stiglitz, Andrei Shleifer from the US, Layard from Britain, Anders Aslund from Sweden. Others, often no less important, worked behind the scenes, such as John Williamson and John Odling-Smee in the IMF. It was Odling-Smee, head of the IMF's European II Department, who wrote in the IMF's house magazine in September 1998 that the impact of the Asian crisis on Russia was 'relatively modest' and that 'growth...is expected to rise'—which was rather unfortunate given that a few days before speculative capital had flooded out bringing down the rouble and a bubble economy.[9]

But the issue is not simply the passports of the advisors. Most of the policy-makers and advisors have had local passports. The most notorious is Anatoly Chubias in Russia who presided over the corrupt privatisation process. 'They steal and steal and steal,' he calmly announced. 'They are stealing absolutely everything and it is impossible to stop them. But let them steal and take their property. Then they will become owners and decent administrators of this property'.[10]

It was in Russia that the corruption was worst, and it didn't stop at Russians. In 1999 the Harvard economist Andrei Shleifer, who had helped plan the privatisation process in Russia, was awarded the American Economic Association's John Bates Clark Medal in 1999 to outstanding young economists. But he was already under investigation for insider dealing and a leading co-worker had been sacked. Then in January 2000 Harvard University shut its prestigious Development Institute which had run much of the US policy advice to Russia, with the US government claiming back $120 million in penalty payments as the authorities charged that Harvard employees had 'abused their positions as high-level and trusted advisors to, and on behalf of, the United States in Russia'. No such claims, however, were admissible in Russia where Chubais and others had presided over 'a thieves banquet'. Under pressure in the political sphere he jumped across to run one of the huge companies he had helped to create.

But the real corruption here was the intellectual justification for the transition and the theft of power within it. What had worked (or failed to work!) elsewhere would work in the East. 'Most of the logic behind the standard stabilisation package applies to Eastern Europe as well,' wrote a prominent group of economists in 1990. Within this the willingness to allow the old state capitalists to appear as market capitalists was often breathtakingly brazen. In Russia, for example, Shleifer boasted that under his privatisation plans 'the single most important benefit that the managers received in their privatisation programme [was that] within certain guidelines, they, rather than any ministerial or other government officials, had almost complete control over the strategy for privatising their firms'. *The Economist* called Russian privatisation 'the sale of the century', but it was more the 'giveaway of the century'. It wasn't much better elsewhere. In 1990 the same Western economists, speaking of Poland and Czechoslovakia, suggested that 'the practical issue may not be how much control to give workers, but how much to take away'. Of course they regretted this, but the logic of the market economy was supposed to sweep all objections before it: 'Although democratic ownership is highly desirable (indeed essential to the political success of privatisation), large shareholders are necessary for efficient management'.[11]

In the end the scale of the crisis that all this created caused even some insiders to question what they were doing. It was Stiglitz, former chief economist of the World Bank, who broke first, blowing the whistle on some of the insider processes. But the response of the others was sometimes vitriolic. For Aslund 'Stiglitz is a striking embarrassment to himself and the World Bank. Without knowing anything he mouths any stupidity that comes into his head'.[12]

These squabbles, however, are of little comfort to workers across the former Soviet bloc who are faced with an everyday

> *The Economist* called Russian privatisation 'the sale of the century', but it was more the 'giveaway of the century'

struggle for survival. Many have simply closed their doors tight against the world, but resistance does exist. Developing it is more difficult because three problems have to be overcome. The first is the dulling impact of the crisis itself, which has put enormous strain on people. The second is the organisational confusion. Trade unions under the old regimes were state-run bureaucracies. New trade unions quickly sprang up after 1989 but they struggled to find a space to organise and many became trapped in the top-down process of transition. Whether as new or reformed old-style unions, therefore, it is taking time for more stable and responsive organisations to emerge, and there are problems everywhere. This has very often thrown workers back on more informal local organisations. The ups and downs of industrial struggle in Russia are set out in the table below.

Striking in the transition: the Russian strike pattern 1991-99[13]

Year	Number of strikes	Number involved (thousands)	Work days lost (thousands)	Average duration (days)
1991	1,755	238	2,314	9.7
1992	6,273	358	1,893	5.3
1993	264	120	237	2.0
1994	514	155	755	4.9
1995	8,856	489	1,367	2.8
1996	8,278	664	4,009	6.0
1997	17,007	887	6,001	6.8
1998	11,162	531	2,881	5.4
1999	7,285	238	1,827	7.7

These statistics show that even in Russia not everything is passive and demoralised. The confusion of 1992-93 can clearly be seen, so too can the struggle against the devastating impact of the transition, the accumulation of unpaid wages etc in 1994-98. But then also the impact of the crash of 1998 is clear. These Russian statistics show the small scale, often guerrilla nature of much industrial conflict. Going beyond this requires a third element everywhere.

This is ideas. The disorientation of the past decade needs to be overcome and it is here that the anti-globalisation movement offers a new chance. 'Their globalisation' has helped bring down some of the barriers between East and West but 'our globalisation' offers the only way forward. There have been some lurches towards nationalism—most notably in the former Yugoslavia. This remains a danger everywhere. But so far nationalism has not been the general response to the crisis. People still believe that they were hemmed in for long enough. What they need is the example of a different kind of internationalism to the internationalism of global capitalism. Some people came from Poland to protest with those in Prague, and a trickle of Russians interested in the anti-globalisation movement has begun. What is true everywhere is that the people of the former Soviet bloc have been victims of a globalisation experiment that stands as an indictment to the claim that the market can improve the world.

Mike Haynes lectures in European Studies at Wolverhampton University. He has written widely on the transition in the former Soviet bloc.
le1958@wlv.ac.uk

Notes

1   United Nations Development Programme, *Transition 1999 Regional Transition 1999: The Human Cost of Transition, Human Development Report for Central and Eastern Europe and the CIS* (United Nations, 1999).

2   R Layard and J Parker, *The Coming Russian Boom: a Guide to New Markets and Politics* (Free Press, 1996).

3   United Nations, Economic Commission for Europe, *Economic Survey of Europe, 1999*, no 2 (United Nations, 1999), p4.

4   'From Solidarity to "Crumbling Bastions",' *World of Work* (ILO)

-    no 37, December 2000; *Financial Times*, 12 May 2001.
- 5 Quoted in B Gwertzman and M T Kaufman (eds), *The Collapse of Communism* (Random House, 1990), pp225-226.
- 6 Quoted in M Edwards, 'Siberia: In From the Cold', *National Geographic*, vol 177, no 3, March 1990, pp13-14.
- 7 'From Solidarity to "Crumbling Bastions",' *World of Work* (ILO) no 37, December 2000; *Financial Times*, 12 May 2001.
- 8 United Nations Development Programme, as above.
- 9 *Finance and Development*, vol 35, no 3, September 1998, pp15-16.
- 10 See M Haynes and P Glatter, 'The Russian Catastrophe', *International Socialism* 81 (Winter 1998), pp45-90.
- 11 O Blanchard, R Dornbusch, P Krugman, R Layard, L Summers, *Reform in Eastern Europe* (MIT Press, 1991), pp1, 32; M Boycko, A Shleifer and R Vishny, *Privatising Russia* (MIT Press, 1995), p80.
- 12 Quoted from *The Economist*, 18 September 1999, p81, in M Goldman, 'Reprivatising Russia', *Challenge*, May-June 2000, p29.
- 13 Compiled from *Russian Economic Trends* (various).

Sites

- ▶ **www.icem.org/campaigns/no_pay_cc/** 'Pay Us Our Wages' the ICEM, the International Federation of Chemical, Energy, Mine and General Workers' Unions. Much broader than its title suggests.
- ▶ **www.trud.org/index7.htm** Semi-official Russian trade union site.

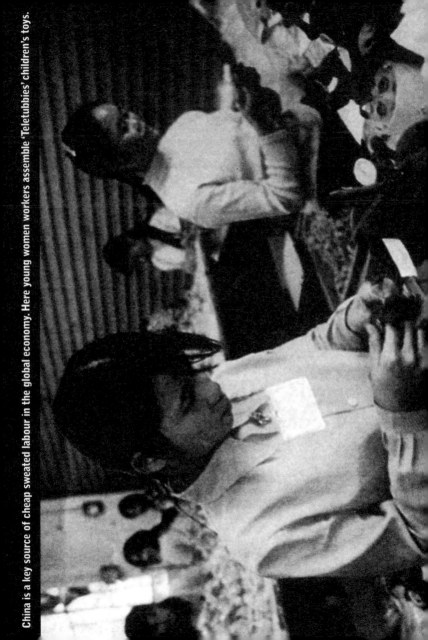

China is a key source of cheap sweated labour in the global economy. Here young women workers assemble 'Teletubbies' children's toys.

China
Helen Shooter

● ● ● ● ● ● ● ● ● ● ● ● ● ● ● ● ● ●

The deal between the US and China that paves the way for China's entry into the World Trade Organisation (WTO) was finally signed on 15 November 1999 just two weeks before Seattle. China's rulers were jubilant. Business leaders in Motorola and Boeing were pleased their lobbying of the US government over the deal had paid off. China's entry had been discussed for 14 years and there are still negotiations to finalise the deal. It will bring misery to the vast majority of the 1.3 billion people in China. They have already had some experience of what the free market means—millions have lost their jobs, and workers and the rural poor have had their living standards savaged.

The number of labour disputes in Shanghai has been rising by more than 40 percent each year for the last three years

China is a one-party state. There are no free elections or independent trade unions. Protests are often met with armed force—soldiers massacred the students and workers in Tiananmen Square in 1989. Yet ordinary people in cities and rural areas have held strikes and protests against the effects of the market.

The number of labour disputes in the major city of Shanghai has been rising by more than 40 percent each year for the last three years, according to government-funded newspaper *China Daily* in March this year. In 1999 government records officially showed there were 100,000 demonstrations—about 270 a day—which was a 70 percent rise on the previous year.

The *International Herald Tribune* reported in July last year:

> The unrest since the beginning of this month has ranged from one end of China to another and across the social spectrum. While there is nothing new about industrial and rural unrest in China, the number of incidents seems to be increasing rapidly.

This unrest is not as yet a self conscious movement against capitalism. But China's rulers are pushing through economic reform and privatisation with the same gusto as Western governments, which will target embittered workers and the poor for even more pain.

Free market reforms have had a dramatic effect on workers in China even before the WTO allows multinationals to let rip. The first wave of market reforms came in 1978 introduced by Deng Xiaoping. The same man went on to order the troops to fire on the students and workers protesting in Tiananmen Square in 1989. Deng turned to the market to solve the economic problems left by Mao. China was poverty-stricken with a stagnating economy that could not compete with Western countries. Deng's plan was to open up China to the global market. 'To get rich is glorious,' was his slogan. The Chinese economy became one of the fastest growing economies in the world. From 1980 to 1985 there was massive growth in industry and agriculture. People's standard of living improved dramatically.

'The status of workers has changed so much. Now we say that workers are like umbrellas. When it's raining, they are used. And when it's not, they are put aside'
— laid off worker, Beijing, 22 July 1999

But once the full force of the market reforms kicked in, workers and the rural poor saw those gains eroded. Rampant inflation in the cities meant cuts in real wages and agriculture stagnated because of lack of investment.

The government also created 'Special Economic Zones' to lure foreign investment. These zones spread to around 20 coastal cities offering tax concessions, free land and buildings, and low wages. They are the sweatshops for Nike and Reebok that we see today. As Cai Chongguo from *China Labour Bulletin*, an independent journal based in Hong Kong, explained in 1999:

> The Special Economic Zones were presented as China's 'window to the world'. But the reality is sweatshops, over-exploitation, untold misery. Peasants are forced to migrate to the zones and the cities, where they are plunged into conditions of indescribable squalor.
>
> Many of you know about some of the fires in the sweatshops. Hundreds of women were killed unable to escape for lack of safety codes and regulations. These are the abominable conditions of exploitation foisted upon us by the multinational corporations through their 'free trade' agreements.

China's rulers today want to use the WTO to open up China's economy even further. President Jiang Zemin and prime minister Zhu Ronghji are privatising the state-run enterprises which employ two thirds of China's urban workers. In the process they are destroying the benefits—the Iron Rice Bowl—that workers in these industries were entitled to. Those benefits included pensions, housing and medical care.

The government ruled that from 1997 these industries could cut back pensions, from 1998 they could no longer allocate subsidised housing to workers, and from 2000 all social welfare would be phased out. This is devastating the lives of workers and the poor as the government tears up the old 'cradle to grave' welfare system.

The government admitted in 1999 that there are at least 300 million Chinese—a quarter of the population—officially living in poverty. Many of those in dire poverty live in rural areas. In some remote areas in China like Sichuan the infant mortality rate reaches 300 deaths per 100,000 people, a level comparable to sub-Saharan Africa. Yet when millions of the rural poor flock to cities desperate for work the government's market reforms have driven unemployment up. Some 57 percent of homes in urban areas are at subsistence level compared to the 5 percent of households classed as rich, according to a survey last year by the non-governmental organisation Asia Monitor Resources Centre.

The rich have gained much from the market reforms. The sons and daughters of the top political leaders, the company bosses and the army chiefs enjoy luxurious lifestyles. Their beds have been feathered by corruption and raking in money from deals with foreign firms that want to get into China's market.

At the same time China's rulers pump out the same lie as institutions like the WTO—that only the market can improve the status of the poor. But as Shen Jiru, director of the top government think-tank the Chinese Academy of Social Sciences, admitted in November 1999, there would be 'considerable pain' as the number of redundancies in state enterprises rises and the gap between rich and

'Over 2,000 workers blockaded the main road of Huainan city in Anhui province for five days from 28 June 1999 against the closure of a paper manufacturing plant.

The factory was privatised in 1998 and each employee was forced to buy shares or face being laid off.

The paper factory workers had surrounded and refused to release the factory's top managers at the beginning of the protest. On the second day the city's mayor, who is a former director at the plant, sent in over 200 riot police.

They were forced back by the sheer number of workers.

Some 500 workers from the Huainan Electronics factory joined the workers' road blockade on 1 July after they appealed for solidarity. The joint action meant the sit-in stretched back over 500 metres.

In the early hours of 2 July the mayor ordered over 2,000 armed riot police to brutally attack the workers. Later that same morning at least 5,000 workers held an outraged protest through the streets against police violence.

The number of marchers swelled as workers in nearby factories joined in support. "Down with corruption!" "We demand a livelihood" read the workers' banners. Again the police had to use force to beat back the protesters.'

— Han Dongfang,
China Labour Bulletin

poor widens. The *Times* warned in October 1999, 'If legions of workers were to become unemployed, party leaders would soon face much more serious opposition than they did during the student protests of 1989.'

Protests

The protests sparked off across China take two forms, according to *China Labour Bulletin* in May this year:

> One is the defensive struggle in the older industrial areas where workers are often fighting for wage arrears, pensions and welfare entitlements.
>
> The other is the struggle going on in the Special Economic Zones. These are much more spontaneous and are often over working hours, forced overtime and unpaid wages. The latter are mostly dominated by migrant workers.

Below is a list of some of those protests:

► *February 2000:* More than 20,000 miners from the Yangjiazhangzi mine in Liaoning province and their families attacked government buildings and fought with police for three days. It was the biggest case of unrest in years in a province that has seen some of China's most serious protests. They were angry at mass sackings caused by the mine going bankrupt and the derisory redundancy package they were offered. They burned cars and blocked a railway line. Armed police were sent in and fired shots into the air to quell the protest.

► *May 2000:* Some 5,000 steel workers blockaded a main road into Liaoyang city in Liaoning province. They were angry that they had not been paid for over a year. Their action forced the officials to agree to pay them three months wages.

► *June 2000:* Young and old protesters against water cuts blockaded the road in Shenyang, the capital of Liaoning province. 'I used to think protests happened only in other countries, but now they are happening right in front of me,' said Wang Rui, a 24 year old protester. Some 500 families in a housing block had no water for 10 days because the money they paid to a state-owned company for water bills went missing. Taxi drivers said demonstrations were so common that Shenyang radio stations gave updates on 'man-made roadblocks' almost every morning.

► *July 2000:* Thousands of Chinese villagers rioted in Shandong province over access to drinking and irrigation water. Around 100 people and 40 police officers were injured in the riot. One police officer was killed, according to the Hong Kong based Information Centre of Human Rights and Democracy. The people were furious that work on a reservoir meant their water would be completely cut off.

► Some 1,000 workers surrounded the factory they worked for in Chengdu in Sichuan province for seven days after they discovered it was going bankrupt and they all faced redundancy. The factory made uniforms for the Chinese army. Its managers began selling off land the company owned to make money and for gambling in real estate deals. But the workers heard that they would not get paid and began the protest. Many of them are retired workers whose pensions could be axed if the firm collapsed.

► Over 10,000 primary school teachers gathered in the north-eastern province of Jilin to try to march to Beijing to fight for their jobs. They wanted to petition the government for help after local officials announced reforms would threaten their jobs. Some 1,000 security officers blocked the train and bus stations. Police beat up and seriously injured many of the teachers to prevent them getting to Beijing.

► *December 2000:* Workers blockaded a main rail line in north east China after the Daqing No 2 construction company had refused to pay the 8,000 workers' wages for two years.

► *January 2001:* Hundreds of workers from the Jilin Industrial Chemicals group in Jilin province blockaded a local highway for three days in temperatures as low as minus 25 degrees centigrade. They were protesting at the factory's closure and the 4,000 workforce being thrown out of work. One worker said, 'The point is that as long as we do not have the right to organise, we are going to be sacrificed by the exploiters. What gives me hope is that the strikes and demonstrations that are taking place all over China today are teaching workers that they have to organise and unite.'

Students

One of the biggest student protests since Tiananmen Square in 1989 took place in Beijing University last year.

A student, Qiu Qing-feng, was raped and killed as she walked home to her campus accommodation in a remote rural suburb. Her fellow students blamed the university and police for the death. As one leaflet distributed round the campus said, 'You have provoked the death of one of our sisters. You spend plenty of money on your own offices but you are ready to sacrifice students' security.'

Some 2,000 students began a candlelit vigil and sit-in on 23 May demanding that the college authorities allowed a memorial service to be held. Their protests spilled over into a second day. Another 500 students

At least 41 primary school children and three teachers were killed at a school in Fanglin village, Jiangxi province, in March after a massive explosion brought the building down.

The children were forced to assemble fireworks despite protests from their parents. School officials said the work brought funds into the school.

China has one of the lowest rates of education funding amongst developing countries. The Fanglin tragedy shows what can happen when business interests dominate in underfunded public services.

'News reports from the scene say that the school engaged in this business because of funding shortfalls. That is no excuse,' said David Bull, executive director of UNICEF.

'The explosion may have been unintended but this was no accident. The deaths were entirely preventable.'

demonstrated, demanding the resignation of the Beijing's police chief. That same evening around 2,000 students shouted down the university vice-president at a meeting, saying, 'Do you have any conscience?' The university caved in over the memorial service, and 3,000 students attended before marching round the campus. The protest became an outlet for raising other grievances like general living conditions and rising tuition costs.

Students were also behind the angry demonstrations against the US bombing of the Chinese embassy in Belgrade during the 1999 Balkan War. The government allowed these to go ahead but soon curbed them, worried they could attract elements 'who may use the occasion to disturb social order'. China's rulers are always mindful that students were the spark for the 1989 Tiananmen Square protests that rocked the government.

Conclusion

Governments across the globe are driving through privatisation and attacking social welfare. China is one of them. China's rulers have already been enthusiastically pushing through these policies. But as *Business Week* admitted in November 1999, 'The WTO deal would give Beijing cover for the tough restructuring necessary to fix its fragmented and inefficient industries.' So there is much more pain to come for China's workers and rural poor.

A report by the Public Security Ministry in 1998 and 1999 revealed then that senior police officers were recording a rise in unrest. The police said most protests in the cities were sparked by the failure of state-owned enterprises to pay wages and pensions, return money taken from workers, or provide support for laid off workers.

One officer summed up the feeling of the protesters:

If we don't create a disturbance our problem won't be addressed. If we create a small disturbance we'll get small redress. If we create a big disturbance we'll get big redress.

Ding Xinfa of Jiangxi's police department described how in the first half of 1998 there had been 'numerous' protests across the province, including protesters organising roadblocks, holding up trains and attacking government and party headquarters. Ding warned that if the number of protests increased 'the possibility grows greater and greater that disturbances will spread from one workplace to others, and across industries and districts.'

China has been hailed as an example of a successful, dynamic market economy. But ordinary people's anger is fuelled by the enormous growth in inequality that the market has brought—the yawning gulf between the rich coastal provinces and the inland regions, between urban and rural areas. They see a growing middle class getting fat off business deals while the mass of the population is being told to tighten their belts. Significant numbers of people have begun to fight back. Crucially this has happened in the countryside as well as the cities. One example is a protest by more than 1,000 farmers in Zhangzhou in Fujian province in November last year. They marched to the local government offices and demanded the resignation of county officials. They were protesting at the increase in taxes on bananas, a crop most farmers in the area depend on.

Protests in China have not gone beyond struggles over immediate concerns to the wider questioning of the whole system that we saw in Seattle and on other such mobilisations since.

But for most of the last 50 years ordinary people in China have been told their society was an alternative to Western countries and the free market. China's rulers have always argued the priority was to compete with Western countries in economic and military terms. That has meant various political strategies of which workers and the poor have been victims. The latest economic restructuring driven by WTO entry conditions is about trying to make workers pay again.

Unrest in both the countryside and the city did not happen in 1989. That is something we have seen emerging today. Inside those protests are the forces that could pose a political challenge inside China—something its rulers are all too aware of.

Helen Shooter is a journalist for *Socialist Worker*.
helens@swp.org.uk

Kurmila Devi, member of a Dalit Sena cell, during weapons training

India
Sam Ashman

● ● ● ● ● ● ● ● ● ● ● ● ● ● ● ● ● ●

An alliance between Teamsters and Turtle kids—that phrase has come, for many, to sum up the remarkable unity between trade unionists and environmentalists on the streets of Seattle in 1999. But where are these turtles that many were protesting about? They are off the coast of the east Indian state of Orissa, and they are being killed by shrimp trawlers which are also destroying the livelihoods of the local fishing communities. This is just one of a huge number of issues associated with globalisation that have mobilised millions across India in the last decade, producing one of the most vocal and powerful movements of resistance anywhere in the world.

Today India is the World Bank's largest single borrower. Loans committed to India in 2000 amounted to $1.8 billion; interest paid to the bank in the same year was $647 million. India is also a member of the World Trade Organisation (WTO). Since 1991 successive Indian governments have followed a World Bank/International Monetary Fund (IMF) programme of neo-liberal reforms, known in India as the New Economic Policy. The prescription is the same as elsewhere: cuts to government subsidies, privatisation, the removal of barriers to the free flow of capital, orientation on an export economy. In 1991 real spending on health, education and social spending was immediately and savagely cut. This structural adjustment has been embraced, even relished, by India's elite.

What are the results after a decade? Deepening poverty, and a growing divide between rich and poor. Around 400 million of India's population of 1 billion people are officially recognised as poor. The number of those who are illiterate today is greater than the entire population at independence from Britain in 1947. Thanks to structural adjustment the poor have to spend more money to buy less food. Unemployment is rising, as is destitution.

Around 400 million of India's population of 1 billion people are officially recognised as poor

The issues

There is a whole range of issues which are affecting farmers, workers, the poor, and indigenous or 'tribal' communities in India:

▶ *Agriculture:* Multinational agribusiness corporations are attempting to gain control of vital resources. They want to introduce genetically modified (GM) seeds, and to put patents on them. That means farmers, instead of saving seeds from year to year, will be forced to buy new seeds every year. One US multinational, Rice Tec, has even gained a patent on Basmati, a rice grown in India for centuries, and others have tried to patent turmeric! Leading anti-globalisation spokesperson Vandana Shiva calls this 'blatant biopiracy'.

Resistance is huge. Farmers in both Andhra Pradesh and Karnataka burned Monsanto's crop trials. Some 3,000 villages have pledged to never obey laws that create monopolies on seed and to not adopt GM seed. Resistance succeeded in blocking Monsanto at the trial stage and to insist on a 5-6 year ecological assessment before seeds and crops are allowed to enter the market.

▶ *Dams:* India is the third largest dam builder in the world; since independence 3,300 big dams have been constructed, their reservoirs uprooting millions of people. But still 250 million do not have access to safe drinking water and over 600 million lack basic sanitation. For over 15 years the people of the Narmada Valley have been fighting plans to construct 3,200 dams along the Narmada river, displacing hundreds of thousands of people in the process.

The scale of resistance forced the World Bank to pull out of the project in 1993—one of the few occasions in history when the bank has been forced to withdraw from a project. But the state government of Gujarat insisted on pushing ahead. Work on the biggest dam, the Sarda Sarovar, was delayed for six years because of a legal challenge. But the Supreme Court of India ruled in favour of the dam at the end of 2000 and work began again. The judgement sparked protests across the country.

► *Power:* The struggle against Enron has become symbolic of the struggle against globalisation in India. Enron is the largest single gas supplier in the US, a giant multinational with close links to the CIA and US government officials. It is now building a $2.8 billion power plant in Maharastra which will supply electricity for double the current price. It is the single largest foreign project in India. In 1995 the state government cancelled the project as mass protests erupted across the state. Six months later it invited Enron (with Bechtel and General Electric as junior players) back. The Maharashtra State Electricity Board is now pledged to buy high-priced power from Enron, whether there is demand for it or not and even if cheaper power is available from its own power plants. Enron even won an assurance that the project would not be nationalised. Wrangling over the deal continues.

► *Water:* Monsanto, among others, is out to launch a new water business in India. It plans to earn millions by the year 2008. It has begun this process by buying a stake in Water Health International and has also launched a joint venture with Indian giant conglomerate Tata to provide distribute and service water systems.

► *Aquaculture:* Hundreds of rural communities are fighting the devastating effects of commercial aquaculture shrimp farms. The industry produces shrimps and prawns for export. It was hailed by the World Bank and the Indian government as a triumph for neo-liberalism in the early 1990s. But large tracts of mangroves and wetlands are destroyed, local people are deprived of their access to the sea and previously common lands, the surrounding soil is made increasingly saline and useless, groundwater is depleted, and the sea is polluted by waste.

► *Toxic waste dumping:* Over 400 million tons of toxic waste is produced every year—90 percent of it by OECD countries. India has become a major dumping ground for hazardous wastes from the US, Australia, Canada, Germany and Britain. The Indian government accepts these toxic imports despite the fact that they infringe domestic laws and international treaties barring exports from rich to poor nations of substances known to be harmful to human health and the environment. For companies in the West it is cheaper to

'First rich landowners came in and offered people 50,000 rupees an acre to sell their paddy fields. Usually our land would sell for 1,000 rupees an acre. It was hard for people to resist that much money. Then bulldozers came in and knocked down all the trees and ploughed up all the fields. Afterwards they built huge concrete jetties out to the sea and pumped sea water into the ponds they had created. Within a year our wells were full of salt and we had swarms of mosquitoes in our village. We are caught between the large fishing trawlers that have taken away our ability to fish and the large aquaculture farms that have taken away our ability to farm. We have nothing left to do except stay and fight.'

—Govinda Ma, villager in Andhra Pradesh

circumvent environmental regulations and higher disposal costs at home by shipping hazardous wastes to the Third World for disposal. The results involve enormous health and environmental problems in those countries least able to deal with them.

► *Climate change:* A cyclone off the coast of Orissa led to devastation and tens of thousands of deaths in 1999, and to widespread fears that global warming was responsible. The power sector in the state had just been privatised but the multinational AES insisted the state government paid to rebuild the network.

► *Child labour:* there are an estimated 60 million to 100 million child labourers in India, despite child labour being illegal. They are employed mainly in the carpet industry, cutting and polishing diamonds for big firms like De Beers, in the glass and glassware industry, and in footwear.

Resistance

'We oppose the profit-oriented New Economic Policy with its attendant liberalisation, privatisation and globalisation because it marginalises and even excludes a majority of people and exhausts the resources of the nation for the sake of the accumulation of profit.

We, therefore, propose that India quits the WTO. We propose that India refuses to submit to any conditionalities and structural adjustment programmes imposed by the World Bank, IMF, and similar international institutions.

Foreign debt must be universally written off.

We support the legal protection of people's right of access to common property, resources of forests, common land and water. We oppose the present industrial policy which abandons social responsibility and devalues human labour.

We oppose the irresponsible policy of lockouts in the organised sector and support the takeover of units by the workers.

We stand in solidarity with the struggles of the Dalits (untouchables) to secure fundamental human rights and justice. We strive for the protection and equal participation of Muslims and all other religious communities in our nation. We demand comprehensive global nuclear, chemical, and biological disarmament.'

—from the founding statement of the National Alliance of People's Movements (NAPM). Over 10,000 people from grassroots organisations all over India pledged to fight globalisation at a NAPM public meeting in Delhi in 1993

As we have seen resistance is enormous, and there are many other examples. US multinational Du Pont was forced out of the state of Goa after a campaign against its plan to relocate a factory there. The local community withstood vicious beatings by the police, and the shooting dead of one activist, until they won. When James Wolfensohn, president of the World Bank, visited India at the end of 2000 he was met by protests at every turn. So too was Bill Clinton in April 2000, though the police did their best to prevent the protesters reaching him.

It is important to note that strikes have tied together opposition to neo-liberalism throughout India. I will conclude with just a few examples:

- ▶ *January 2000:* 90,000 power workers in Uttar Pradesh struck against plans to privatise electricity. They won a 12 month delay. In July 2000 the World Bank threatened to withdraw loans unless the privatisation went ahead.
- ▶ *May 2000:* A one-day general strike was supported by 30 million workers. It was called by all the trade unions in India, except those affiliated to the right wing Hindu chauvinist BJP. The strike was against price rises, cuts in fertiliser subsidies, the privatisation of public utilities, attacks on Muslims and other minorities, the World Bank, the IMF and the WTO, the opening up of the economy to multinationals, and the introduction of tuition fees
- ▶ *August 2000:* 20,000 telecom workers struck against plans to privatise the sector, then 400,000 struck over the same issue in September.
- ▶ *December 2000:* 1 million bank workers struck for the day against privatisation, 600,000 postal workers struck for pension rights for part time workers, power workers

struck for the day against World Bank/IMF pressure to privatise the sector.

- ► *April-May 2001:* two month strike by workers at Balco aluminium against privatisation.

- ► *April 2001:* millions of workers join a one-day strike across the state of Maharashtra, which includes the business centre of Mumbai (Bombay), against 'the onslaught of globalisation, privatisation and liberalisaton'. The strike is also against proposed changes to labour laws in the name of 'labour flexibility' that will allow employers to lay off workers at will and to introduce more contract labour.

- ► The strike was called by 50 trade unions and nine political parties, and included an unholy alliance of the left and the right wing Shiv Sena. Even so, the strike succeeded in uniting mill workers, teachers, bank workers and street hawkers. One trade unionist said, 'A hawker is often a worker who has lost a job. But when he goes vending he gets caught and is forced to pay fines. Teachers are not getting their salaries. Besides they suffer from the uncertainties of the contract system. Earlier all these people were looked upon as partners in the creation of wealth. Now we are all seen as dispensable means of production. We don't count.'

Sam Ashman is a journalist for *Socialist Worker.*
samashman@hotmail.com

Daewoo Motors workers swing iron pipes at riot police blocking them from ... ing the protesters inside the company's factory in Seoul. Protests occurred after Daewoo Motors laid off 1,751 workers, a step it said was necessary to make it more attractive to General Motors.

East Asia
Giles Ji Ungpakorn and Tom O'Lincoln

●　●　●　●　●　●　●　●　●　●　●　●　●　●　●　●　●　●

The Asian economic crisis of 1997 is the single most important issue which stimulated the anti-capitalist mood in East Asia. Despite attempts by the apologists for international capitalism to blame the crisis on Asian crony capitalism, the overall effect of the crisis was to shatter the myth that the capitalist free market would bring unending prosperity to the region. In many countries new generations of people are searching for more just and civilised alternatives to capitalism. However, due to specific conditions within each country, the nature of the impact of the crisis in terms of political awakening varies greatly within the region.

In countries where the government policy has relied on the free market for some time (such as Thailand or the Philippines) people are searching for alternatives to what the Thai radicals call the system where 'whoever has the longest arm grabs the most'. However, at this stage, much of this anti free market mood is tinged with economic nationalism, a tension that exists throughout much of East Asia in one form or another. It is something which must be recognised and dealt with by activists within the region and outside.

In countries with authoritarian regimes, where government economic policies relied more on the role of the state in a heavily protected economic system (eg Indonesia), or in countries where the population perceived the state to be 'socialist' or monopolistic (eg Vietnam or Burma), reaction to the crisis has often pushed many people into calling for more free market policies. Experience from Eastern Europe suggests that when the true nature of the market is experienced these illusions will eventually be shattered.

Already we can see this disenchantment in Vietnam, where overt political opposition is suppressed under a Stalinist regime which is opening the country up to the free market. These policies are causing vast inequalities. The result is rural unrest among ethnic minorities and peasants and strikes by urban workers in foreign-owned factories. Although those involved may not see themselves as part of the anti-capitalist wave, their struggles are undoubtedly against the effects of capitalism and the market.

Indonesia

In May 1998 the Indonesian government announced that, on International Monetary Fund (IMF) instructions, it would slash subsidies on basic goods. Prices were set to skyrocket. The rich profiteered while the poor faced new suffering. A fuse had been lit. Within two weeks Jakarta erupted in riots, the dictator Suharto fell from power, and the price hikes were retracted. A year later, under so-called democracy, another government tried to lift the subsidies, but backed down when students came into the streets followed by the urban poor. In mid-2001 the government was still having trouble meeting the IMF's demands.

The unrest that brought down Suharto stemmed from the 1997 monetary crisis. In early 1998 a mass student movement emerged, and eventually occupied the parliament buildings in May, around the same time as the riots. The problem in May was that the students had few links to the workers and poor; the riots lacked leadership and were manipulated in a racist direction. Even so, the fall of Suharto opened up a space for further struggle. Far left groups began to take shape around the campuses.

In November these groups united and mobilised hundreds of thousands of urban poor behind them, in what briefly looked like a challenge for power. Because there was political leadership, no race riots took place. However, the weakness at this time was the lack of a coherent labour movement able to take the mobilisation forward. This is partly because the huge industrial proletariat is new, partly because its bargaining power is diminished by the reserve army of labour from the villages, and partly it reflects the 1965 crushing of the Communist movement. Building the labour movement remains the central task for those fighting to create

a mass anti-capitalist movement today. There are dozens of national union groups and many more at local level trying to do this.

Political clarification is another vital task. As in Eastern Europe during the 1980s, the liberal politicians who assumed leadership of the democratic struggle against Suharto were free marketeers, welcoming IMF policies. These included Megawati (daughter of Sukarno, Indonesia's independence leader), and Muslim figures Amien Rais and Abdurrahman Wahid (who became president in 1999). Prominent economist Kwik Kian Gie, Megawati's advisor, was the first to call for IMF intervention. There is still a strong tendency, even on the far left, to orient to one or another of these leaders. But now that these politicians are in power it is much clearer how free market policies hurt the people, as subsidies are lifted, prices rise and wages fail to keep up. The people watch appalled as the politicians do deals with the army and squabble over the spoils of power.

As for imperialist agencies, Bonnie Setiawan, Jakarta-based programme officer from the non-governmental organisation (NGO) network INFID has told the IMF's Indonesian representative John Dodsworth to his face, 'You are not really doctors helping patients... you are the butchers hacking up people's economies any way you please.'

The anger is there. Now it's a matter of anti-capitalists using that to develop an independent mass movement of workers, peasants, students and the poor.

South Korea

A year before Indonesia's unrest South Korea saw students and workers taking to the streets in response to the 'reforms' demanded by the bodies of international capitalism. As President Kim Young-sam issued the statement, 'We will do our best to boost international confidence by honouring the terms of the agreement with the IMF,' people gathered in the thousands to voice their dissent. 'The government and rich company owners ruined the economy, and now they tell us to take all the pains... We never will!' 'We oppose IMF trusteeship! Abolish the IMF agreement!' 'Arrest [President] Kim Young-sam for ruining the economy!' they shouted.

In response to the uproar over the demands of the $57 billion IMF loan to South Korea, the Citizens' Coalition for Economic Justice stated, 'It is a totally justifiable reaction on the part of the Korean people to suspect that the IMF bailout was used as a golden opportunity for the US and Japan to push their own agenda onto a Korea on its knees.' It is this kind of understanding, articulated as the battle between nation-states, which reflects the nationalist anti-capitalist mood throughout much of Asia. It is an anti-imperialist instinct which risks being hijacked for nationalist platforms.[1]

Vietnam

Because most people associate the old command economy run by the Vietnamese Communist regime with 'socialism', they believe that the alternative must be the capitalist free market. For this reason it will take a few more years of experiencing the real effects of the free market before significant numbers of people come to question global capital in a systematic manner. Already inequality and hardship is increasing as a result of 'market reforms'.

The regime opened the economy to the world market under a process called '*doi moi*' in 1985, yet it claims to be 'building a market economy under socialist principles'. What this means in practice is opening up to the market while attempting to maintain the dictatorship of the Communist Party.

Free market policies are resulting in growing inequalities, rural unrest and strikes by urban workers. These struggles can be regarded as part of the

rising tide of struggle against globalisation, even though the participants may not view it in this manner themselves.

Another interesting sign of resistance is the growing body of modern Vietnamese literature, by independent writers, which shows how money and the market distort human relationships.

Malaysia

The effects of the 1998 crisis resulted in Mahatir Mohamad's authoritarian government turning further to economic nationalism and increased state regulation. At the same time the democratic opposition is lead by jailed ex deputy prime minister Anwar Ibrahim who is in favour of the IMF! There are contradictions on both sides. Mahatir's government is not really against foreign investment and global capital. He simply wants to protect Malaysian capital from the worst excesses of the market. Similarly the Reformasi movement against the authoritarian nature of the regime, which is lead by Anwar, is made up of many people who are not particularly in favour of the IMF or global capital and stand to be at the sharp end of any moves to increase the dominance of the free market.

Thailand

'People's groups should unite to form a political party. The issuing of announcements and denunciations is neither enough nor effective in solving the problems of farmers and the poor.'
—Somkiat Pongpaiboon, The Assembly of the Poor

'There is an urgent need for the common people to come together in order to strengthen their power and establish funding institutions or cooperative groups to support themselves. We should also have our political party.'
—Somsak Kosaisuk, railway workers' leader

The anti-capitalist movement in Thailand is still concentrated at the level of alternative ideas to global capital rather than large demonstrations or strikes. There has been a groundswell in support of economic nationalism, opposition to privatisation and a search for 'community-based' self-sufficient economic models.

Economic nationalism and community economics cannot solve the problems of urban workers and poor peasants, and are not true alternatives to the market. Nonetheless the fact that large numbers of people are looking for alternatives to global capital is a positive aspect.

In addition there has also been revulsion at the way the previous Democrat Party government attempted to solve the economic crisis by massive spending

Effects of the crisis in Thailand

▶ The first half of 1998 saw a 12.6 percent decline in earnings and 4.4 percent decline in hours worked.
▶ 300,000 school children dropped out of school due to poverty in 1998.
▶ Average real incomes fell by 10 percent from 1997 to 2000.
▶ 73 percent of the labour force earn less than 5,000 baht per month (£78).
▶ The poorest 20 percent account for 3.8 percent of income, the wealthiest 20 percent for 58.5 percent.

—Thai government and World Bank figures

to bail out the rich. The IMF supported this use of government funds to bail out the private banking sector and the estimated cost has reached 1.2 trillion baht, resulting in a massive increase in public debt. A public backlash against these policies resulted in a landslide victory at the polls for the Thais Love Thais Party of telecom tycoon Thaksin Shinawatra in January 2001. The poor voted for Thaksin's party because he promised some form of universal healthcare, a village development fund and a moratorium on farmers' debts. However, not surprisingly, Thaksin's government is not prepared to tax the rich to pay for these benefits. This will cause problems in the future if the hopes of workers and peasants are raised and then not fully met.

On the positive side, Thailand is a relatively open society with a free press. Opposition and socialist organisations can work openly. There are a number of issues around which activists are fighting. These are: universal healthcare, dam building and land use, the environment, unemployment insurance, health and safety at work, and human rights (including the issue of the death penalty). However, the political nature of the NGO movement and the legacy from the Maoist Communist Party of Thailand mean that there are too few links between organised workers and the new anti-capitalist mood. Community economics also offers nothing to urban workers and cannot therefore be a rallying point.

The Philippines

The Philippines economy was hit by a crisis in 1983-85 and then again in 1990-92. For this reason it did not suffer so badly from the 'bubble effect' of rapid speculative growth in the late 1990s like Thailand or Malaysia. The impact of the Asian crisis was therefore much less pronounced.

In the first half of 2001 the struggle between two factions of the Philippines ruling class, led by Joseph Estrada, on the one hand, and Gloria Arroyo, on the other, has resulted in political instability. The left in the Philippines, once dominated by the Maoist Communist Party of the Philippines and its armed wing, the New Peoples Army, has been hopelessly split. This explains why groups of workers supported the ousting of Estrada while some urban poor defended him. Despite Estrada's populist rhetoric, which claims to support the poor, both he and Arroyo support IMF policies. Estrada is associated with ex-dictator Marcos and his cronies while Arroyo comes from an elite family dynasty. Unless an alternative political focus emerges, based on class politics or opposition to global capital, anger against the system will continue to be channelled behind one or other group of elites.

Japan

The world's second largest economy and dominant regional power spent most of the 1990s in an economic slump as the hangover from the speculative party of the previous decade dragged on. The Asian crisis of 1997 sent already low gross domestic product (GDP) growth rates plunging in 1998 to minus 2.8 percent as a percentage change over the previous year. While not as bad as other Asian economies like Hong Kong (- 5.1 percent), Malaysia (- 7.5 percent) or Indonesia (- 13.2 percent), the crash led to a wave of bankruptcies and layoffs, a jump in the suicide rate, and helped to further expose Japan's heavily-indebted financial institutions, which had invested in many of these countries.

GDP returned to weak growth the following year but the fall-out still lingers in a number of ways. The crisis forced Japan's ruling class to face up to the size of the problems in its financial sector. In the ten years until 1999 financial institutions registered 87 trillion yen ($791 billion) in loan losses. Japan's assets are shrinking at an unprecedented rate and the country's banks, with collateral tied to declining land values and a diving stock market, are buried under a mountain of bad debt. The 1997-98 episode pushed many large financial institutions over the edge.

For most of the 1990s the government's approach to the slump has been to protect the financial sector from collapse and pump billions of yen into the economy to prevent it from declining further. However, in the aftermath of 1997 a significant section of the ruling class now wants to push far more institutions into bankruptcy as a form of shock treatment to rid the country of the problem once and for all. The ruling LDP, in an echo of the Thatcherite logic it seeks to emulate, admits that this will cause much more unemployment and social pain.

Voices within the ruling class calling for more free market policies have grown more insistent and powerful in the last three years. The business newspaper *Nikkei Shimbun* advocated in June 2001 the privatisation of everything from Tokyo International Airport to the National Parliament (Diet) building. Current prime minister Junichiro Koizumi has warned he will push ahead with selling off the massive post office savings system and further deregulate telecommunications and banking.

The great danger of the current political mood in Japan is the rise of nationalism. Some elements of the small but vocal extreme right, dominated by Tokyo's mayor Shintaro Ishihara, argued that the currency crisis was a US-led Western plot to further damage the Japanese economy, which at one stage looked like it might overtake the US. With no end in sight to the restructuring, corporate failures and unemployment, there is a real possibility such messages could sink in and take root in a weary population. Koizumi too has been stoking nationalism by promising to visit Yasukuni Shrine, final resting home to some of Japan's fascist leaders.

Powerful trade unions associated with the telecommunications and consumer electronics industries are still a significant barrier to the full scale implementation of privatisation policies, but on the question of whether there is an anti-capitalist mood in Japan the answer is probably no. There has been some success in organising anti-debt protests around the Jubilee Drop The Debt campaign but the main show of force for the left is the annual May Day rallies around the country which bring thousands of trade unionists and their families out on the streets for a largely ritualised show of strength.

There has been nothing in Japan to compare with the protests, riots and revolutions in other Asian countries, nor with the new anti-capitalist movement that jolted the right out of its complacency when it broke through in Seattle. What there is, however, in abundance is massive discontent and anger with the apparent disintegration of a system that exacted enormous sacrifices from workers as it promised to deliver the benefits of security, peace and prosperity. And it is this discontent that must be built on by socialists before the right begins to play its familiar tune.

Privatisation

Privatisation of state utilities (electricity, water, transport and telecommunications), universities and hospitals is an issue facing workers across East Asia and is closely linked to the further penetration of the free market.

Apart from the quest for massive profits and reduced government spending for the poor, privatisation is part of a generalised attack on employment standards. This is because state employees are well unionised and have managed to achieve guarantees of secure employment, good wages and decent fringe benefits such as free hospital treatment. All these things should be viewed as basic human rights, but under the neo-liberal economic nightmare the bosses hope to sweep such rights aside. Whether they achieve their nightmare depends on the state of class struggle. The whole public argument about privatisation relies on one great contradiction. It is claimed that privatisation will increase efficiency because of the introduction of market forces, yet the 1997 Asian crisis itself was brought about by the problems of free market capitalism and the inefficiencies of the private sector. Furthermore, in order to manage the private sector debt crisis, many governments have embarked on a process of wholesale nationalisations of failing private banks and have effectively assumed the private debt.

In Malaysia privatisation under economic boss Diam Zainuddin has been dubbed 'crony privatisation' with state enterprises being sold off cheap to government party politicians and their close friends. Both Mahatir and Anwar were involved. When Radicare, a private hospital maintenance company associated with Anwar, took over a large hospital in the capital, the electricity failed. One businessman was quoted in the *Far Eastern Economic Review* as saying that profit was the only motive for buying up state enterprises, 'Most of us thought [that when the private companies failed] someone, maybe the government, would carry the can later.'

One issue which effects students is the privatisation of universities in Thailand and Indonesia. The World Bank, Asian Development Bank and IMF are all pushing for state universities to become 'autonomous'. The main aim is to reduce state funding for universities, raise fees and attack employment conditions. This has become an issue in the student movement.

The struggle against privatisation depends on political mobilisation of workers, not reasoned argument. The free marketeers contradict their own theories constantly, using the state to prop-up their business interests when it suits them. In Thailand the trade unions have conducted trench warfare to delay privatisation, but often the argument is posed in nationalist terms, as though sales of state enterprises to local indigenous capitalists would be any better than to multinational companies.

Conclusion

The East Asian region of the world economy encompasses a variety of different forms of capitalist organisation of production: from state capitalist Vietnam, through the state-directed capitalism of South Korea, to Singapore, which is highly integrated into the world capitalist market. The crisis that has ripped through them since 1997 has exposed the weaknesses of each of these models. It has also fuelled a complex set of social and economic struggles.

So populist politicians in Thailand and the Philippines have been able to tap the desperation of particularly the urban poor. The crisis has brought bitter divisions among the various ruling classes. An argument in Malaysia about whether to respond to the crisis by greater state intervention or further opening up to the world market resulted in authoritarian leader Mahatir Mohamad jailing his own deputy prime minister. Pro-democracy activists across the region face a strategic challenge: how to address the economic concerns of the mass of people who are suffering both from corrupt, repressive regimes and from the neo-liberal policies demanded by the IMF.

The general sentiment of revolt among the working classes and poor unites the region, but it is expressed in often contradictory ways. This means there is enormous political upheaval as different forces try to impose their own strategies for escaping the crisis. The organised working class is at the heart of solving all the problems people face. But for that to happen, the bitterness at what capitalism is doing to people needs to be channelled, and attempts by sections of the ruling classes to gain support for their own strategies for preserving capitalism need to be challenged.

That is true the world over, but it is especially poignant in the countries of East Asia. For here a sharp economic crisis (comparable to the 1930s in some countries) has posed for anti-capitalists the central political and strategic questions which characterised the most stormy periods of the last century: the role of workers and the impoverished masses, the struggle for democracy, the nature of socialism, nationalism, war and ultimately revolution.

Giles Ji Ungpakorn is a founding member of Workers' Democracy (Thailand) and has written two books in English about Thai politics.
Giles.U@chula.ac.th

Tom O'Lincoln is a founder of the international socialist current in Australia. He is the author or editor of several books on Australian labour history and social issues, and has also translated John Molyneux's 'What is the Real Marxist Tradition' into Indonesian. Tom edits an Indonesian language e-mail newsletter and website.
red_sites@hotmail.com

Notes

1   Bonnie Setiawan, 'Saatnya Mengusir IMF' (Time to Kick out the IMF), on the Indo-Marxist internet mailing list.

Texts

- ▶ K S Jomo (ed), *Tigers in Trouble. Financial Governance, Liberalisation and Crises in East Asia* (Zed Books, London, New York, 1998).
- ▶ Abduhl Rahman Embong and Jurgen Rudolph (eds), *Southeast Asia into the 21st Century* (Penerbit Universiti, Kebangsaan, Malaysia, 2000).
- ▶ C Manning and P Van Dierman, *Indonesia in Transition* (Zed Books, 2000).
- ▶ *International Socialism 78, 80.*
- ▶ *The Journal of Contemporary Asia.*
- ▶ W Bello, S Cunningham, and Li Kheng Poh, *A Siamese Tragedy: Development and Disintegration in Modern Thailand* (Zed Books, 1998).
- ▶ Giles Ji Ungpakorn, *Thailand: Class Struggle in an Era of Economic Crisis* (Workers' Democracy, 1999).
- ▶ B Reid, 'The Philippine Left: Political Crisis and Social Change', *Journal of Contemporary Asia* (2000).

Sites

- ▶ **www.anu.edu.au/polsci/marx/ interventions**
  Marxist Interventions
- ▶ **www.focusweb.org**
  Walden Bello's organisation 'Focus South'
- ▶ **members.nbci.com/indomarxist/ index.htm**
  Indo-Marxist site
- ▶ **arts.anu.edu.au/suarsos/**
  Suara Socialis (Socialist Voice), International Socialist Tendency

Anti World Economic Forum demonstration, Melbourne, 11 September 2000

Australia, New Zealand and Melanesia
David Glanz

● ● ● ● ● ● ● ● ● ● ● ● ● ● ● ● ● ●

Neo-liberalism, known in Australia as economic rationalism, has ripped through the lives of the country's workers and students for 18 years. Since 1983, first Labour governments and now the current Liberal (conservative) government of John Howard have privatised and deregulated, presiding over a massive upwards shift of wealth.

The richest 1 percent owns about 20 percent of private wealth, the richest 10 percent owns half, and the poorest 30 percent have no net wealth. Between 1993 and 1999 the number of millionaires went from 71,700 to 208,000. Meanwhile, real incomes for the majority have dropped, with the median figure falling 12 percent in 14 years. The Australian Bureau of Statistics reported at the beginning of 2001 that 30,000 working households

The richest 10 percent own half the wealth and the poorest 30 percent have no net wealth

have gone without meals, 31,000 have been unable to afford heating, and 22,000 have sought help from charities.

Australian governments have conducted one of the biggest privatisation exercises in the world, selling the national airline and bank, half of the telecom business, airports and the national rail network. In the state of Victoria—where the economic rationalist experiment has been pursued most vigorously—gas, electricity generation and distribution, public transport and some prisons are all in private hands. In 2000 the federal government introduced a regressive 10 percent consumption tax, the GST, while simultaneously shifting billions of dollars from public education and health to the private sector.

Work has become more precarious for many, with more than one in five in casual jobs. Women workers have been particularly hard hit. In 1998 they earned on average $246 less per week than men. Migrant women are 90 percent of out-workers in the clothing trade and earn an average of $2 an hour—about 70 British pence or just over one US dollar. All workers have lost out under the draconian Workplace Relations Act, which strips basic conditions and limits legal industrial action.

Many indigenous people continue to live in Third World conditions, with a life expectancy 15-20 years less than the general population. Infant mortality is three to five times higher, and the incidence of diabetes is four times higher. At the 2000 Sydney Olympics the Australian government hailed Aboriginal athlete Cathy Freeman; meanwhile the unemployment rate for indigenous people is nearly five times higher than for other Australians, and indigenous people are 17 times more likely to be arrested. To rub salt into the wounds, the Liberal government refuses to apologise for past injustices, in particular for the systematic removal of indigenous children from their families—the 'Stolen Generations'.

The tide turns

The tide began to turn in 1998. The trade union movement beat back an attempt to smash the waterside workers' union, with mass pickets defying anti-union laws and police, and shutting down much of the docks. Major militant protests forced Pauline Hanson, leader of the racist One Nation party, to abandon public meetings. An attempt to open the Jabiluka uranium mine within the World Heritage Area of Kakadu National Park, fiercely opposed by indigenous traditional owners, brought thousands on to the streets. In retrospect, it was one of the first stirrings of the anti-capitalist mood.

Regional struggles reinforced the radicalisation. On the Papua New Guinea island of Bougainville traditional owners forced the closure of the Rio Tinto owned Panguna mine. In West Papua the resistance movement faced not only the Indonesian army but mining giants Freeport and Rio Tinto. And the resistance of the East Timorese, whose oil was being plundered by Australia and Indonesia, was a beacon. The massacres following the 1999 independence referendum provoked huge solidarity rallies in Australia, with industrial action by workers on the waterfront and at airports.

On national breakfast TV a presenter and an activist discuss whether bosses or workers create the nation's wealth

Anger with economic rationalism at home and neo-liberalism overseas finally coalesced in Australia's 'Seattle'. Over three days in September 2000 some 20,000 people blockaded a World Economic Forum summit in Melbourne. Hundreds of business delegates were left stranded. Prime Minister Howard made it in only by police dinghy and Bill Gates had to fly in by helicopter. Their joint address to 4,000 high school students was cancelled.

The events of 11 September (S11) marked the arrival of the movement. It took a major step forward when, on 1 May 2001 (M1), activists blockaded stock exchange buildings in every state capital. In Melbourne the peak trade union body organised its first 1 May march since the Second World War. Construction and manufacturing workers struck to join it. The unity march between strikers, blockaders and environmental activists became a triumphant 10,000-strong festival.

At the time of S11 most of the media referred to the protests as 'anti-globalisation' while many activists talked of an anti-corporate mood. By M1 the term anti-capitalist was everywhere. Media interviewers asked movement spokespeople why they blamed capitalism. On national breakfast TV a presenter and an activist discussed whether bosses or workers created the nation's wealth. One government minister desperately asserted that the protesters were mistaken—after all, capitalism was simply another word for freedom.

The anti-capitalist movement has not yet, however, taken a unified form. S11 was organised through central collectives in each city, plus a constellation of affinity groups. The S11 collectives, heavily influenced by socialists, morphed into M1 collectives and are once again growing over into organising points for the next big mobilisation, the Commonwealth Heads of Government Meeting (CHOGM) in Brisbane in October 2001. Environmental activists, with Friends of the Earth the most prominent group, organise as a Green bloc but in liaison with the central city collectives. Anarchists and their sympathisers organise separately. In mid-2001 there were the first moves towards cohering the movement on the campuses, with a national student anti-capitalist conference in Sydney.

The key flashpoints

▶ *Uranium:* In 1996 the newly elected Liberal Australian government scrapped the policy restricting uranium mining to three sites. Mining corporations quickly proposed dozens of new projects; there are 56 known uranium deposits in Western Australia alone. The newly opened Beverley mine in South Australia uses in-situ leaching to extract the ore. Sulphuric acid is pumped down to the deposit, dissolving it so it can be pumped to the surface for processing—an obvious risk to underground water supplies. Two other concerns are the plan for a radioactive waste dump in South Australia and the proposal to build a replacement nuclear reactor at Lucas Heights in outer suburban Sydney.

The national focus though has been on Jabiluka, the land of the Mirrar people, and at the heart of one of the most important wetland areas in the country. Resistance has taken many forms. The Mirrar have withstood enormous pressure, using limited veto powers over elements of the mine's construction to slow down the project. Activists have organised protests around the country, including a blockade of the mine site and a 5,000-strong rally in Melbourne in 1998.

Also in Melbourne, protesters blockaded the offices of North Ltd (since bought by Rio Tinto) over several days. All up, nearly 600 have been arrested during the campaign. The Jabiluka cause has been supported by a range of unions and was discussed at the 2000 conference of the Australian Council of Trade Unions. Rio Tinto announced in early 2001 that plans for the mine were on hold for a decade; for the Mirrar and their supporters this concession is not enough and the campaign continues.

Friends of the Earth, the Australian Conservation Foundation and the Wilderness Society are all active nationally on uranium issues. The Gundjehmi Corporation is the voice of the Mirrar. Sydney People Against a New Nuclear Reactor (SPANNR) is campaigning against the Lucas Heights project and has groups in seven suburbs.

▶ *Refugees*: Australia is the only industrialised country with a policy of mandatory detention for asylum seekers who arrive without a visa, a policy begun under Labour and intensified under the Liberals. About 3,000-4,000 so-called 'boat people' land each year, the majority coming from the Middle East and Afghanistan. They are mostly held in remote, desert detention centres while their applications are processed. Some spend years in what even a former Liberal prime minister called 'hell holes'. Children have been born and brought up in the camps. Even when the refugees are released, their visas are valid for just 30 months, they have limited access to welfare, and cannot bring family members to join them. Meanwhile white Zimbabwean farmers are warmly welcomed and overseas businesspeople can effectively buy residency rights.

This blatantly racist policy is stirring enormous outrage. Many people can see that the more the Liberal government pushes economic rationalist policies, the more it needs scapegoats. For many in the anti-capitalist movement the hypocrisy of capital being free to roam the globe while its victims are imprisoned is particularly compelling. The issue has even won unusually good coverage in the 'quality' media, including Rupert Murdoch's flagship, *The Australian*.

The resistance has been spearheaded by the detainees themselves. There have been break-outs, hunger strikes and riots. On M1 2001 some 500 detainees at the Port Hedland camp demonstrated in solidarity with the stock exchange blockades thousands of kilometres away. Amnesty International has run a campaign including protests outside government offices. Activists have set up Refugee Action Collectives in most state capitals, which called a national day of action in June 2001. Thousands, including union peak bodies, MPs, Greens and human rights activists, have supported an RAC open letter demanding an end to mandatory detention, full rights for refugees and funding for a settlement.

► *Forests:* Australia is one of the largest per capita producers of greenhouse gases in the world. Yet land clearing continues at a frenetic pace, especially in Queensland. Meanwhile state governments continue to permit the clear-felling of native forests for woodchip exports, endangering localised species such as owls. Regrowth trees need a lot of water, reducing flow into rivers and reservoirs. Widespread land clearance also raises the water table, bringing salts to the surface and creating wastelands.

Australia was one of three developed nations allowed to increase its greenhouse gas emissions under the 1997 Kyoto protocol. Its 'challenge' under the agreement was to limit emission increases to 8 percent above 1990 levels. Even this was too much for the Liberal government. When President Bush junior scuppered the Kyoto protocol in early 2001, Prime Minister Howard cheered the decision as 'good for Australian business'. Australian emissions had by then increased 16 percent on 1990 levels.

Concern about global warming has led to a jump in sympathy for forest activists. There has been supportive media coverage of actions including blockades and tree-top sit-ins. The logging of old-growth forests in Western

Australia and land clearance in Queensland became major election issues in early 2001, contributing to landslide Labour victories. In Victoria residents and tourism-dependent businesses have united against logging in the Otways region. However, because most campaigning takes place in the forests rather than the cities, the numbers involved are still small. Support for clear-felling by the forestry workers' union and occasional violence by union members against forest activists means the question of how to unite to save the forests remains controversial.

▶ *Indigenous rights:* Australia was founded on dispossession and genocide. More than two centuries on, indigenous people are proud to declare they have survived. With just 2 percent of the population they are, however, grossly over-represented on every negative social indicator. The courts have finally acknowledged Aboriginal prior ownership of the continent and opened the way to claims of native title on crown land, but new restrictive laws make even this minor gain difficult.

Growing numbers of non-indigenous people are disgusted. In 2000 nearly 1 million people across the country rallied for reconciliation. Most want the government to apologise to indigenous people and there is a growing call for a treaty. At progressive public meetings it is becoming customary to acknowledge that the participants are on Aboriginal land or to have a welcome ceremony by an indigenous representative.

There are frequent local struggles by indigenous nations over land use and access, but there is no united indigenous voice. The national Aboriginal and Torres Strait Islander Commission (ATSIC) is government-funded and distrusted by many indigenous activists.

▶ *Fair trade:* Australian activists joined the worldwide campaign against the Multilateral Agreement on Investment (MAI) and have taken up the campaign against the World Trade Organisation (WTO). The national mobilisation against CHOGM in October 2001 is calling for the

Commonwealth nations to pull out of the latest WTO round, to be launched in Qatar in November.

The union movement in particular has taken up the slogan 'Fair trade, not free trade.' In the past Australian unions called for tariffs to 'defend jobs'; now this is often coupled with demands for union rights and restrictions on child labour in countries which compete for Australian markets. This position straddles two camps; for some it is a coded call for protectionism, while for others it marks a real desire for international solidarity. The challenge for the anti-capitalist movement is to engage with the debate and pull the unions into the internationalist camp.

There is also a growing anti-sweatshop campaign. The textile workers' union has established the Fairwear campaign, with church and community support. This has raised awareness, especially among students, leading to campaigns and blockades against Nike.

Voices of opposition

The anti-capitalist movement is growing and with it unity across differing sectors. The miners' union campaigns against Rio Tinto, not just for its union-busting policies, but for its appalling track record on environmental and indigenous rights. The manufacturing workers' union supports protest at CHOGM, as does Jubilee Australia, which campaigns against Third World debt.

> **The challenge for the anti-capitalist movement is to engage with the debate and pull the unions into the internationalist camp**

Meanwhile nine socialist organisations have collaborated to launch a Socialist Alliance to put an alternative to economic rationalism at home and neo-liberalism overseas at the next federal election.

While activists are aware of, and angry about, the predatory corporations like Nike and McDonald's and their backers in the WTO or International Monetary Fund (IMF), most understand that the Australian government does locally what the IMF or WTO does globally. Many of the same people who took part in S11 or M1 come not only to blockades of Nike or Starbucks but to protests against the Liberal government's policies on refugees or education. In the 18 months following Seattle the face of Australian radicalism has changed almost beyond recognition.

New Zealand/Aotearoa

New Zealanders suffered one of the harshest neo-liberal experiments in the world, under Labour from 1984 to 1990 and under National until 1999. Real incomes fell by between 5 and 20 percent for three fifths of the population. Communities were ruined by cutbacks and privatisation. The 1991 Employment Contacts Act destroyed entire trade unions.

The election of a Labour government in 1999—and of seven Green MPs under a proportional electoral system similar to Germany's—changed little for ordinary people but symbolised the mood for change. With the term 'market' a swear-word, workers have begun to return to the unions. The peak trade union and student bodies have endorsed a socialist-initiated campaign for the freedom to strike.

Activists are organising to turn the anti-capitalist mood into a movement. The first anti-capitalist conference, in September 2000, attracted 150 people, a substantial achievement in a country of 3 million. A delegation, including Green MPs, attended S11 in Melbourne. Around 300 marched in Auckland on M1 2001 and activists held the first ever May Day rally in Palmerston North. Students have launched Globalise Resistance clubs in Auckland and Palmerston North, with more planned in Christchurch, Wellington and Hamilton.

No Human Is Illegal is campaigning for the rights of asylum seekers and so-called 'overstayers', often Pacific islanders who are also trade union members. Activists are linking the issue of workers' freedom to strike with the potential to take industrial action against deportations. There will be another anti-capitalist conference in September 2001 with activists heading to Brisbane to join the CHOGM protests.

Melanesia

The impact of neo-liberalism has been especially harsh for developing nations in Melanesia, which includes Papua New Guinea (PNG), the Solomon Islands, Vanuatu, Fiji and Kanaky (New Caledonia), and the Pacific. UNICEF reports that 1,100 Pacific women die each year from pregnancy-related causes and 19,000 children suffer preventable deaths.

The biggest economy, PNG, has taken a battering. With prices for its coffee, oil and mineral exports trending down, the IMF is demanding ever more austerity and privatisation. In return for standby loans the PNG government is selling a large bank and insurance company, the national airline, the harbour board, telecom and electricity companies, is capping public sector wages and cutting jobs. In March 2001 troops mutinied against IMF-imposed cutbacks to the military budget. They won support from trade unions and students.

Fiji, heavily reliant on sugar and gold production, has also suffered from low prices. In 1998 its economy contracted by 2.3 percent. Along with other Pacific island nations, it is in danger of losing control of the locally grown kava plant to US and German pharmaceutical corporations anxious to exploit its medicinal properties.

But the greatest devastation is to the region's forests. The IMF, World Bank and WTO all encourage industrial logging as an export industry. Corruption means mainly Malaysian and South Korean companies can clear-fell at will and pay minimal taxes. In the Solomon Islands a Malaysian company has already logged half the forest and is moving in on the rest. In the mid-1990s logging activist Martin Apa was murdered on Pavuvu island. In PNG the government retains just 2.75 percent of logging income through taxes. A communalist coup in Fiji in May 2000 and continuing near civil war in the Solomons make organising difficult.

David Glanz helped organise the S11 protests in Melbourne. He is a member of the national executive of the International Socialist Organisation and is currently writing a book on anti-capitalism in Australia.
dglanz@netstra.com.au

: Sites

- ► www.sll.org/ml
- ► www.melbourne.indymedia.org
  Indymedia Australia
- ► www.foe.org.au
  Friends of the Earth Australia
- ► www.vicnet.net.au/~rac-vic
- ► www.socialist-alliance.org
  Socialist Alliance Australia
- ► www.jubilee2000.org.au
  Jubilee 2000 Australia
- ► vic.uca.org.au/fairwear

ACTORS

Italian and Spanish Ya Basta! contingents marching to the conference centre to disru the meeting of the IMF/World Bank, Prague, 26 September 2000

DIRECTORY

The exciting reality that there are more of 'us' than there are of 'them' really hits home when you try to compile a list of key organisations in the anti-capitalist movement. To say that we have been selective is a serious understatement—that we should explain our methods of selection is therefore important.

US> We have tried to highlight those organisations which have had a fairly high profile vis-à-vis the major anti-capitalist demonstrations, at the same time as trying to find a cross-section of different types of organisation to represent the breadth and diversity of the movement. Smaller and more focused groups may be mentioned in the websites listed at the end of many of the articles. We have restricted ourselves to English language sites which tend to be based in Britain and North America. Organisations with international networks like ATTAC, Friends of the Earth, Indymedia and the International Socialist Tendency are a good place to start if you are interested in getting more information on anti-capitalist groups in a particular region.

THEM> The driving forces of corporate globalisation are multinational companies. The IMF, World Bank and WTO are their facilitators, and governments are their allies. We have provided a brief profile of the unholy triumvirate — IMF, WB and WTO — followed by a description of five of their notorious ringmasters: Walmart, McDonald's, Nike, GlaxoSmithKline and Shell. The role of governments has been illustrated in the regions section above and will not be dealt with again here.

A

ACT UP▶Aids Coalition To Unleash Power is a diverse group of individuals committed to direct action to end the AIDS crisis. They have been outspoken in their demand for AIDS treatment drugs to be made available and affordable to those who need them both in the US and elsewhere. They advise, inform and demonstrate. ACT UP members have been protesting in the streets since the 1980s, and in 2000 organised for people with AIDS to travel to the demonstrations in Washington. Their website banner says, 'Our job is not to be invited to coffee or to schmooze at a cocktail party… Our job is to make change happen as fast as possible, and direct action works for that.'
www.actupny.org

ADBUSTERS▶is 'a global network of artists, writers, pranksters, students, educators and entrepreneurs who want to advance the new social activist movement of the information age'. Their aim is to 'topple existing power structures and forge a major shift in the way we live in the 21st century'. To this end, they publish a magazine specialising in subverting gimmicks—slick parodies of corporate messaging. This may not be the shortest or surest route to a revolutionary change in society, but 'culture jamming' is an important part of the propaganda struggle, and Adbusters are fighting it with great humour and a very good sense of design.

www.adbusters.org see also www.subvertise.org

ALLIANCE FOR SUSTAINABLE JOBS AND THE ENVIRONMENT▶is a coalition of environmentalists, trade unionists and others who came to world attention in Seattle as the 'Turtles and Teamsters' who united. Six months earlier a group of environmentalists and the United Steelworkers of America joined forces to confront the CEO of Maxxam Corporation, to demand that the company be held accountable for its impact on working people, communities and the environment. Recognising their common interest in making corporations more accountable for their behaviour worldwide, they formed the alliance and wrote a formal statement, dubbed 'The Houston Principles', which is available online. This statement encourages people to hold group corporations accountable for their actions with a stronger and more unified voice.

enshrined in the Universal Declaration of Human Rights and other international standards. In particular, Amnesty International campaigns to free all prisoners of conscience; ensure fair and prompt trials for political prisoners; abolish the death penalty, torture and other cruel treatment of prisoners; end political killings and 'disappearances'; and oppose human rights abuses by opposition groups. Amnesty has been very active in the Free Mumia campaign and was at the forefront of exposing Shell Oil's appalling record in Nigeria. The organisation is an extremely valuable resource for the anti-capitalist movement.

www.amnesty.org

ANARCHIST FEDERATION▶is an organisation of class struggle anarchists who aim to 'abolish capitalism and all oppression and create a free and equal society.' They believe in the direct action of the working class and reject any attempts at reform through parliament or national liberation movements. They are also reluctant to get involved with unions given that they are 'part of the capitalist system'. They are in favour of 'a united international anarchist movement.' Due to the fragmented nature of many anarchist organisations, it is difficult to know what kind of presence they have had on the major anti-capitalist demonstrations.

www.afed.org.uk

ATTAC▶the Association for the Taxation of financial Transactions for the Aid of Citizens was founded in France in 1998 by a group of citizens, associations, trade unions and newspapers. The idea for the organisation came from a 1997 editorial article by Ignacio Ramonet entitled 'Disarm the Markets' which appeared in *Le Monde diplomatique*. ATTAC advocates the imposition of a Tobin Tax, which is a tax on speculative transactions in the exchange market proposed by the Nobel prize-winning American economist James Tobin. ATTAC works to ban currency speculation, tax capital revenue, punish fiscal paradises and 'recapture the spaces of democracy lost to the financial sphere'. The organisation advocates citizens taking 'militant action 'to encourage governments' to live up to their responsibilities. ATTAC is a large and heterogenous organisation with elements of greater and lesser radicalism. Their main spokesperson, Susan George, has provided much inspiration to the anti-capitalist movement.

www.attac.org

C-E

COLORLINES▶is an independent US-based magazine which covers a huge range of race issues relating to the anti-capitalist movement, including poverty, workfare, environmental justice, immigration, interracial unity, the prison/industrial complex, reproductive rights, bilingual education, labour organising, campaign spending, corporate welfare, consumer racism, postcolonialism, biracialism, brutality and violence, geopolitics, identity and strategy. They recently did a special feature on 'Race Across Borders: Immigrant Movements' which examined the intersection of racial justice, immigrant rights and US labour unions' new pro-immigrant stance.
www.arc.org/C_Lines

CONFEDERATION PAYSANNE▶is an environmental group led by José Bové, a sheep farmer from Millau in south west France jailed in August 1999 for leading a raid on a McDonald's under construction in Larzac, and put on trial for destroying genetically-modified corn. His action against McDonald's was in response to the US decision to impose a heavy tariff on Roquefort cheese because the EU refused to import American hormone-treated beef. Bové and other French farmers handed out Roquefort in Seattle, and gave speeches against Monsanto and other major corporations.
www.confederationpaysanne.org

CORPORATE WATCH (UK)▶is a radical research and publishing group based in Oxford, which coincidentally has the same name as the US organisation. Corporate Watch (UK) was set up in late 1996 to support activism against large corporations. It has a research team who investigate all aspects of the corporate world for people and groups campaigning against corporations. They specialise in in-depth analysis of corporate structures rather than criticising corporate behaviour. In so doing they hope to help activists strategically target weaker points in companies. They aim to 'push the boundaries of both corporate accountability and the campaign movement'.
www.corporatewatch.org.uk

CORPORATE WATCH (US)▶previously known as TRAC (Transnational Resource and Action Center), is a San Francisco based organisation which educates and mobilises people through their website, and campaigns on environmental and labour issues. Their website has a searchable archive which is a fantastic resource for finding out the lowdown on corporate offenders. One of their most famous reports revealed Nike's sweatshop conditions in Vietnam and resulted in considerable mainstream media attention. Corporate Watch has done a great deal to keep up the profile of corporations behaving badly.

the WTO meeting at Seattle in 1999. There was discussion at the time of the groups staying organised after the event in order to create a continental network of activists 'fighting capital-directed governments' and 'publicising radical visionary politics and culture'. Their mission statement reads, 'We are committed to overcoming corporate globalisation and all forms of oppression. We are part of a growing movement united in common concern for justice, freedom, peace and sustainability of all life, and in a commitment to take direct action to realise radical visionary change.'
www.cdan.org and www.directactionnetwork.org

DROP THE DEBT > is based in London and is a short-term successor to Jubilee 2000. It ran a short-life campaign to win a 'New Deal on Debt' by the time the G8 world leaders met in Genoa in July 2001. Drop the Debt has called for deeper debt cancellation for more countries, including 100 percent debt cancellation from the IMF and World Bank for the poorest countries in Africa, Latin America and Asia. Drop the Debt is supported by Oxfam, UNISON, the WDM and many other organisations, and sent between 1,000 and 2,000 campaigners to the Genoa demonstrations.
www.dropthedebt.org

EARTH FIRST! > is a non-violent direct action deep ecology movement which 'rejects the anthropocentric (human-centred) worldview of industrial civilisation'. Earth First! was founded in 1979 in response to 'a lethargic, compromising, and increasingly corporate environmental community.' Earth First! believes in a wide range of methods from grassroots organising and involvement in the legal process to civil disobedience. They have an 'End Corporate Rule' campaign which focuses on corporations' threat to democracy, and environmental and social justice. They are members of PGA (see below) and were active at the Prague demonstrations.
www.earthfirstjournal.org/primer/

EARTH ISLAND INSTITUTE > prepared more than 500 sea turtle costumes for Seattle. Sea turtles are a prime symbol of WTO threats to environmental laws, since a WTO tribunal ruled that the US Endangered Species Act which requires shrimp to be caught with turtle-excluding devices was 'an unfair trade barrier'. The Earth Island Institute has published the *Earth Island Journal* since 1982 when it was a class project at Stanford University. The journal has exposed such diverse (and perverse) consequences of capitalism as the use of rendered cats and dogs as major ingredients in commercial pet foods, US military plans to use the ionosphere as a weapon of war, and links between the Mexican tuna industry and cocaine importers. Not for the faint of heart.
www.earthisland.org

FIFTY YEARS IS ENOUGH▶began their campaign in 1994, the year that marked the fiftieth anniversary of the World Bank and IMF. They have brought to light some of the most damaging effects of World Bank policies and development projects. Most of the organisations that backed this campaign were later active in the preparations for Seattle and continue to be in the movement. Among them are the Environmental Defense Fund, Food First, Friends of the Earth, Global Exchange, Greenpeace International, the Institute for Agriculture and Trade Policy, the Institute for Policy Studies, the International Rivers Network, Oxfam America, Oxfam Canada and Probe International.
www.50years.org

FOCUS ON THE GLOBAL SOUTH▶recognises that structural adjustment programmes and other neo-liberal economic policies have had a devastating effect on countries throughout the Southern hemisphere, increasing economic inequality, corruption and environmental degradation. Focus argues that these policies, imposed by the IMF and World Bank, have 'crippled the state as an agent of development and protector of the community'. They therefore advocate the creation of links between local, community-based, national, regional and global 'paradigms of change'. The main focus of the organisation is Asia, but they coordinate their research with organisations based elsewhere.
www.focusweb.org

FRIENDS OF THE EARTH▶was founded in 1971 to campaign around issues of pressing environmental concern. There are now 61 Friends of the Earth member groups which campaign internationally and locally to protect the environment and create sustainable societies. They place considerable emphasis on grassroots activism. They were present in Seattle and can be expected to keep up the pressure elsewhere. Their analysis of environmental problems is rooted in their understanding of global free market economics and unsustainable free trade practices. Their strategy is mainly one of public awareness raising.
www.foe.co.uk (UK) and foei.org (international)

GLOBAL EXCHANGE▶is a US-based organisation which combines activism and research. They edit books, publish pamphlets and flyers, and promote community activism. Global Exchange organises tours to cities like Tijuana, Mexico, to demonstrate the adverse effects of free trade and globalisation. Its two main founders, Medea Benjamin and Kevin Danaher, are constantly speaking and agitating on issues ranging from World Bank and IMF policies to sweatshop labor and the power

and organisations from many strands of the anti-capitalist movement: environmentalists, socialists, anarchists, trade unionists, students and others. GR has organised a number of successful speaking tours, attended by thousands throughout the UK, highlighting the major issues at stake in the anti-capitalist movement. They have also organised actions over the patenting of AIDS treatments, Gap's sweated labour and George Bush's Star Wars. GR was one of the key coordinating groups at the May Day 2001 protests in London and was active in mobilising for the G8 summit in Genoa.
www.resist.org.uk

GREENPEACE INTERNATIONAL▶is renowned for its militant actions to defend the environment against free trade and corporate devastation. In April 2001 in Quebec City, Greenpeace sent up a hot air balloon to breach the 2.5 mile chainlink fence that encircled the 34 presidents of the Americas who were intent on setting up the Free Trade Area of the Americas. Then a month later, when President Bush announced his pro-corporate energy policies, Greenpeace dumped a truckload of coal in front of vice-president Dick Cheney's residence in Washington DC. Greenpeace has long advocated direct action and civil disobedience in the cause of environmental protection.
www.greenpeace.org

INDYMEDIA▶is a network of collectively run media outlets for 'the creation of radical, accurate and passionate tellings of the truth.' Indymedia was established by various independent, alternative media organisations and activists specifically to provide grassroots coverage of the WTO protests in Seattle in 1999. With networks all over the world, and centres even in politically sensitive areas like the Middle East, Indymedia is an invaluable source of independent media coverage.
www.indymedia.org

INPEG▶many of the protests against financial institutions have been coordinated by different groups coming together to mobilise and organise for a short period—J18 (Global Carnival Against Capitalism), A16 (Washington), S11 (Melbourne), N30 (Seattle), S26 (Prague). These groups only exist for a short duration, but many still have an ongoing web presence—an example being INPEG, which coordinated the Prague protests against the IMF and World Bank.
www.inpeg.org

J-M

JOBS WITH JUSTICE▶is the social movement arm of the AFL-CIO. It works through coalitions of labour, community, religious and constituency organisations to fight for workers' rights and economic justice. The organisation was formed in 1987 by industrial and service-sector unions to allow organised labour to work more effectively in wider campaigns against sweatshops and for a living wage. JwJ has played a critical role in organising actions around all the major mobilisations since Seattle. For A16 in Washington DC, JwJ secured key labour endorsements from major US unions such as the steelworkers' union, UNITE! (the textile workers' union) and the service employees' union. JwJ activists organised local teach-ins, rallies and direct action from Knoxville to Tucson, bringing together labour, student and environmental organisations. In solidarity with the S26 protests in Prague, JwJ issued a call to 'localise the movement for global justice', asking organisations to plan actions around local labour disputes. By the time of the mobilisation against the FTAA in Quebec in April 2001, JwJ had developed a national network of activists who helped organise over 80 local actions in cities across the US.
www.jwj.org

JUBILEE PLUS▶based in London, is an official successor organisation to Jubilee 2000. Jubilee 2000 was very successful at highlighting the enormous human costs of high levels of unpayable debt in the world's poorest countries. With roots in the biblical concept of Jubilee, the campaign gathered an enormous global movement of charities, churches, businesses and trade unions calling on the world's richest nations, the G8, along with the IMF and World Bank, to forgive debts and abandon the structural adjustment policies that have decimated social services and impoverished millions of people in the Third World. In May 1998 Jubilee 2000 helped organise 70,000 people who formed a human chain around the G8 leaders as they met in Birmingham. Jubilee Plus continues Jubilee 2000's work in providing clear and thorough analyses, news and data on the subject of debt. (See also Drop the Debt.)
www.jubileeplus.org

LABOR NOTES▶has served as a forum for union activists since 1979. Labor Notes is for people who want to 'put the movement back in the labor movement'. They publish a monthly magazine which prints news about grassroots labour activity and 'problems facing the labor movement that top union leaders don't want to print'. The organisation is highly critical of trade union officials who hold back or compromise the position of more progressive grassroots members. Labor Notes believes that if the labour movement is to grow in numbers and power it must confront this issue head-on. Every two years

rights, and improve their wages and conditions. It includes Oxfam and all major UK textile unions, as well as alternative trading organisations and small solidarity groups. Members are committed to drawing attention to the plight of garment workers around the world, campaigning for the improvement of working conditions in the garment industry, including the right to representation and to organise, encouraging retailers to extend their responsibility for working conditions in all stages of production, and promoting fairer trade and supporting alternative trading networks. LBL's campaigns include the Ethical Trading Initiative and the Clean Clothes Campaign.
www.labourbehindthelabel.org

LEFT TURN▶ is a US-based network of revolutionary socialists and anti-capitalists active in struggles against globalisation, imperialism, police brutality and unfair labour practices. Left Turn chapters hold educational events and meet regularly to discuss issues facing the movement for social justice. The one idea that unites the organisation is the belief that 'through our collective efforts a better world is possible'. Left Turn was born in the aftermath of the Seattle rebellion, and supports all efforts to unite and broaden the anti-capitalist movement so that we can more effectively challenge the rule of corporations. Left Turn believes that the promise of the movement lies in the coming together of students, who have sparked a worldwide revolt, with the working class, who have the power to shut down the entire system.
www.left-turn.org

LESBIAN AVENGERS▶ are a direct action group focused on issues vital to lesbian survival and visibility. This is the group which linked arm in arm with the steel workers in Seattle. They support direct action, which for them means 'turning our political ideals into concrete confrontation'. They conduct letter writing campaigns, visibility actions and guerrilla publicity campaigns, all the while 'flaunting their lesbionic outrageousness'. They have occasionally worked with ACT UP.
www.lesbianavengers.org

MUMIA ABU-JAMAL▶ is an award-winning Pennsylvania journalist who has been on death row since 1982. He was wrongfully sentenced for the shooting of a police officer. He has written a book entitled *Live From Death Row*, as well as a number of other political essays available online. He has been a key activist in the movement against the death penalty within the US and abroad. He has done a great deal to highlight issues of police racism and corruption. The Free Mumia campaign has supporters worldwide, including large numbers of student organisations and Amnesty International.
www.freemumia.org

N-R

NATIONAL LABOR COMMITTEE▶ is 'a human rights advocacy group dedicated to promoting and defending the rights of workers'. It was founded in 1981 to oppose the US government's interventions in Central America. They conducted fact-finding labour delegation tours to the region, and they helped to protect threatened trade unionists and human rights activists through circulating reports and initiating emergency response campaigns. In the last few years they have expanded their scope to address the economic issues that are shaping the context for human rights and social justice in Latin America, with a focus on trade policy and international labour standards. They have organised high-profile campaigns against Wal-Mart, Gap and Walt Disney. They are an important source of research for United Students Against Sweatshops.
www.nlcnet.org

OXFAM▶ based in Oxford, conduct research and campaign on a wide range of social justice issues. Recently they have been at the forefront of research into the implications of TRIPS, an international intellectual property law dealing with pharmaceutical patents. TRIPS would prevent poor countries manufacturing their own cheaper versions of medicines for life-threatening diseases. Oxfam have produced a number of extremely hard-hitting reports on this subject which are available on their website. Their research and writing on pharmaceutical patents is first class, and lays bare the fundamental flaws in a corporate system of healthcare for profit. Their strategy has been one of moral pressure and reasoned argument vis-à-vis GSK and the rest of the industry, along with overall public awareness raising.
www.oxfam.org.uk

PEOPLE AND PLANET▶ was originally called Third World First, and was set up in 1969 to raise money for overseas aid. They now exist to 'educate and empower students to take effective action on the root causes of social and environmental injustice'. They are an important campaigning organisation among students. They stand for an end to world poverty, the defence of human rights and the protection of the environment. There are People and Planet groups at over 70 percent of UK universities and colleges, and 150 People and Planet groups in sixth form and further education colleges.
www.peopleandplanet.org

PEOPLE'S GLOBAL ACTION▶ is a network of grassroots movements united against globalisation. In early 1998 movements from all continents met in Geneva and launched a worldwide coalition of resistance against the global market, a new alliance ... and ... support called the People's Global Action Against Free Trade and the WTO.

today!' 'Hey NAFTA, hey NAFTA—we know what you're afta!' A fluid group of pranksters who dress up and chant radical—sometimes overtly anarchist—songs to dances at most US anti-capitalist events. Some of their cheers can be found at the website below, and you are invited to add your own.

www.a20.org/cheerleaders.cfm

RAINFOREST ACTION NETWORK▶works to protect the Earth's rainforests and support the rights of their inhabitants through education, grassroots organising and non-violent direct action. Within North America alone there are now over 150 Rainforest Action Groups (RAGs) associated with RAN. Their most important campaign at the moment is the 'Campaign for a Sane Economy' which recognises that while the obvious culprits are the corporations extracting oil and felling trees, these corporations are fuelled by a global financial system that finances and profits from destructive activities. Citigroup, the largest financial institution in North America, is a key financial player in many of the world's most destructive projects. The goal of the Campaign for a Sane Economy is to bring social and environmental accountability to all aspects of Citigroup's business practices.

www.ran.org

RECLAIM THE STREETS▶came together to campaign and organise direct action against roads being built in the mid-1990s. They are best known for the 'street parties' they organised, as well as for being part of the J18 'Stop the City' protests in 1998, and their involvement in the London May Day 2000 protests when they organised 'Guerrilla Gardening' outside Parliament in London. Until recently they were the European coordinators for the People's Global Action network.

www.reclaimthestreets.net

RUCKUS SOCIETY▶based in the US and formed in 1995, trains activists in the skills of non-violent civil disobedience to help environmental and human rights organisations. They argue that effective protest does not always happen spontaneously, and 'often requires careful planning and preparations, and the participation of experienced activists'. They run 'action camps' which combine physical and mental training for such things as communicating with the media and dealing with the police in a non-violent way.

www.ruckus.org

S-Z

SIERRA CLUB► is one of the oldest environmental organisations in the US, founded in 1892. They conduct campaigns through grassroots advocacy. They were outspoken in their attacks on Shell Oil's practices in Nigeria, and they joined with Amnesty International to investigate human rights abuses against environmental activists worldwide. The Sierra Club worked closely with the Clinton administration and caused controversy in the US Green movement when they backed Gore rather then Nader in the 2000 election.
www.sierra.org

SOCIALIST ALLIANCE► is an electoral alliance offering a left alternative to New Labour, challenging the government on everything from its privatisation of London Underground to the scapegoating of asylum seekers. The Socialist Alliance is made up of ex Labour Party supporters, and individuals and organisations from Britain's far left. The Socialist Alliance ran in the general election for the first time in July 2001 and contested around 100 seats. The Socialist Alliance in England and Wales, and the Scottish Socialist Party got the best result for any party left of Labour in the post-war period. The Socialist Alliance organised for many of its members to attend the protests against the G8 summit in Genoa.
www.socialistalliance.net and www.welshsocialistalliance.org.uk

SOCIALIST WORKERS PARTY► is the biggest revolutionary party in the UK. The SWP is a member of the Socialist Alliance, and many of its members are involved with Globalise Resistance. The SWP is part of the International Socialist Tendency, which is a network of revolutionary socialist organisations throughout the world. The organisation stresses the need for the mass mobilisation of workers to fundamentally change society, to put 'people before profit' once and for all. The SWP has been present at the major demonstrations in Nice and Prague, and worked with a variety of organisations to mobilise more than 1,000 people for the G8 summit demonstrations in Genoa.
www.swp.org.uk and www.socialistworker.co.uk

UNDERCURRENTS► is an 'alternative news service distributed via video' in the UK. Undercurrents Foundation, the organisation's charitable wing, has regular training workshops for video activists here and abroad. Undercurrents Productions does not have charitable status, in order to continue producing politically radical video coverage with a focus on international direct action. The organisation has been involved with negotiations between police and journalists for the helmeted individuals act together to facilitate free movement and communication during protests, helping to stop attacks on demonstrators such as baton charges, horse charges, and CS gas sprays. Based on principles of libertarian solidarity, they aim to promote mutual respect and protection among demonstrators. News reports that the police have been battering Wombles certainly seem to fit well with one of Susan George's suggested strategies — that we make the authorities appear as ridiculous as they are.

www.wombleaction.mrnice.net

WORLD DEVELOPMENT MOVEMENT▶ is a network of individuals and local groups campaigning against world poverty.

WDM's current campaign focus is the abolition of GATS. It also campaigns more generally for debt cancellation. WDM strives for change through its research, by lobbying decision makers, raising public awareness and mobilising members of the public to influence the political process.

www.wdm.org.uk

YA BASTA!▶ their Spanish name (which means 'Enough!') was inspired by the Zapatistas' first statement to the world in January 1994. The 'Tute Bianche' ('White Overalls') are part of this movement, first appearing in Milan in 1994 when the right wing mayor accused the Leoncavallo Centre of having no support. To make themselves immediately identifiable some people started wearing white overalls. Autonomists generally choose to have very little to do with trade unions and the traditional parties of the left. Overall they could be described as anarchists, although some supporters use Marxist terminology and analysis. Belonging to an autonomist movement doesn't involve any official membership or financial commitment — the 'movement' simply mobilises over issues they feel strongly about.

www.yabasta.it

ZAPATISTAS▶ the Ejército Zapatista de Liberación Nacional (Zapatista National Liberation Army) carried out an armed occupation of the state capital in the Chiapas region of Mexico on the very day in 1994 that NAFTA's launch was announced. They have become an important symbol of resistance to globalisation. In 1996 the Zapatistas called for a series of continental and intercontinental 'encounters', which led to a historic gathering in Chiapas at the end of July 1996. Over 3,000 grassroots activists and intellectuals from 42 countries on five continents came together to discuss the struggle against neo-liberalism on a global scale. There are a huge number of organisations and activities associated with the Zapatistas, but a guide can be found at the website below.

www.eco.utexas.edu/faculty/Cleaver/zapsincyber.html

World Bank: Founded 1944.
HQ: Washington DC.
Director: James Wolfensohn, US, investment banker.
Members: 177 countries.
Staff: 8,168 in DC and 2,445 overseas.
Assets: US$200 billion.
Loans: (in 2000) US$28.9 billion to over 80 countries.

The World Bank was established at the Bretton Woods conference in 1944, towards the end of the Second World War. The stated aim was to create a stable world order avoiding the economic

IMF: Founded 1947.
HQ: Washington DC.
Managing Director: Horst Kohler, Germany, banker and finance minister.
Members: 183 countries.
Staff: 2,500 worldwide.
Assets: Access to World Bank funds.
Loans: (at Jan 2001) US$65.3 billion to 91 countries.

The IMF was set up in 1947 to give financial assistance to member countries with balance of payments problems, to support policies of adjustment and reform.

WTO: Founded 1995.
HQ: Geneva, Switzerland.
Director-General: Mike Moore, New Zealand, ex-Prime Minister (Labour).
Members: 140 countries.
Staff: 500 in Geneva.
Budget: 127 million Swiss francs.

Growing irritation with state involvement in the borrowing countries led in 1995 to the replacement of GATT (General Agreement on Trade and Tariffs) by the deeply proactive World Trade Organisation (WTO).

rules across the globe through a series of highly secretive international trade tribunals.

The method is through the imposition of carefully drawn up structural adjustment programmes (since Seattle, renamed poverty reduction and growth facilities) for the borrowing nations. The programmes all impose heavy reductions in public expenditure, slash workers' rights and wages, privatise state facilities, and bring in the multinationals. Governments cooperate or lose the loans.

• • • • • • • • • • • • • •

Decision making (all 3 agencies): The semblance of democracy is completely false, since voting is on the basis of financial contribution. Broadly, the rich nations (US, Germany, Japan, UK and France, have over 40 percent of the votes. Secondly, World Bank/IMF representatives from all countries are usually unelected bankers. Thirdly, WTO tribunals can overrule national laws where they conflict with WTO policy.

settlement was to head off the spread of 'Communism' and anti-colonialism. The Bank makes loans for large infrastructure projects such as roads, dams and power plants.

From the beginning this opened the way for transnational corporations to obtain construction contracts, thus funnelling the money back into the coffers of the richest nations. Meanwhile the recipients of the loans are crippled by interest payments, the burden falling heaviest on the poorest inhabitants. For the last 20 years the bulk of new loans have been made to service debt — that is, to repay interest on existing loans.

include surveillance of its members' economic policy strategies, and guidance in implementing reforms. In the early post-war political climate the World Bank/IMF, though generally disapproving, was somewhat vague about the involvement of the state in managing projects, but by the 1970s it was mirroring and leading the growing neo-liberal project.

▶ Eric Toussaint, *Your Money or Your Life*, Pluto, 1999. Excellent on the history and practices of the institutions.

▶ Websites: The institutions all have their own comprehensive sites. The best critical ones are: www.50years.org and www.globalexchange.org

CORPORATIONS

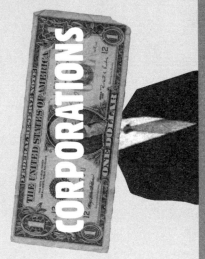

ROYAL DUTCH SHELL

Shell Oil is the largest oil corporation in the world — every day it produces 1 million barrels of petroleum from Nigeria alone. Corporate Watch lists a number of reasons for boycotting the company.
▶Shell has devastated the environment of the Niger Delta. ▶Shell has imported arms for the Nigerian military. ▶Shell has paid the Nigerian military to conduct operations in Ogoni. ▶Shell helicopters have been used to ferry Nigerian military troops. ▶Shell bribed witnesses at Ken Saro-Wiwa's trial.

Ken Saro-Wiwa was a Nigerian writer and environmental activist who was hung in November 1995 after a military tribunal found him guilty of helping to kill four Ogoni elders. There isn't a human rights or environmental protection organisation in the world which doesn't believe Saro-Wiwa was executed because of his campaign to help the Ogoni people.

He and others protested against environmental problems caused by Shell's oil spills and toxic gases, and the killing of 2,000 local people by the Nigerian military in the space of a few years.

Shell made $30 billion from oil in Ogoni between 1958 and 1995, while 500,000 people in that area have had no water, electricity, schools, roads or hospitals. Injustice on this scale requires a repressive military regime to keep down dissent. As a 1994 memo from the Nigerian chairman of internal security to the military administrator of the Ogoni territory reads, 'Shell operations still impossible unless ruthless military operations are undertaken for smooth economic activities to commence.' Official documents show that Shell imported Beretta handguns and ammunition to supply the Nigerian police through a company called Humanitex Nigeria. Shell spokespeople have acknowledged this purchase.

The Sierra Club has done a good job of keeping Shell's crimes in the public conscience. It is up to us to make sure that Shell doesn't get away with it. We can use trade union and activist links to do so. Shell has played a leading role in moves by the oil industry to derecognise trade unions in the UK.

GLAXOSMITHKLINE

At the end of 2000 Glaxo Wellcome merged with SmithKline Beecham to create GlaxoSmithKline (GSK). In 1999 the combined group had pre-tax profits of $6.8 billion. GSK has manufacturing sites in 41 countries and its products are sold in almost 140. It has the highest global sales in key anti-infectives, respiratory products and vaccines, all of which are important in the control of AIDS and pneumonia.

South Africa has an AIDS epidemic which is ravaging 4.2 million of its citizens. Its government appealed to its own constitution to justify manufacturing cheaper drugs to help treat the disease.

The government was able to do this through the manufacture of cheaper generic drugs, bringing down the cost of treatment by 80 percent in four years, halving the mortality rate in just three years.

As you can imagine, GSK will see them in court.

But we will be there too.

It is important to recognise that companies as big as GSK, with monopolies on products which many of us require to survive, cannot be challenged by consumer politics. Nor are they particularly susceptible to moral pressure even when framed in business terms.

Campaigners have encouraged GSK to

It was taken to court by pharmaceutical companies including GSK. Partly due to a well fought campaign the companies lost their case. The fact that they launched it in the first place is a serious cause for alarm.

More disturbing still is that the companies' lawsuit was strongly backed by vice-president Gore. Why? Because the pharmaceutical industry, led by their trade group, the Pharmaceutical Researchers and Manufacturers Association, wanted him to back it. As a Democratic congressman remarked, 'PhRMA doesn't need to lobby. The industry is in the White House already.'

And if drug companies were inside the White House before, it looks as if they own

expand its 'philanthropy portfolio'. They have remarked on it running an enormous 'reputation risk'. But the bottom line for a corporation that profits from illness and suffering, disease and death are simply market opportunities.

The bottom line for people is that their needs are met and their lives are improved. It is up to the people who make these drugs to refuse to make them if they do not save the lives of the people who need them. It is up to all of us to protest at the current state of affairs.

it now. GW donated over $1 million to the Republican Party in the US elections, and PhRMA, its main lobby group, spent nearly $24.4 million in campaign money on the Republican Party. As the *Guardian* reported, the wager paid off. PhRMA now has grateful Republicans running the White House, Senate and House of Representatives, and it deploys one lobbyist for every two members of Congress.

All of which will be useful when GSK moves next to attacking Brazil, where the government has threatened drug companies' profits through a policy of universal access to anti-viral drugs. This is a policy which benefits nearly all AIDS patients in the country.

All the information on corporations given here can be obtained from www.corpwatch.org and www.mcspotlight.org

WALMART

In 1998 David Glass, the CEO of Walmart, outlined the company's objective: 'First we dominate North America, then South America, then Europe, then Asia.' By 2001, Walmart had become the largest retailer in the world, with 3,000 US stores, and chains in Britain, Germany, China, Korea, Mexico, Brazil and Argentina. It opens a new megastore every two days. With 25,000 people on its payroll, Walmart is the single largest employer in the US after the federal government.

Al Norman, founder of a group called Sprawl Busters, explains the company's method, 'Walmart operates on a saturation strategy. They place stores so close together that they become their own competition. Once everyone else has been wiped out, they're free to thin out their own stores. Walmart currently has over 390 empty stores on the market today. This is a company that changes stores as casually as you or I change shoes.'

Speaking of shoes, Walmart is one of the largest retailers of goods and clothing produced by child labour and under sweatshop conditions.

Since Walmart espouses the philosophy that workers are part of the corporate family, we can only assume they mean poor and distant relations. Jobs with Justice report that one third of Walmart employees work part time with no benefits or job security, many of them restricted to 28-hour weeks so that they remain ineligible for benefits of any kind.

Walmart defeated every unionisation attempt made since it was founded in 1962—until 1997, when an Ontario Labour Board found the company had made threats of closures to workers trying to unionise. The vote against unionisation was therefore judged invalid, and the United Steelworkers were certified to represent the employees. This groundbreaking result meant that Walmart had to deal with a union for the first time in any of its 2,736 stores.

We need to make sure this is a situation it gets used to.

NIKE

In 1997 Nike got a nasty surprise when Corporate Watch exposed unsafe working conditions at plants that manufacture its goods in developing countries. An inspection done by Ernst and Young in Vietnam found inadequate safety equipment and training, encouragement of excessive overtime, and exposure to chemicals, noise, heat and dust exceeding the standard level by ten times. They also found that personal protective equipment such as gloves and masks were not provided each day.

Nike responded with a PR whitewash and claimed to have learnt its lesson. The company is aware of the damage to its brand image of the protests against its practices, and last year claimed that the campaigners have focused on 'the right issue, but the wrong company.'

Yet, also last year, labour rights investigators found Nike workers in China forced to work 12 hours a day, seven days a week for poverty wages. In Thailand and Cambodia there were reports of forced overtime, union-busting and abusive treatment. In Indonesia it was found that workers were being pinched and slapped, having their ears pulled or having to stand for hours in factory yards, a practice known as 'being dried in the sun'. Nike clothing workers interviewed earned less than $33 a month. We've got the right company.

Phil Knight, chief executive officer of Nike, subtly threatens that jobs will be lost if Nike is not allowed to conduct business as usual:

'We fundamentally believe and are demonstrating that human rights and good business practices can peacefully coexist. We are only trying to accomplish what makes sense for Nike and the workers who depend upon manufacturing jobs in the US and around the world.'

The crucial point which Phil Knight has missed is that it is Nike which depends on the workers who make its goods and not the other way round—it is strikes and occupations which will drive this point home.

PEOPLE NOT PROFIT

McDONALD'S

McDonald's has been under attack on many of the anti-capitalist protests. It may not be difficult to understand why, but it is difficult to explain why—without being sued.

In 1990 Helen Steel and David Morris of London Greenpeace (unrelated to Greenpeace International), produced and circulated a leaflet criticising McDonald's business policies and practices. They then spent the better part of a decade defending those words in the 'McLibel battle'.

The case against these activists is one of many which McDonald's has pursued to try and create a climate of intimidation amongst its critics, to put them out of business and/or to force them to apologise. It

then uses the apologies as propaganda to claim its innocence.

An example is made of certain organisations or individuals in order to prevent others from speaking out against McDonald's on such issues as low wages, anti-union policies, rainforest devastation or the lack of nutrition in fast foods—accusations which a small unprofitable publishing company wouldn't dream of making in the pages of its guide to the anti-capitalist movement.

Instead we will tell the story of McDonald's censorship strategy and hope we get away with it. If not, please send your cheques to: Bookmarks McLibel Support Fund, 1 Bloomsbury Street, London WC1B 3QE. Many thanks.

McDonald's is one of the most litigious companies in the world. It has invoked libel laws against national daily papers and TV channels, local press, a wide variety of Green groups, trade union organisations, a theatre group and many individuals. A few examples are listed on the www.mcspotlight.org website, which we wouldn't suggest anyone visits.

Some of the critics which McDonald's have attempted to silence include:► Vegan Action, who produced McVegan T-shirts with the slogan 'billions and billions saved' replacing McDonald's 'billions and billions served'. ► The publishers of a Polish primary school handbook entitled *Biology for Man and Environment* which linked McDonald's with rainforest destruction.

► *Scottish Fayre*, a play which satirises the fast food business and aims to 'highlight the appalling working conditions many young people have to endure in the fast food industry'. ► And many more.

The great complexity and expense of libel battles have forced many to back down from their statements, pay huge compensation costs, go broke, or even pulp books (ouch!)

Given all these lengthy legal battles, it is a wonder the company has any time left to make its delicious, nutritious, environmentally-friendly burgers.

But a little more needs to be said. McDonald's is a popular restaurant because its inexpensive fast food fits in well with our

poorly-paid, overstretched lives. It is a major employer because we live in a world where people are forced to compete for extremely poorly-paid jobs.

McDonald's size makes it an obvious target, but many smaller, even family-owned, companies have worse employment practices due to a lack of standardisation and accountability. This is where the arguments against big multi-nationals versus small local companies begin to break down, and we need to deepen our critique of transnational corporations into a critique of capitalism itself—including a lambasting of anyone who claims capitalism leads to greater freedoms of speech and information!

A part of the 100,000 strong union demonstration parades through Nice, December 2000.

Unions
Kim Moody
● ● ● ● ● ● ● ● ● ● ● ● ● ● ● ● ● ● ● ●

Almost half a decade before the inspiring confrontations at Seattle, Prague, Nice, Seoul and Quebec, mass political strikes and demonstrations by workers and their unions on almost every continent revealed the social depth of opposition to the impact and institutions of capitalist globalisation. While the 1995 strike of public workers in France and the massive demonstrations that paralysed the country were among the most visible of these actions, they were only one of dozens of such brief upheavals that swept such dissimilar nations as France, Canada, Korea, Taiwan, Spain, Greece, Indonesia, South Africa, India, and Argentina, to mention only a few. They had in common opposition to neo-liberal policies imposed in the name of globalisation.

These were to be only the first wave in a rising arc of working class resistance to the consequences of international corporate capital's push for power and access in every corner of the world. In South Korea an almost unbroken chain of mass strikes of both a political and economic character that began in 1996 continue even today (2001). In 2000 similar, if briefer, mass strikes swept Nigeria (as they had in 1994), India, Uruguay and Argentina. In 2001 Argentina erupted twice in general strikes against the government's neo-liberal policies. One of the most successful of these uprisings, mentioned previously in this book, was in Bolivia, where workers and peasants conducted a mass strike, surrounded the capital, and forced the reversal of the privatisation of the country's water system.

These and other working class mass actions against capitalist globalisation were mostly national in scope. Although some of the federations and unions involved maintain active international contact, these actions were not linked or coordinated across borders or seas. Yet neither were they strikes against local employers, of whatever nationality, or solely against their national governments even when those were the immediate targets. They were strikes against the consequences of globalisation as they were experienced in different countries. To one degree or another, they reflected the relative immobility of the working class. The very position in production and accumulation that gives this class the power to shut down society, roots it geographically. Its massive numbers and limited income prevent it from quickly moving over great distances. A massive march of tens of thousands on the capital in the end only represents a tiny proportion of the working class of any nation. But its ability to act in its place along with its majoritarian numbers gives it a social weight and power that is denied to all other classes except possibly the ruling class itself.

What a contrast to the highly mobile, disproportionately youthful core of the global justice movement that caught the world's attention in Seattle, moved on to Washington and other US sites, to Prague, Nice, and London, and then to Quebec City. What gives this 'movement of movements', as Naomi Klein describes it, its impact is the mobility of its activists, across the globe and in the streets, and their tactical audacity. This combination of mobility and audacity, with its ability to disrupt the business of elite globalisers has caught the imagination of millions and moved the consequences *and* methods of capitalist globalisation way up on the agenda of social movements—including organised labour—the world around. It has also raised questions about the very system that has spawned international economic integration under corporate domination, and the elite political forces attempting to accelerate this domination and spread it into every crevice of life on Earth.

Yet by itself, and despite its ability to breach police lines, this 'movement of movements' lacks the social weight to carry out the very task it has set itself—the dismantling of the mechanisms of capitalist globalisation. This is not to say that the actions from Seattle to Quebec have had no effect. As Gerard Greenfield of the Canadian Auto Workers points out, there has been a shift in the discourse of the elite. Labour rights, environmental standards, and the worldwide fight against poverty now decorate the rhetoric of many trade officials, corporate bosses, and publications from the World Bank to the World Trade Organisation (WTO). WTO commissar Mike Moore went so far as to pull out his old New Zealand Labour Party credentials to proclaim himself a leftist. But as a naively bitter memo from the International Confederation of Free Trade Unions recently noted, the WTO is back to its old agenda

By itself, and despite its ability to breach police lines, this 'movement of movements' lacks the social weight to carry out the very task it has set itself—the dismantling of the mechanisms of capitalist globalisation

having learned nothing from Seattle. If the shift in discourse is superficial and temporary, the attention that the emerging movement has focused on the process of corporate globalisation is more enduring and potentially far reaching in its implications.

As scores of activists and analysts alike have stated, the great need is to pull these two forces together: the mobility and audacity of the movement in the streets with the social weight and numbers of the organised working class. 'Teamsters and Turtles, together at last,' was the slogan that celebrated that momentary unity in the streets of Seattle and projected such an alliance as the future of the global justice movement. Yet that prospect has largely turned to disappointment.

In Washington, London, Prague, and even at the World Social Forum in Brazil, labour's big battalions were notable mainly by their absence. Even in Seattle only a few thousands of the 30,000 the AFL-CIO union federation brought to demonstrate joined the action that disrupted the WTO ministerial meeting. The Canadian unions brought several thousand to Quebec City, but marched away from the confrontation. Only some US unions and local central labour bodies in the Northeast US organised for Quebec at all. Many individual union activists joined the fray at the fence, but one of them was moved to write an open letter titled 'Where were the unions?' The huge turnout by European labour in Nice in December 2000, estimated at from 50,000 to 80,000, was certainly an impressive sign of internationalism. But even here, the activist confrontations and customary teargas response came the day after the unionists marched.

The great need is to pull these two forces together: the mobility and audacity of the movement in the streets with the social weight and numbers of the organised working class

Given the realities of the US labour movement, there is more than a little irony in the frequent citing of Seattle as the global precedent for uniting labour with the environmentalists, direct action enthusiasts, student anti-sweatshop activists, animal rights advocates, anarchist youth, and other issue-oriented groups that form the active core of this movement of movements. This would have required not only a continuing series of massive mobilisations such as the AFL-CIO carried out in Seattle, but also a politics and audacity that is largely missing at the commanding heights of most US unions. To place such a burden on the shoulders of the US labour bureaucracy is to guarantee failure.

This is not because US unions were unwilling to fight their 'friend' Bill Clinton on matters of trade and international economic policy. They had, in fact, engaged in a long series of such fights from NAFTA, through the WTO, and two fast-track efforts by Clinton, both of which they beat. Though, of course, as the 2000 US elections drew closer, the labour leaders dropped everything to campaign for arch globaliser Al Gore. Nor was labour's inability to forge a confrontational coalition because US union activists flinch from conflict. One had only to see the massive confrontations mounted by US workers against police lines from the Pittston coal strike of 1989 through the first year or so of the Detroit newspaper strike of 1995 to know better. No, it is because the politics and practices of US business unionism, which still rule in most unions, preclude such an alliance on any basis unacceptable to the majority of union leaders.

A look back at Seattle is instructive about the reality of the Teamsters and Turtles and the future of organised labour in the growing global justice movement in North America. The big brigades that broke from the respectable, 'permitted', AFL-CIO march were Teamsters, Steelworkers and Longshore workers. The dock workers were from the west coast union, the International

The politics and practices of US business unionism, which still rule in most unions, preclude such an alliance

Longshore and Warehouse Workers Union (ILWU). This is a union with a long history of left leadership not typical in the US. It had struck earlier in 1999 for a day in support of a new trial for Mumia Abu-

Jamal, the radical African-American journalist on death row in Pennsylvania. A couple of years before that the ILWU struck for a day in solidarity with the Liverpool dockers in Britain. Most of the dockers in Seattle were from the region. Similarly, many of the members of the United Steelworkers of America (USWA) who joined the fight were locked-out strikers from Kaiser Aluminum in Washington state, a few hours drive from Seattle. They had been through a long struggle at that plant and had already forged an alliance with environmentalists fighting to save old growth forests in the region from cutting by Kaiser's parent company, Maxxam Corp. In other words, these too were seasoned troops mostly from the area.

Perhaps the most significant group, however, were the Teamsters who broke from the official march. Most were members of Teamsters Local 174 in Seattle. The president of Local 174 at that time, Bob Hasegawa, is an Asian-American leader of the rank and file union reform organisation Teamsters for a Democratic Union (TDU). This was an exemplary and highly democratic local union that aggressively organised new members and regularly mounted solidarity actions for other groups of workers in the city. It actively participated in the national rank and file movement in the Teamsters of which TDU formed the core. Joining leaders and members of Local 174 were other TDUers and reformers from the Pacific Northwest and other parts of the country. Later in the evening many of these Teamsters joined other workers and residents in defending the inter-racial and largely gay neighbourhood of Capital Hill from police attack. As one Teamster wrote to TDU's newspaper, *Convoy-Dispatch*, 'It was rank and file members and reform leaders who were in the streets when the going got tough.'

At least three things stand out: first, those workers who joined the action in the streets were mostly people who had been through some kind of struggle recently and who rejected to one degree or another the norms of US business unionism; second, they were rank and filers or local level officials at most; and, third, most of the militants of the day were from the region around Seattle. The top leaders gave speeches, played it safe, and flew back home. There was also a political difference between the top leaders and ranks in Seattle, even at the main, legal rally. Another TDUer described this in a letter to *Convoy-Dispatch*:

> **'It was rank and file members and reform leaders who were in the streets when the going got tough'**

> At the big labour rally, whenever a speaker called for getting labour protections in the agreements, the response was lukewarm. But whenever a speaker called for getting out of the WTO altogether, the crowd went wild with enthusiasm.

The crowd even cheered when a South African miner quoted Karl Marx in a call for the workers of the world to unite.

While the US is an extreme case, the tensions between workplace and rank and file militants facing the real and accelerating pressures brought on by globalisation, on the one hand, and high level union leaders bogged down in 'social partnerships', far more accustomed to negotiations and comfortable hob-nobbing with the business elite than confrontations, are likely to exist in many of the developed capitalist countries. Evidence of this can be found in the statements and actions of various international trade union bodies, notably the International Confederation of Free Trade Unions and the various International Trade Secretariats, which are worldwide federations of unions in specific or related industries. For the most part, they are dominated by the big union federations in the US,.

The top leaders gave speeches, played it safe, and flew back home

UK, Germany and Japan. Typically, their statements and protests are free of confrontational or abolitionist language and call for labour rights to be included in any trade agreements and a place at the table of multilateral organisations or meetings. They are, for the most part, muted protests from the aggrieved (junior) social partners of developed capitalism.

It is also in the countries of the economic North that the global justice movement, the 'movement of movements', has emerged so far. Perhaps for this reason many in the movement seem scarcely aware of the mass strikes and brief upheavals mentioned above that have swept so many countries of the economic South—another rift in the potential global alliance capable of taking on the enablers of globalisation. In any case, the movement's primary roots in the developed capitalist countries is definitely one reason why the alliance with labour is frustrated over and over as it comes up against the likes of the AFL-CIO hierarchy. It is unlikely that the leaders of labour federations such as the British TUC, the German DGB, or Japan's Rengo, with their faith in 'social partnership', would behave much differently. The alliance that almost seems most natural, that between the global justice activists and the more active unions and labour federations of the South, is, at least geographically, the hardest to pull off.

As if to make matters worse, the various forces currently fighting capitalist globalisation focus on different aspects of it. Looked at as a process, globalisation can be broken down into four phases. First is capitalism's inherent drive to expansion rooted in accumulation and competition. This is the powerful reality hidden behind neutral-sounding 'market' forces. Second, is the political process in which the major economic powers, usually led or pushed by US corporations and political leaders, negotiate trade and investment agreements, bend the multilateral institutions (IMF, World Bank, WTO etc) to their current needs, and generally accelerate the process of uneven development that leaves the world's majority in poverty. The third phase involves passage or ratification of the various agreements and policies at the national level, such as the ratification of Maastricht and NAFTA or that of the Free Trade Area of the Americas (FTAA) in a few years when and if it is finally negotiated. Fourth and last is the implementation of these policies at the national level, such as structural adjustment programmes, WTO rulings or neo-liberal policies in general.

So far the highly mobile 'movement of movements' has focused on the second, negotiating phase, while North American and European unions seem most active around the ratification phase. Most of the mass strikes whether in the South or North, on the other hand, have been reactions to implementation at the national level. Thus, in addition to differences in mobility and social weight, there is also a divergence of targets. So far at least, none have focused on phase one, the capitalist system itself—an admittedly daunting task given the often hidden and geographically vast character of the system itself. While there is an emerging consciousness that capitalism is at the root of the matter, there is only a small wing that characterises itself as anti-capitalist. How then can these separate movements, rooted labour and footloose activists, workers of the North and the South, all so seemingly out of step with one another, be pulled together and develop more of a common view of the roots of the problem?

In the most literal sense of all acting in unison, they probably can't. What is far more important for now, as in any potential coalition, however, is an awareness of the common enemy. This was the simple secret behind the alliance of steel workers and environmentalists in Washington state who united against Maxxam Corp. It was what inspired a few thousand of the more conscious workers in Seattle to bolt the official march and join the fight in the streets. The most obvious shared enemy are the multinational corporations (and by implication the capitalist system they represent) that are behind the political processes that have advanced international economic integration far beyond what ordinary market forces could accomplish. Not far behind are the political parties that ratify and implement the policies that increase the power of corporations over the rest of us and allow them to reorganise national economies in their own interest. With few exceptions this includes the traditional parties of the working class in the developed capitalist nations.

The second step is to turn the activist core (s) of the movement away from its (their) exclusive focus on elite meetings (phase two) toward other aspects of globalisation, such as national ratification or implementation. The attacks on the elite meetings are important and have awakened millions

What is important now is an awareness of the common enemy

and have awakened millions to a deeper realisation of the forces behind their declining living standards and worsened working conditions, but if the global justice movement remains focused exclusively on following governmental ministers and multilateral bureaucrats from one meeting to the next, the likelihood of such an alliance of audacity with social weight is slim. A post-Quebec poll showed that one out of five Canadians said they would have liked to join the protests in Quebec. Jobs, family, geography, and lack of money dissuaded them from doing so. One of the new developments around the Quebec City mobilisation was the number of local and regional demonstrations across the US and Canada. This allowed thousands to participate, even if at a less dramatic level, rather than remain passive observers.

A third aspect of how to forge an alliance of global justice and trade union activists involves the realisation that labour or the unions are not a monolith. The dynamism that came from the unions in Seattle and again in the local mobilisations in the US Northeast for Quebec came from the ranks and the local unions, not the top bureaucracy. The organising in the Northeast was carried out above all by Jobs with Justice, a grassroots, labour-based, and highly activist coalition. There is an opportunity facing the different elements of the movement in US in the fight against 'fast track', the legislative devise that will smooth the way for ratification of the

FTAA. This is strategically important because if the FTAA can be defeated or derailed in the US it will become useless to capital everywhere. The point here is not that we don't want the AFL-CIO or the Canadian Labour Congress to mobilise for big demonstrations, even if they do it in a less than confrontational way. The reality is that only the unions can turn out these kinds of numbers. If, however, organisers of the various events have created links to rank and file union activists, the conventional character of such labour demonstrations can be altered, as they were in Seattle and Quebec.

The fourth dimension of building a durable alliance with organised workers is, of course, internationalism.

> **If organisers of the various events create links to rank and file union activists, the conventional character of such labour demonstrations can be altered, as they were in Seattle and Quebec**

Here again the trade union bureaucracy can be a weak link in so far as it clings to a protectionist outlook, as most in the developed capitalist world do. Globalisation and the movement against it is opening a lot of minds to an internationalist perspective. This too was evident in Seattle and Quebec where international delegations were cheered. Yet two of the most important international initiatives in the Western hemisphere, the World Social Forum held in Brazil and the Hemispheric Social Alliance that met in Quebec prior to the confrontations to talk of alternatives to capitalist globalisation, had very little trade union presence. Again the answer to this lies in the fact that official labour, the trade union bureaucracy, is unlikely to play more than a token role in such things, while the activist rank and file is constrained by its very class position.

There is an enormous opportunity in the Western hemisphere in the next few years to begin to test ways to bring together a coalition of global justice activists and workers in the fight against the FTAA. This can be fought at both the negotiations and ratification level, nationally, and in joint international actions. Most of these actions will necessarily be national or local, which would allow for greater involvement of rank and file workers and local trade unionists. In Latin America, where many of the mass strikes of the last few years have taken place, the more left wing unions will continue to be central. It is even possible that hemispheric coordination could occur through the Hemispheric Social Alliance or the World Social Forum if they deepen links with union activists.

What is most encouraging about the role of unions in the movement as it has unfolded is that despite all the barriers to working class participation in the high profile events, including the conservatism of the bulk of the union leadership, thousands of trade union activists have found their way to them and to the front-lines where consciousness, like the action itself, moves swiftly and fluidly from yesterday's ideas to tomorrow's awareness of who the enemy really is.

Kim Moody works with the independent monthly publication *Labor Notes* and is a member of the US socialist organisation Solidarity.

hundreds of students converging with other protesters in Oxford Circus shortly before being encircled and held for eight hours by the police, with no access to food, drink or toilets. London, May Day 2001.

Students
Joel Harden and Brandon Johnson
● ● ● ● ● ● ● ● ● ● ● ● ● ● ● ● ● ●

'Activism is my schooling—it is my university.'

These were the words of a Purdue University student after he had helped shut down the World Trade Organisation (WTO) meetings in Seattle, campaigned against sweatshops, and returned from the anti International Monetary Fund/World Bank protests in Washington DC.[1] His words are not unique—thousands upon thousands of students across the globe are waking up to activism and taking their voices to the streets. As they challenge the world's injustices they are beginning to learn what will be necessary to end those injustices for good.

Student activism is, of course, nothing new. From the heady days of 1968 to the present, students have figured prominently in struggles for a better world. Indeed, the exciting spirit of resistance today—particularly the anti-capitalist mood within the broader anti-globalisation movement—has resonated loudest on campus. Here calls for reforms to trade deals have won less support than arguments surveying the ruins of capitalism itself. Amidst the teargas and riot police in Seattle, Melbourne, Prague, Buenos Aires or Quebec City, there were few cries for 'corporate responsibility'. The most popular slogans are revolutionary claims: 'This is what democracy looks like', 'Our world is not for sale', 'Human need, not corporate greed', 'A better world is possible'.

But, contrary to popular fiction, student revolts do not arise spontaneously. Be it from high prices in Indonesia, vicious para-militaries in Colombia, ruthless pharmaceutical companies in South Africa, or a barricaded trade meeting in Quebec City, there are material reasons why waves of student unrest take place. The real question for us now is how student activism can be mobilised into an unstop-pable force to change soci-ety. To do that, solidarity must be painstakingly forged between student radicals and those who produce the world's wealth, the working class. Students are enormously impor-tant to transforming society—they can provide an agitational spark that can inspire millions to act. But capitalism will only be brought to its knees by the brain and muscle that moves its gears.[2]

The window of opportunity provided by today's anti-capitalist mood will close if we are unprepared to deepen the links between students and workers

The positive news is that an openness exists today as never before to foster a spirit of internationalism and solidarity that can unite students, workers and their allies the world over in a com-mon cause—to fundamentally change society. From Seattle to Seoul, from Belgrade to Jakarta, massive waves of protest have arisen where workers and students (among others) have shown their collective strength. The post-Seattle period is one where unprecedented alliances have been forged between union mili-tants and campus radicals.

But this solidarity remains uneven and will not last forever. The window of opportunity provided by today's anti-capitalist mood will close if we are not prepared to deepen the links between students and workers. Examples reviewed here will tes-tify to the fact that much more must be done to push student poli-tics in a direction that will yield lasting rewards. The challenge for us now—as it was for those before us—is to convey the arguments and generate the kind of political focus to make it happen.

Students and capitalism

Though the precise experience of students may differ from country to country, historically they have held a particular place in society.

Traditionally higher education was solely the preserve of the elite and the tiny middle class strata that served its functional needs. Indeed, for many years most students were regarded as proud defenders of the status quo, frequently fighting 'on the side of reaction: in Paris in June 1848, in Russia in 1917, in Germany in 1919-23 and 1930-33'.[3]

But the changing needs of capitalism have also changed the face of student politics. A widened layer of personnel was needed by business to help facilitate the processes of mass production and consumption of the post-war economic boom in the West. In countries with tuition fees, grants and loans were extended to war veterans for higher education. In countries without fees, streaming systems were relaxed somewhat to provide greater access to the credentials necessary for an emerging professional workforce. Women and ethnic minorities were seen in higher numbers on campuses, although whites and men from professional or middle class backgrounds remained over-represented in the ranks of the student movement compared to others from poor or working class families.

During this post-war expansion students were met with the same contradictions that remain to this day. On the one hand, they were told to develop their capacities as critical thinkers. On the other hand, they saw universities and colleges operate as 'education factories' run by functionaries who worked hand in glove with those provoking imperialist wars, sanctioning dictatorial regimes, or suppressing dissent on campus. This contradiction would create a smouldering discontent that exploded the world over in 1968.

The tremors of this ground-shaking period were felt from all corners of the globe. In May 1968 France ground to a halt with 10 million workers on strike. Students there initiated a conflict that nearly led to the ousting of president Charles de Gaulle. The anti-war movement raged in Europe and North America, the 'Hot Autumn' in Italy shortly after saw unprecedented mass action. Students and workers in Czechoslovakia bravely took on a Stalinist regime. Pakistan saw the emergence of a near-revolution, and Mexico City was a scene of daily street fights between Olympic promoters and dispossessed workers and students. It was a time when a cauldron of dissent nearly bubbled over, when the establishment trembled at the thought of where the activity in the streets might lead.

For the most part, the days of 1968 gave way to either wild ultra-left currents or passive identity politics among campus activists. Though minimal gains were made with the emergence of new social movements, the academy quickly reacted to channel the legitimate questions students were raising into the bizarre and rudderless world of postmodernism.

The atomising and often alienating milieu of higher learning still regroups people from different walks of life, though with soaring fees and deepening poverty this is quickly changing. It is unquestionable that a creeping elitism is taking over as the costs of higher education continue to sky-rocket. Many students are trapped in a cynical situation—a degree or diploma is necessary for even a modest foothold in society, but the cost is prohibitive to the extent where massive levels of debt or inordinate hours of part-time work are necessary to bear the cost.

> **The academy quickly reacted to channel the legitimate questions students were raising into the bizarre and rudderless world of postmodernism**

But today's anti-capitalist mood has provoked a shift away from the single-issue campaigning and parochialism that marked student politics during much of the 1970s, 80s and 90s. In the West, as the reach of today's insatiable markets has spread extensively on campus, an ideological war is being waged by a growing minority of students who name capitalism as the source of their problems. Elsewhere, students are gaining the confidence to take on dictatorial regimes that rightly fear the agitational role campus radicals are playing.

Students and revolution: Indonesia and Serbia

In Indonesia in 1998 and Serbia in 2000 students played a major role in urging forward oppositional movements. At the same time, both revolutions ultimately fell short of their aims, and both hold important lessons for student radicals trying to build a revolutionary mass movement today.

Indonesia 1998

> 'Indonesia is rich in raw materials yet the people live in misery. The people can no longer afford to eat or buy medicine. This is all the fault of the system—this is what we have to smash.'
> —Cecep Daryus, Indonesian student leader[4]

Mass demonstrations broke out shortly after President Suharto had rigged yet another parliamentary election in 1997. Strikes were widespread and rioting was rampant in the streets of Jakarta, as upwards of 1 million people held the streets. Early 1998 also saw major waves of protest in Indonesia, as rising prices and high levels of unemployment battered the country. Violence spread through the industrial heartlands after riot police attacked student demonstrators.[5]

As the protest wave built, the Indonesian military warned students not to take their demonstrations off-campus. The advice was ignored. Students gained more support as the attacks on them increased. When Suharto announced in May that democratic reform would come only in 2003, the barometer of campus unrest shot through the roof. It intensified twofold as the government announced it was cancelling subsidies for fuel and electricity prices due to an IMF directive. Workers everywhere began to move into action.

The ten days in mid-May 1998 that followed contained the moments most will remember from the Indonesian Revolution. These were the moments when military officers at times showed open sympathy with the uprising, often urging looters to 'take turns' to ensure a fair distribution of a warehouse's supplies. Whole sections of Jakarta burned, costing many lives. At first most students, in the name of non-violence, refused to join in. But on 19 May over 30,000 occupied the main parliament building in Jakarta. Workers sent representatives to support the initial occupation, and joined the students' call for Suharto to step down.

Most people know the result of the Indonesian Revolution—Suharto's resignation and replacement by B J Habibie, a close supporter of the old regime. Less known is the fact that a vigorous debate broke out inside the student occupation of the parliament building about whether workers or the poor should be allowed into the building. Sadly, the leadership of the occupation fought bitterly against the unity position, ordering that pamphlets backing the idea were torn up and a cordon put in place to physically block workers and the poor from joining the students.[6] The failure of a united voice between students and workers meant that the largest demonstrations during the Indonesian Revolution were co-opted by liberal opportunists desperate to restore order, even if that meant supporting Habibie.

Serbia 2000

'We did it on our own. Please do not help us again with your bombs.'
—Serbian student[7]

Students were the initial force to challenge Serbian president Slobodan Milosevic's rigging of the September 2000 elections. Students had been a thorn in Milosevic's side for some time, but in an organised fashion for only two years. In 1998 a spirited wave of dissent was raised against the Serbian government's proposed 1998 University Act. The new legislation allowed the state the right to directly appoint deans or rectors to oversee all faculty hirings. The act also compelled professors to sign thinly-veiled declarations of support for the Milosevic regime. Over 150 professors were fired as a result of the act.

The faculty of philology in Belgrade was a particular target. The neo-fascist Serbian Radical Party—among the three parties in Serbia's ruling coalition—appointed an ultra-nationalist dean to the faculty, who used his arbitrary powers to sack most of the world literature department. The students in the faculty responded with months of protests. Within these events emerged a small group of activists who referred to themselves as Otpor! (Resistance!) Otpor! and others managed to get rid of the appointed dean and force the reinstatement of the fired professors.

The confidence arising out of this experience was clearly infectious. Otpor! began to mobilise in a serious way, often using the weapons of satire and comic theatre to confuse their opponents. Sometimes students would amass in large numbers to play the board games Monopoly or Risk in public venues, emphasising how Milosevic was toying with their future. When Milosevic once declared himself a national hero, Otpor! printed stickers and badges in mass quantities that read 'I am a national hero'.

Otpor!'s campaign for free expression and democratic elections won broad support. Voya Brovic, Serbia's most famous actor, took a famous curtain call with his fist raised while donning an Otpor! T-shirt. A statement Otpor! released on the advent of Milosevic's 58th birthday, 20 August 2000, is emblematic of the anger they were heaping on the Milosevic regime:

> Thank you for the childhood you have taken from us, for the unforgettable war scenes you have given us, for all the crimes you have committed in the names of the Serbs, for all the lost battles... Thank you for the unforgettable convoys of our brothers, for the sound of the air-raid sirens, for all the lives lost in vain... Happy birthday, Mr President. May you celebrate your next one with your nearest and dearest on a deserved holiday in The Hague.[8]

Otpor!'s goal was to build a broad coalition that sought to mobilise the vast majority who detested Milosevic.[9] As one activist put it:

> Milosevic controls the media, and he has 20 percent of the people in his pocket. The rest of the country hates his guts and knows he is an evil tyrant. It's our job to motivate those 80 percent.[10]

But Otpor! faced a problem. While most Serbians detested Milosevic, there was little enthusiasm for the opposition parties which were frequently just as corrupt and often collaborated with the existing regime. Laura Secor recalls the popular message Otpor! representatives would convey when speaking at opposition events in the run-up to the 24 September elections:

> When Otpor! representatives attend rallies organised by the SPO (Vuk Draskovic's Serbian Renewal Party) or other parties, they win thunderous applause for demanding accountability from the opposition

leadership. 'If you betray us again,' an Otpor! spokesperson is reported to have announced at one opposition rally, 'next time we will bring 10,000 of our people'."

When Milosevic tampered with the 24 September elections Otpor! took the lead in street protests. High school students were seen everywhere. The army was split up to its highest levels as high-ranking officers headed off to lobby the powerful Kolubara miners to join or avoid the activity in the streets. Strike action was proliferating in all corners of Milosevic's embattled regime, and many recognised that the Kolubara miners would be the force that decided where the activity would lead. The miners began striking despite police intimidation, and tens of thousands of supporters flocked to their aid.

Students and workers accomplished what NATO's 78-day bombing campaign had failed to deliver— ousting Milosevic from power

The Kolubara miners and thousands of other workers joined the revolution. Parliament was set ablaze and the national television station taken over, while police and security forces countered with little or no resistance. Milosevic's regime had been toppled, and many of his sympathisers were driven out of their posts. Students and workers accomplished what NATO's 78-day bombing campaign had failed to deliver—ousting Milosevic from power. This was done in three days, and not one bridge, school or hospital was damaged.

Otpor! has begun to steadily unravel from within since the revolution, due in large part to internal disagreements about the way forward. The weakness for Otpor!—much like it was with the Indonesian students—was its failure to base its organisational strategy on a process of building unity with workers and other allies. Students proudly sought out workers in the heat of the battle, but little effort was made to extend the reach of Otpor! into the ranks of the working class. This unnecessary polarisation has left Otpor! isolated and incapable of being a serious threat to the Kostunica government. Since coming to power Kostunica's liberal opposition has moved quickly to condemn the worker-management experiments which had become commonplace during the revolutionary fervour.

Plan Colombia: building solidarity in perilous circumstances

In contrast to the experiences of Indonesia and Serbia, in Colombia student organisations are bravely attempting to build solidarity with workers, peasants, radicalised groups and insurgents in what may be the world's most dangerous conditions. Currently Colombia holds the dubious distinction of having the highest rate of assassinations of trade unionists and student activists. In 1999 half the union leaders assassinated in the world were Colombians. Since 1987 five presidential candidates have been assassinated, as have 3,500 opposition activists. Last year over 130 student leaders were killed. The latest reports indicate that 35 student activists have been killed since early January 2001.[12]

As is the case for Indonesia, the greatest problem facing Colombians today is not just their terrible poverty but the wealth of resources in their homeland. Colombia's oil reserves, ideal position for canal construction, and gold, platinum, silver, bauxite, manganese, radioactive cobalt, zinc, chrome, nickel, copper, exotic wood and large fishing resources are significant enough to gain attention from investors the world over. For some, given the global concern about the finite nature of currently tapped oil reserves, Colombia represents an oyster in need of imperialist pliers.

Enter Plan Colombia. Touted as a high-financed 'war on drugs', Plan Colombia is a thinly veiled war on the ordinary Colombians who stand in the way of profitable resources. (See Mike Gonzalez's piece in this volume for more details.)

Seen in its true context, Plan Colombia is nothing more than an attempt to finish off the havoc that trade liberalisation started. After pushing peasants into the drugs trade, Plan Colombia intervenes to displace those trying to eke out an existence, and others for daring to stand in the way of lucrative mega-projects. The crop-spraying and forced displacement of people is discriminate, however, primarily targeting the resource-rich areas in Bolivar, Cauca Valley, Quindio, Caquetá, Putumayo, Meta, Casanare and Chocó.[13] Making matters even worse, well over 8,000 paramilitaries are active in Colombia, engaging in sickeningly brutal attacks on anyone organising to resist displacement, while the government sits on its hands (indeed, many insist, with convincing evidence, that the government is the puppeteer behind the paramilitaries). Understandably in such conditions, guerrilla insurgency has been a feature in Colombia for many years, and popular militias have fought bitterly to stave off the aggression of imperialist forces.

The role students are currently playing in this perilous environment is nothing short of astounding—they are working to build solidarity between the local communities under attack and the guerrillas. ANDES (Andean High School Association), ACEU (Colombian Association of University Students), JUCO (Young Communists of Colombia) and OCLAE (Continental Organisation of Caribbean and Latin American Students) are groups that have actively fought to bring together the very people in Colombia the state and paramilitaries are trying to tear apart. Three days of action have been called for summer 2001, all of which aim to bring together workers, students, peasants and guerrillas desperate to beat back Plan Colombia.

In November 2001 the OCLAE general secretariat meeting is to be held in Colombia. The meeting will be followed by a field trip to a guerrilla zone, to live and engage in dialogue with guerrillas for approximately a week. This activity is typical of the work already under way by ANDES, JUCO, OCLAE and, to a lesser extent, ACEU. There is a real push among student militants to organise national and international forums, 'colluqs', to build solidarity with guerrilla groups, particularly the FARC (Revolutionary Armed Forces of Colombia). This is doubtless the reason they have been targeted by paramilitaries and death squads. In the bravest of circumstances, Colombian students are providing a lead for their counterparts elsewhere.

North America and Europe: students on the move

'Think the WTO is bad? Wait till you hear about capitalism!'
—placard in Seattle

'After a long slumber, student activism is waking up.'
—Ralph Nader addressing 1,500 students at the University of Wisconsin

The events of Seattle were an appropriate beginning to a new century where an exciting optimism is taking hold. North America and Europe is alive and well with the exuberant spirit of anti-capitalist politics on the campuses. What is more, as many have noted, the internationalism witnessed in student protest in Europe and North America is providing a means to break down old divisions. The spirit of anti-capitalism has set the tone for a reassessment of the boundaries that had previously thwarted an internationalist sentiment. On 26 September 2000 in Prague, Macedonians marched with Greeks, Basques with Spaniards, Poles with Russians. Between 20 and 21 April 2001 in Quebec City, French and English-speaking militants united to tear down security barricades.

There were important campaigns that set the stage for the onset of today's anti-capitalist mood. By the mid-1990s US student activism woke up over the issue of sweatshop labour. Students were shocked to learn of the conditions their school's garments were being produced in, and they rejected the notion that their only recourse against the brutality of sweatshops was individual consumer power. They began to realise that, if they mobilised and united with workers' organisations, other tactics were possible. By July 1998 activists from over 30 different schools came together in New York to establish an organisation that would help coordinate anti-sweatshop campaigns from campus to campus. United Students Against Sweatshops (USAS) was born.

And it was born fighting. By January 1999 students at Duke University occupied to get full disclosure over the university's licences. They won. Georgetown University students followed suit by occupying the president's office and winning full disclosure as well. UW-Madison then upped the stakes, winning not only full disclosure but also a living wage study and a clause on women's rights. By Spring 2000 USAS had over 200 affiliated campuses. Currently they are campaigning for a Worker Rights Consortium (WRC), an independent advisory board seeking to regulate the activities of companies producing school garments in cooperation with workers' rights organisations in the global South. By May 2000 some 47 schools were affiliated with the WRC.

The international movement to save imprisoned Black Panther

'People are drawn in by the horror stories, but then they start seeing how the whole system works'
—Maria Roeper, a sweatshop activist at Haverford

Mumia Abu-Jamal from state execution has been an important pole of international solidarity. Activities in support of Mumia have taken place in more than 100 cities worldwide—from Brazil to Antarctica, and in more than 45 cities throughout the US.[14] Students in defence of Mumia were linking up with lesbian-gay-bisexual-transgender and AIDS action groups such as the Simon Nkoli Queer Crusaders for Mumia.

As Bob Lederer of the Crusaders would say, 'If Mumia can be executed without ever having had a fair trial, it sets a dangerous precedent that would make it easier to heighten repression against all types of activists. That's one reason groups which rarely work together are united in action today.' This came as he and other Queer Crusaders leapt over police barricades to protest at the US Supreme Court. Demonstrators too were learning a valuable lesson—direct action works. Left to the courts, Mumia would probably have little hope, just as, left to patient petitioning in university boardrooms, battling sweatshops would be less effective. Movements were evolving.

Other campaigns, too, have provided inspiration and focus. Ralph Nader's campaign during the recent US presidential elections provided a voice for thousands of students politicised in anti-capitalist activity. In Canada and Quebec students figured in mass labour protests and rallies protesting against cuts to social programmes. In Europe the anti-nuclear movement has seen sizeable student involvement, along with campaigns against genetically modified organisms and soaring tuition fees. May Day 2001 was as raucous an affair as ever, with thousands of students celebrating the traditional workers' holiday in diverse fashion in Europe and elsewhere.

'We are training an entire generation to think differently about capitalism'
—Laurie Kimmington from SLAC (Student/Labor Action Coalition, a Yale affiliate to USAS)

Conclusion

It would be false to assume that the impulse to build solidarity is automatic for students as they radicalise in a period such as ours. The recent revolutions in Serbia and Indonesia reveal the necessity for students to be organised in a way that builds solidarity with workers. The Teamster-Turtle alliance struck in Seattle has created the potential to bring the fight against international capitalism to a level not seen in decades. Students, workers and others are more open-minded than ever before to arguments about alternatives to capitalism. Those sceptical about the resonance of today's anti-capitalism would do well to consider the words of Beverley Young, whose 22 year old son was arrested during the June 2000 protests in Windsor, Ontario in Canada against the proposed Free Trade Area of the Americas:

Students at the University of North Carolina held a nude-optional party titled 'I'd Rather Go Naked Than Wear Sweatshop Clothes'. Syracuse students biked across campus nude under the same principle

> Our young people have things to say about the world they will inherit. I'm proud of my son. I tried to instil in him the ability to think for himself, to question things. He has become an independent adult with the passion to believe he can make a difference. Your children, too, have opinions and ideas that could change the world. It's time we listened. Why am I writing this? To try to make Canadians realise what a truly apathetic bunch we've become—and ask if this is really what we want our country to be? Something is amiss in our society and our government: do we care?[15]

People do care. They are deeply concerned about the ruinous poverty, chronic unemployment, rampant bigotry, environmental degradation and costly wars that come with capitalism's insatiable search for profit. The task for socialists is to relate to this sentiment and mobilise it into action. The opportunity before us is exciting, but it will only last as long as the commitment to building solidarity remains. Mobilising people in greater numbers will

315 STUDENTS ANTICAPITALISM

require activists to maintain an open mind in appealing to others to join the struggle. The fight for a better world must not become the preserve of the most informed.

The most significant power our opponents have today is not their economic clout but the ability to divide citizens against each other, to split natural allies and diffuse dissent. The 'Spirit of Seattle' is latent in every human being who realises the present state of affairs is both unjust and unsustainable—who realises that a better world is possible.

Joel Harden is a PhD candidate in Political Science at York University, Toronto, Canada. His research focuses on the politics of the anti-globalisation movement, and the potentials for the anti-capitalist current within it.
thatcommie@hotmail.com

Brandon Johnson is an activist in Left Turn, US. He was an organiser for the Nader election campaign in 2000 and spent a year in the UK during which he built for the protests in Prague and Nice.
bj9@ukc.ac.uk

Notes

1. 'Activism Is My University.'
   Contributing student producers: Jeremiah Johnson, Phil Nardiello, Kelly Skiver, James Shaw, Kyle Thomas.http://www.cnn.com

2. As more students work an increasing number of hours to pay for their educational costs, or become active in unions as campus workers, a proletarianisation of student politics is taking place in many countries. Indeed, the line between 'workers' and 'students' is progressively less clear. A recent study conducted by the Centre for Research on Work and Society at York University (Toronto, Canada) revealed that over 70 percent of the 35,000 students there worked more than 24 hours a week. Nonetheless, while the proletarianisation of student life is a reality, this does not mean that students can be understood as a class. The student movement is a reflection of class society, with higher fees and declining access for working class families having an impact on the tenor of campus politics.

3. Chris Harman, *The Fire Last Time: 1968 and After* (Bookmarks, 1998), p39. Harman's book is essential reading for any student activist interested in learning what the battles of 1968 and after have to teach us today. Grant Brookes and Dave Colyer's *Students and the Education Factory* (New Zealand, Socialist Workers Organisation Pamphlet) is also worth reading to grasp the impact of students' struggles under capitalism.

4. In Clare Fermont, 'Indonesia: the Inferno of Revolution', *International Socialism* 80 (Autumn 1998), p4.

5. Ibid, p15.

6. 'Three Interviews with Workers'

Representatives and Socialists in Indonesia', *International Socialism* 80 (Autumn 1998), p40.

7 In Lindsey German, 'Serbia's Spring in October', *International Socialism* 89 (Winter 2000), p13.

8 From Joe Rubin, 'The Kids Who Could Topple Milosevic', *Mother Jones*, 22 September 2000. http://www.otpor.net/news/ The reference to The Hague refers to the fact that Milosevic was indicted by the International War Crimes Tribunal for his wars waged in the Balkans. Sadly absent from the indictment were any of the foreign leaders who waged the vicious 78-day bombing campaign in 1999 under the bogus auspices of helping Kosovan Albanians.

9 This decision was sometimes controversial when many nationalists and members of the Orthodox Church who had once supported Milosevic were drawn into Otpor!'s fold. Sonja Licht, a leading Otpor! activist, explained the strategy thus: 'My opinion is that one should go into the broadest possible coalition now, making absolutely sure that you don't let into that type of coalition people who are chauvinist, racist, fanatics, fundamentalists of any sort.' Laura Secor, 'Rage Against the Regime', *Lingua Franca*, vol 10, no 6, September 2000.

10 Ibid.

11 Ibid.

12 Hector Mondragon, 'US Fuelling the Fires in Colombia', http://www.freespeech.org/agp/colombia Strong thanks is also given here to Elizabeth Carlyle, Canadian spokesperson for the International Union of Students, who provided much of the text here about student activities in Colombia.

13   Hector Mondragon, 'US Fuelling the
     Fires in Columbia'.
14   In the springs of 1999 and 2000
     students at Evergreen College, Antioch
     College, the University of California at
     Santa Cruz, and Brooklyn Friends High
     School all invited Mumia Abu-Jamal to
     give taped speeches at their graduation
     events. See www.freemumia.org for
     more information.
15   'Proud of my Protester Son',
     Maclean's Magazine, 1 July 2000, p18.

Anarchists
Michael Albert

● ● ● ● ● ● ● ● ● ● ● ● ● ● ● ● ● ● ●

Like most social movements, anarchism is diverse. Most broadly an anarchist seeks out and identifies structures of authority, hierarchy, and domination throughout life, and tries to challenge them as conditions and the pursuit of justice permit. Anarchists work to eliminate subordination. They focus on political power, economic power, power relations among men and women, power between parents and children, power among cultural communities, power over future generations via effects on the environment, and much else as well. Of course anarchists challenge the state and the corporate rulers of the domestic and international economy, but they also challenge every other instance and manifestation of illegitimate authority.

So why wouldn't everyone concerned that people ought to have appropriate control over their lives admire anarchism? Problems arise because from being 'opponents of illegitimate authority' one can grow movements of incomparable majesty, on the one hand, and movements that are majestically unimpressive, on the other hand. If anarchism means mostly the former, good people will admire and gravitate toward anarchism. But if anarchism means mostly the latter, then good people will have reservations or even be hostile to it. So what's the not so admirable or even distasteful version of anarchism now? And what is the admirable version? And do even the admirable strands incorporate sufficient insight to be successful?

Distasteful 'anarchism' is the brand that dismisses political forms per se, or institutions per se, or even plain old technology per se, or that dismisses fighting for reforms per se, as if political structures, institutional arrangements, or even technological innovation, all intrinsically impose illegitimate authority, or as if relating to existing social structures to win immediate limited gains is an automatic sign of hypocrisy.

Institutions that permit people to express their humanity more fully and freely are not abominable at all, but part and parcel of a just social order

Folks holding these views presumably see contemporary states' use of force and rule to subjugate the many, and deduce that this is an outgrowth of trying to adjudicate, or legislate, or implement shared aims, or even just to cooperate on a large scale, per se, rather than seeing that it is instead an outgrowth of doing these things in particular ways to serve narrow elites and what we need is to fulfill the functions more positively.

They see that many and even most of our institutions, while delivering to people needed organisation, celebration, food, transport, homes, services etc, also restrict what people can do in ways contrary to human aspirations and dignity. They wrongly deduce that this must be the case for all institutions per se, so that instead of institutions we need only voluntary spontaneous interactions in which at all times all aspects are fluid and spontaneously generated and dissolved. Of course, in fact, without stable and lasting institutions that have well-conceived and lasting norms and roles, advanced relations among disparate populations and even among individuals are quite impossible. The mistake is that while institutional roles that compel people to deny their humanity or the humanity of others are, of course, abominable, institutions that permit people to express their humanity more fully and freely are not abominable at all, but part and parcel of a just social order.

The situation with technology is similar. The critic looks at assembly lines, weapons, and energy use that despoil our world, and says there is something about the pursuit of technological

The issue isn't to decry and escape technology per se, but to create and retain only technologies that serve humane aims and potentials

mastery that intrinsically breeds these sorts of horrible outcomes, so we'd be better off without technology. Of course, this misses the point that pencils are technology, clothes are technology, and indeed all human artifacts are technology, and that life would be short and brutish, at best, without technologies. So the issue isn't to decry and escape technology per se, but to create and retain only technologies that serve humane aims and potentials.

And finally, regarding reforms, the debilitating orientation notices that with many reforms the gains are fleeting, and elites even manage to reinforce their legitimacy and extend their domain of control by first granting and then domesticating and then eliminating the advances. But again, this doesn't result from change or reform per se, but from change conceived, sought, and implemented in reformist ways that presuppose and do not challenge system maintenance. What's needed instead isn't to have no reforms, which would simply capitulate the playing field to elites, but to fight for reforms that are non-reformist, that is, to fight for reforms that we conceive, seek, and implement in ways leading activists to seek still more gains in a trajectory of change leading ultimately to new institutions.

It shouldn't be necessary to even discuss the above addressed 'bad trajectory' of anarchism and its anti-political, anti-institutional, anti-technology, and anti-reform confusions. It is perfectly natural and understandable for folks first becoming sensitised to the ills of political forms, or institutions, or technologies, or first encountering reform struggles, to momentarily go awry and blame the entire category of each for the ills of the worst instances of each. But if this confusion were to thereafter be addressed naturally, it would be a very temporary one. After all, without political structures, without institutions per se, and/or without technology, not to mention without progressive reforms, humanity would barely survive, much less prosper and fulfill its many capacities.

But, of course, media and elites will take any negative trajectory of anarchism and will prop it up, portraying it as the whole of anarchism, elevating the confused and unworthy to crowd out the valuable and discredit the whole. In this context, some of the most extreme (but colourful) advocates of these counter-productive viewpoints will be highlighted by media. The whole unsustainable and objectionable approach will thereby gain far more visibility than is warranted by its numbers, much less by its logic or values, and, thereafter, also a certain tenacity.

What about the good trajectory of contemporary anarchism, less visible in the media? This seems to me to be far more uplifting and inspiring. It is the widely awakening impetus to fight on the side of the oppressed in every domain of life, from family, to culture, to state, to economy, to the now very visible international arena of 'globalisation', and to do so in creative and courageous ways conceived to win improvements in people's lives now, even while leading toward winning new institutions in the future. The good anarchism nowadays transcends a narrowness that has often in the past befallen the approach. Instead of being solely politically anti-authoritarian, as often in the old days, nowadays being an anarchist more and more implies having a gender, cultural, and an economic, as well as a politically-rooted orientation, with each aspect taken on a par with and also informing the rest.

This is new, at least in my experience of anarchism, and it is useful to recall that many anarchists as little as a decade back, perhaps even more recently, would have said that anarchism addresses everything, yes, of course, but via an anti-authoritarian focus rather than by simultaneously elevating other concepts in their own right. Such past anarchists thought, whether implicitly or explicitly, that analysis from an overwhelmingly anti-authoritarian angle could explain the nuclear family better than an analysis rooted as well in kinship concepts, and could explain race or religion better than an analysis rooted as well in cultural concepts, and could explain production, consumption, and allocation better than an analysis rooted as well in economic concepts. They were wrong, and it is a great advance that many modern anarchists know this and are broadening their intellectual approach accordingly so that anarchism now highlights, not only the state, but also gender relations, and not only the economy, but also cultural relations and ecology, sexuality, and freedom in every form it can be sought, and each not only through the sole prism of authority relations, but also informed by richer and more diverse concepts. And of course this desirable anarchism not only doesn't decry technology per se, but it becomes familiar with and employs diverse types of technology as appropriate. It not only doesn't decry institutions per se, or political forms per se, it tries to conceive new institutions and new political forms for activism and for a new society, including new ways of meeting, new ways of decision-making, new ways of coordinating, and so on, most recently including revitalised affinity groups. And it not only doesn't decry reforms per se, but it struggles to define and win non-reformist reforms, attentive to people's immediate needs and bettering people's lives now as well as moving toward further gains, and eventually transformative gains, in the future.

The good side of contemporary anarchism is in various respects too vague to rise above the rest — good anarchism doesn't posit clear and compelling goals

So why doesn't the good anarchism trump the not so good anarchism out of visibility, so to speak, leaving the way clear for most everyone on the left to gravitate toward anarchism's best side? Part of the answer, already noted, is that elites and mainstream media highlight the not so good, giving it far more weight and tenacity than it would otherwise embody. But part of the answer is also that the good side of contemporary anarchism is in various respects too vague to rise above the rest. What's the problem? I think it's that the good anarchism doesn't posit clear and compelling goals.

Anarchism has historically focused on the political realm of life. But even there, even with the long history, the emerging anarchism of today's movements doesn't clarify for us what an anarchist polity could be. Assuming that societies need to fulfill adjudicative, legislative, and implementation functions in the political realm of life, and need to do this via institutions which citizens partake of and constitute, then what should these institutions be? If the bad trend is to say that we favour no political institutions but only spontaneous face to face interaction of free individuals, each doing as they choose with no constraints on them, then what is the good trend's better viewpoint? What kind of structures with what kinds of social roles and norms in an anarchist polity will accomplish political functions while also propelling values that we support?

It is perhaps premature to expect this newly-enlarging anarchism to produce from within a compelling vision of future religion, ethnic identification, or cultural community, or a future vision of kinship, sexuality, procreation, or socialisation relations, or even a future vision of production, consumption, or allocation relations. But regarding attaining, implementing, and protecting against the abuse of shared political agendas, adjudicating disputes, and creating and enforcing norms of collective interaction, it seems to me that anarchism ought to be where the action is. Nonetheless, has there been any serious anarchist attempt to explain how legal disputes should be resolved? How legal adjudication should occur? How laws and political coordination should be attained? How violations and disruptions should be handled? How shared programmes should be positively implemented? In other words, what are the anarchists' full set of positive institutional alternatives to contemporary legislatures, courts, police, and diverse executive agencies? What institutions do anarchists seek that would advance solidarity, equity, participatory self-management, diversity, and whatever other life-affirming and liberatory values anarchists support, while also accomplishing needed political functions?

Huge numbers of citizens of developed societies are not going to risk what they have, however little it may be in some cases, to pursue a goal about which they have no clarity. How often do they have to ask us what we are for before we give them some serious, sufficiently extensive, carefully thought through and compelling answers? Offering a political vision that encompasses legislation, implementation, adjudication, and enforcement, and that shows

> **Public, accessible vision, political and otherwise, which truly serves the whole populace, is precisely what we need**

how each would be effectively accomplished in a non-authoritarian way promoting positive outcomes, would not only provide our contemporary activism much-needed long-term hope, it would also inform our immediate responses to today's electoral, law-making, law enforcement, and court systems, and thus many of our strategic choices. So shouldn't today's anarchist community be generating such political vision? I think it should, and I eagerly hope it will be forthcoming soon. Indeed, I suspect that until there is a widespread component of anarchism that puts forth something positive and worthy regarding political goals, the negative component decrying all political structures and even all institutions will remain highly visible and will greatly reduce potential allegiance to anarchism.

Some will say anarchism has more than enough vision already. Too much vision will constrain ingenuity and innovation. I reply that this is the same type of mistake as dumping political structures, or all institutions, or all technology, or all reforms. The problem isn't vision per se. The problem is vision that is held and owned only by elites and that serves only elites. Public, accessible vision, political and otherwise, which truly serves the whole populace, is precisely what we need.

So what about good anarchism's potentials? I guess I would say that if anarchism has truly recognised the need for culture-based, economy-based, and gender-based, as well as for polity-based concepts and practice, and if anarchism can support vision originating in other movements about non-governmental social dimensions while itself providing compelling political vision, and if the anarchist community can avoid strange confusions over technology, political structures, and institutions per se, and seeks to win non-reformist reforms—then I think anarchism has a whole lot going for it and could well become a main 21st century source of movement inspiration and wisdom in the effort to make our world a much better place.

Michael Albert is author of many books on diverse topics including an emphasis on economic visions beyond capitalism. His primary work is currently with *Z* magazine and the website Znet at www.zmag.org
sysop@zmag.org

The International Socialist Tendency marching in Prague, 26 September 2000.

Socialists
Colin Barker

● ● ● ● ● ● ● ● ● ● ● ● ● ● ● ● ● ●

This is the best time for a whole generation to be a socialist. The perverted top-down 'socialism' of Eastern Europe and Russia has been bumped off by those it oppressed, while the social democratic parties have finally abandoned their fake claims to be socialist. A genuine socialism from below is re-emerging from the shadows. The last few years have seen the rise of vibrant new movements across the globe challenging core institutions of capitalism—the great capitalist corporations, the system of states and their instruments of coordination (World Bank, IMF, G7 and G8, WTO, NATO, etc).

It is not just a matter of the great set-piece demonstrations — Seattle, Prague, Washington, Nice, Porto Allegre, Quebec City, Genoa and so on. For the language of 'anti-capitalism' and the aspiration to a whole new world fits the experience of people fighting a host of seemingly more local issues. For workers made redundant by newly

A genuine socialism from below is re-emerging from the shadows

mobile capital, for environmental and peace campaigners, for AIDS sufferers across Africa, for those facing the sell-off of essential services to private business, and for opponents of every form of barbarism and cruelty, it's not difficult to ask: isn't there something about the very system we live under that demands the widest direct action to bring it to an end?

The new movements are alive with fundamental debates about the most serious issues facing humankind. What are the central problems of modern society? Is another and better world possible? How can we best organise to change the world? What will work, and what won't? In these debates socialists have something to offer, provided they are also ready to listen and learn.

The starting point of such discussion is a basic agreement. What connects all the different evils we find ourselves fighting is the nature of the system we live under. Its name is capitalism. Its core characteristics generate all the major problems we find ourselves contesting.

The first is competition, the war of all against all. This is its driving force. Who says capitalism says competitive accumulation. It is the system, not simply capitalists' personal greed, which compels them to act as they do. Feed on others, or become their food, is the rule. Those who hope to change things by persuading corporate bosses to behave morally are genuine utopians.

The second is class division and exploitation. Capitalism's defenders see it as the natural working out of economic laws. Its socialist opponents insist it is a system of social relationships, which cannot but breed inequality and hierarchy. Capitalism depends on an ever-expanding class of workers. Each, to live, must enter into a contract of unfreedom, agreeing to obey their employer. Each must compete with other workers for the privilege of being bossed and exploited. Each, to eat, must spend her wages on goods produced, not for need, but for profit. Workers for Ford, Nike, Safeway and McDonald's don't simply make cars, shoes, groceries, hamburgers; through their effort and weary sweat they reproduce and fatten the corporation bosses and their system.

Third, capitalism is immensely destructive. Its hierarchical and competitive relations reappear in its system of rival, unevenly powerful but deadly states, machines built for warlike competition and oppression. Capitalist production, by ruthlessly subordinating every consideration to profit, threatens the planet's very ecological balance. Meanwhile, it condemns millions to the sheer barbarism of unnecessary misery, starvation and disease.

The capitalist system absolutely dominates the world, shaping

Since socialism involves an immensely wider democracy than capitalism can ever envisage, those who construct it will determine its shape everything humankind does. It is vast, intricate, global. It confronts its opponents like some mad monster, which can regrow its limbs when it is attacked. We have some-how to confront it as a whole. Fighting it thus poses a profound problem. Where can we find a force, an agency, capable of directly combating and defeating capitalism, of going beyond making mere moral protests at some of its worst features?

Here we need to remember capitalism's final characteristic. Capitalism is also defined by class struggle. That valuable old phrase is a shorthand way of summarising the social antagonisms that also define the system's inner workings. The class struggle is fought from two sides. The ruling class engages, daily, in a battle to control the exploited and oppressed. But the reason it must do so is because it constantly engenders resistance, in a multitude of forms and intensities. It is on that struggle from below that the socialist hope for the future rests.

Socialists have always opposed drawing up detailed blueprints for a future socialist society. And rightly. For since socialism involves an immensely wider democracy than capitalism can ever envisage, those who construct it will determine its shape—in cir-cumstances we cannot know until we are part of that active process. Yet the principles of a future socialism are already implicit in the very demands discovered and voiced in popular struggles. Across the whole face of capitalist society we find conflicts between intrinsic opposites: between the need of rulers to control and exploit, and of ordinary people to form their own power; between the drive for profit and the assertion of human need; between the rights of property and people's rights to the means of life; between the demands of profit-based production and the reproductive needs of nature and humankind alike; between wealth concen-trated at one pole and poverty at the other; between 'political economy' and 'moral economy'; between division and cooperative solidarity; between subjection and humiliation and the struggle for dignity and self-empowerment.

Those fundamental oppositions are between the working rules of capitalism and the principles of a socialist alternative. We can sense the alternative in small ways when we witness the possibilities of cooperative activity—even within such things as the feeding and medical arrangements for large demonstrations, or in the extraordinary network of food provision and support that kept the miners going for a year on strike in Britain in the 1980s. We can see the transformation that people undergo when they begin to take responsibility for organising their own lives and struggles in strikes, in demonstrations, in occupations. The seeds of a different future are present, time and again, in the self-empowerment of people taking action together.

That kind of experience is not peculiar to socialists, but is the property of movements in all their diversity. Socialists bring two distinctive arguments to the movements of today. The first concerns the working class, and the second socialist organisation. Both provoke understandable controversy.

Today the majority of the world's population are workers—a strategy for changing the world that doesn't directly involve that majority will always fail

So far as the working class is concerned, the argument goes, surely it's not the force it used to be? It's shrunk, it's defeated, it no longer has the capacity to change the world. But what's the working class? It's not confined to manufacturing. It's not confined to manual jobs. It's composed of everyone who, in order to live, must depend on earning a wage. In those terms, it's still growing. Shop assistants in supermarkets, computer technicians, teachers, nurses, bank and insurance workers and the like are, in the proper sense, workers. That's one reason why, in country after country, just such workers have been unionising, or would like to. Nor is the working class something, today, confined to the advanced world: the biggest strikes in recent years have been in countries like India, Brazil, Argentina and Indonesia. Today the majority of the world's population are workers—or would-be workers, the unemployed. Some work in sweatshops, others are better paid—just like in Britain or the US. Some are child labourers, others are adults. More and more are women, in every sphere of capitalist production. If capitalism is global, so is the modern working class—even the competition for jobs today is international.

A strategy for changing the world that doesn't directly involve that majority will always fail. Socialism has to speak to every facet of people's lives, and not least their working lives. It has to be about the majority empowering themselves, taking control of their workplaces themselves, putting themselves as people before profit, refusing to obey their bosses. History reveals that movements come in waves. We can easily see the new wave of anti-capitalist demonstrations. However, there are vital signs of another wave building up. Creakingly sometimes, labour movements are reawakening; leftist challenges within unions are more successful; strikes are more popular; the arguments of anti-capitalism have a popular resonance which—if they have not yet translated into practical action—should not be underestimated. In Seattle and Nice and Quebec City, mostly, the organised workers marched separately. That need not always be—Canadian workers are now asking their unions for direct action training. There are multiple possibilities of cross-inspiration and cross-fertilization between the anti-capitalist demonstrators and the workers' movements. Socialists should be encouraging these, not stressing the differences.

The socialist stress on the working class, and its power to change the world, does affect the way we argue about strategies. Putting a brick through the window of Starbucks is a moral gesture, but an ineffective one. Organising Starbucks workers is harder, but more effective—and hurts the Starbucks bosses more. We protest, as we should, outside Gap and other stores about the conditions under which the clothes they sell are produced. But the people who can really change things work in the factories that make those clothes, in the sweatshops and *maquiladoras*. We need to focus on people's lives as producers and not simply as consumers—for there is a power in producers' hands that consumer boycotts can never match. In any case, many consumers can't afford to 'choose', say, Fairtrade products and the like.

We need always to turn to the majority, and to their potential power. It's that which sets a distance between socialists and those who rely only on 'guerrilla' action—for they substitute their own heroism for the difficult task of mobilising millions. To rely always on a militant minority is a form of unconscious elitism, born of impatience and despair. It misses something vital: the sense of excitement, the creative self-transformation involved when workers do begin to stand up to their employers, the initiative and the pleasure in new dignity. Ken Loach's film about union organising among office cleaners in Los Angeles catches something of it. The film's title—*Bread and Roses*—catches something else, that fighting back is not just about more money but is about winning some beauty and joy in life by contesting the dispiriting humiliations of subordination.

> **Fighting back is not just about more money but is about winning some beauty and joy in life by contesting the dispiriting humiliations of subordination**

Doubts about the potential of working class militancy are understandable. We are just coming out of a period of huge knock-backs for working class organisation. But movements among workers, like other movements, come in waves. We have been through a terrible trough, and it takes a new generation to lift its head and shake off past defeats. As they do, at whatever speed and with whatever unevenness, socialists have to be part of that movement, not standing aside. There will be huge battles against the conservatism of the trade union bureaucracies, whose beginnings can be sensed already. Not to be part of them is to miss big opportunities for combining the radicalism of the anti-capitalist movements with powerful new forces.

However, that does require political organisation, the other strand of the socialist argument. Again, suspicions about the very idea of socialist organisation are widespread, and comprehensible. Much of the left fragmented in the downturn years. Those that survived and even recruited new forces, thanks chiefly to the strength of their ideas, were also often damaged by the very process of maintaining some tradition of organisation. They were often inward-looking, strident rather than persuasive, prone to sectarianism, spoiled by their own isolation.

Now, though, the question of socialist organisation presents itself in ways different from those dominant in the dark period of the 1980s and after. Socialists have to change: they must be more open to impulses from without, more discussive in style, more able to relate to a multitude of new issues and arguments. They need to learn new ways of uniting in agreed common action with people who agree with them on many things but not all. Socialist organisations need, of course, to be inwardly democratic. Without internal debate and discussion they cannot develop a shared sense of the diversity of today's movements and the possibilities they open up, or draw on each other's experience in order to be able to argue and act more effectively. Some socialists brought up in the sectarian practices of the past will find the transition difficult; others, those who will make a difference, will embrace the new possibilities with enthusiasm. Reshaping the left will sometimes be a hard task—but it is essential.

> **To invite radical anti-capitalists and militant workers alike to become socialists is to invite them to take their own anger and resistance seriously**

There's a crucial reason. We need both to celebrate and learn from the great movements of the past. May 1968 in France, for example, was one of the great inspirations of the previous generation, and rightly so. Yet there was a problem at its heart. The essentially conservative Communist Party was able to pull the plug on the largest general strike movement in European history. Why? Because the forces of the socialist left at that time were too small, too confused, and too weakly implanted in the factories and other workplaces to be able to challenge the Communist bureaucrats' control. May 68 was glorious, joyous, inspiring—and defeated. May 68 in France was but one example among many from the last great round of magnificent, but ultimately defeated, movements.

We are now living in the dawn of a new period which will witness such great movements and such great moments again. We should be better organised next time, to be able to offer practical alternatives to the conservatism of union bureaucrats, to aid the development of rank and file challenges, to infuse the radical spirit of the new movements into workers' movements and the power of workers' movements into the challenge to the system.

Building socialist organisation now is an essentially visionary process. Opportunity knocks mostly once or twice for each generation. The desire for a better world is spreading fast, the readiness to fight for it is spreading. The convulsive social battles to come will again pose the question: can we so mobilise all the popular forces of society to spring it in the air, and to begin a world that is, in manifold ways, more democratic, more just, more equal, more free?

The heart of the socialist case today is that the possibility beckons. To invite radical anti-capitalists and militant workers alike to become socialists is to invite them to take their own anger and resistance seriously, to think it through to the end, to recognise the possibilities buried in their neighbours and workmates for immense leaps of imagination and hope, and to work together to realise those potentials. It is the largest human project there is, to win back our world.

Colin Barker is a member of the Socialist Workers Party. He teaches at Manchester Metropolitan University.
c.barker@mmu.ac.uk

More than 30,000 people demonstrated in solidarity with striking Danone workers in Calais, France April 2001

EVENTS

A CHRONOLOGY OF ANTI-CAPITALIST STRUGGLES

LOCATION	DATE	TYPE OF ACTION	NUMBERS
Seattle, US	Dec 1999	Demonstration (WTO)	70,000
Nigeria	Dec	Strike (dereg of oil price)	5,000
Argentina	Dec	Strike wave (SAP)	Tens of thousands
Vienna, Austria	Jan 2000	Demo (Anti-Nazi)	250,000
Cochamba, Bolivia	Jan	Demo (water privatisation)	Thousands
Quito, Ecuador	Jan	March of Indians (IMF 'reforms')	40,000
Quito, Ecuador	Jan	Demo (IMF 'reforms')	10,000
La Paz, Bolivia	Feb	Demo (IMF 'reforms')	1,000
Ochomogo, Costa Rica	Mar	Demo (electricity privatisation)	Not known
Hamilton, NJ, US	Mar	Demo (IMF/World Bank meeting)	600
La Paz, Bolivia	Apr	Demo (IMF 'reforms')	3,000
Washington DC, US	Apr	Demo (IMF/World Bank meeting)	30,000
Buenos Aires, Argentina	Apr	Demo (SAP)	Thousands
San José, Costa Rica	Apr	Demo (SAP)	10,000
Lusaka, Zambia	Apr	Demo (SAP)	Not known
Nairobi, Kenya	Apr	March (SAP)	Small
Salsa Region, Argentina	May	Demos & road blocks (SAP)	Thousands
Quito, Ecuador	May (5 weeks)	Strike of Teachers (pay cuts/SAP)	Not known
Honduras	May	Hospital workers strike (SAP)	8,000
Windsor, Canada	May	Demo (IMF)	5,000
Argentina	May	Strike (IMF)	80,000
Malawi	May	March (IMF)	Not known

Location	Month	Event	Number
Millau, France	Jun	Demo (free José Bové)	60,000
Nigeria	Jun	General strike (SAP)	Vast
Ascunsion, Paraguay	Jun	General strike	Not known
Philadelphia, US	Jun	Demo (Republican convention)	20,000
Okinawa, Japan	Jul	Demo (IMF/World Bank)	5,000
Los Angeles, US	Jul	Demo (Democratic convention)	20,000
Bogota, Columbia	Aug	General strike (SAP)	Not known
Honduras	Aug	General strike (SAP)	Not known
Sao Paulo, Brazil	Sep	Demo (SAP)	100,000
Melbourne, Australia	Sep	Demo (IMF/World Bank)	5,000
Prague, Czech Republic	Sep	Demo (IMF/World Bank)	20,000
Dakha, Bangladesh	Sep	Demo (Prague support)	Hundreds
Capetown + others, SA	Sep	Demo (Prague support)	Not known
40 cities, US	Sep	Demo in support of Prague event	Thousands
Boston, US	Oct	Demo at presidential debate	12,000
Mexico City	Oct	Demo	10,000
The Hague, Netherlands	Nov	Demo at climate change coference	Thousands
Nice, France	Dec	Conference	100,000
Porto Alegre, Brazil	Jan 2001	Demo	3,000 +
Davos, Switzerland	Jan	Demo	Thousands
Quebec, Canada	Apr	Demo against FTAA	80,000
Gothenburg, Sweden	Jun	Demo at EU summit	Tens of thousands
Genoa, Italy	Jul	Demo at G8 summit	300,000

▶ This table does not include hundreds, perhaps thousands, of smaller actions on the theme of anti-capitalism. ▶ All numbers given for events are of course approximations! ▶ SAP refers to actions protesting at specific plans of the World Bank/IMF. ▶ Much of this information is extracted from the WDM report States of Unrest.

A young environmentalist faces off with riot police in Seattle November 1999.

Action!
John Charlton
● ● ● ● ● ● ● ● ● ● ● ● ● ● ● ● ● ● ●

The meaning of Seattle

Peasants and small farmers in India have struggled to obstruct big dam construction in India. Workers across Latin America have fought against the attrition of meagre welfare state provisions. Environmental activists have attempted to stop the logging companies destroying the giant redwoods in California and Oregon. Thousands have campaigned to save the rain forests. These are examples of a multitude of actions, large and small, against the effects of neo-liberalism which have taken place across the world for nearly two decades. The courage and determination of these activists has been magnificent but largely their activities remained discrete, failing to cohere into a movement with a single target—the system which was the author of all their rage. In a very short period, still less than two years, there has been a profound shift. People from dozens of campaigns increasingly speak of a common enemy. And, although there are many differences in strategy, tactics and alternative solutions, the debates around these questions are not abstract. They have risen organically from common participation in a cycle of action since the events in Seattle in December 1999.[1]

Back in December 1999 many observers of the Battle of Seattle predicted that there would be an ongoing 'Seattle effect'. So triumphant was the feeling of those participating and those across the globe who watched, that such predictions could simply have been born of excitement and hope. Indeed some cautious spirits at the time minimised the achievements and counselled care. One internet correspondent, drawing attention to the alleged reactionary position of labour union leaders, said, 'We've been here before. I've seen too many false dawns.' But 18 months on, it does seem that the optimists were right. In analysing the succession of events taking place since, Seattle must play a central part in any explanation. A number of factors combined to give that event its resonance across the world.

There were the numbers participating: 50,000 to 70,000 people converging on that northwest city was itself startling given the logistical problems of travelling there from almost every part of North America and the recent modest history of radical demonstrations in the US.

There was the political and social composition of the participants. It brought together dozens of environmental, ecological, Third World debt and social justice campaigns. These were campaigns, which had worked separately for years in pursuit of sometimes quite narrowly defined objectives. In terms of broadcasting the message the presence of campaigners from India, South East Asia, Africa and Latin America ensured that its messages were heard first hand across the planet and not simply via the media, however important that might have been.

There were the labour unions. For more than 50 years, in the grip of reactionary business unionism, workers were steered away from political protest. The ruling class assault and deindustrialisation had ravaged the membership rolls, marginalising union leaders and drawing them into the critical stance which brought some of them to Seattle to protest the effects of liberal economics. No matter that a substantial chunk of them, demonstrating to keep China out of the WTO, brought a tinge of economic nationalism with them. Their very presence in large numbers was in itself significant. However, the thrilling aspect was the charge by rank and file members through lines of their own stewards to join demonstrators being beaten up by the robocops. This was the conjuncture on everyone's lips.

Perhaps most importantly there was the stunning success of

the demonstration in actually preventing the World Trade Organisation carrying out its business. Symbolic it may largely have been, but a victory on the streets over one of the key agents of global capitalism was a moment to be celebrated.

There were also those who argued after Seattle that it was simply another event in a long struggle waged for years by many campaigners. Indeed an Earth First!er speaking at a conference in New York in April 2000 actually argued that Seattle was a disaster to the ecological movement because the focus on it had completely stopped recruitment to his project of creating an alternative and superior society in unspoiled regions of the American west! Some of his disappointment was understandable. He belonged to a varied cohort of activists who had toiled for years to bring to public notice the multitude of crimes against the environment committed by corporations and to peasants and workers in the Third World. In many ways they could be said to be what stood for opposition to the system in the decades following the collapse of the anti-war movement and the growing obsession with identity politics.

Such activists had never given much time to the exploited and oppressed in their own countries. Nevertheless they had often demonstrated resolution and great courage in attempts to prevent the destruction of, say, giant redwoods in Oregon or areas of natural beauty like the woods round Newbury on the North Downs in England assaulted by motorway developers. So some activists felt sidelined. However, the evidence is that many more were like the young woman at Seattle who said, 'I came to save the turtles and left hating capitalism.' She and people like her were taking a first bold step from fighting at the *sites* of spoliation to fighting the corporate power itself as represented by agencies like the WTO, the IMF and the World Bank.

In 'leaving the tree tops', so to speak, protest on these issues was undergoing a qualitative change. Firstly, in terms of those who could take part it became more inclusive. Activism had often required physical fitness, a commitment to direct action, the space in one's life for long-term settlement at a site of action, and it posed a high probability of arrest. For a street demonstration in an urban centre anyone could participate. Activities could range from locking on, through street theatre, to more conventional modes like marches and rallies. Though all could have physical confrontation thrust upon them by the forces of the state no one needed to attend with that as their central presumption.

Secondly, the boundaries between different types of campaign tend to dissolve in the crowd. Even where protesters arrive in separate contingents the very act of meeting with others and sharing a target, both physically and ideologically, produces an interaction across those boundaries. This process of interaction is sharply accelerated where the police intervene. Seattle had all of these characteristics, the latter one massively heightened by the outrageous response of the police and the city authorities. The photograph of the Lesbian Avengers of Santa Cruz linking arms with hard-hatted Teamsters was one of the most powerful images of Seattle and has most certainly contributed to the ongoing impact of the event in the months which followed.

A further important factor is the impetus given to the movement by victory. In the urban setting this too is potentially greater than a victory at a site of depredation. Road protests, for example, may extract concessions from the authorities, but at most they are likely to be minor. Since the struggle is likely to have been long and the participants relatively few, even partial victory is likely to have been exhausting. And its local nature is likely to limit its wider effect and power to generate emulation. The halting of the deliberations of the WTO was achieved by massive numbers in a matter of two or three days in the maximum glare of publicity. The beatings by the police and the mass arrests served to generate anger, not disappointment. The arrested were heroes, not victims. People left Seattle with triumph in their hearts. This was the fuel for moving into further action—the true Seattle effect. They fanned out over America and throughout the world moving within weeks into new coalitions aiming at related or fresh targets.

Eyewitness: Seattle 1999

Those who marched or stood or sat in the streets of Seattle this week made history, and they knew it. And like the great marches against the Vietnam War, or the first sit-ins in the South in the late 1950s, it was not always easy to see just what history was being made, especially for those closest to the events of the time. Teargas, rubber bullets and police sweeps, the object of incessant media coverage, are the outward signs of impending change—that the guardians of the social order have grown afraid. And there's always a little history in that. But perhaps the greatest impact of Seattle will be on the people who were there. Just as anti-war demonstrations and civil rights sit-ins of decades ago were focal points, from which people fanned out across the country, spreading the gospel of their movement, Seattle is also a beginning of something greater yet to come. What will the people who filled its downtown streets take with them back into this city's rainy neighbourhoods, or to similar communities in towns and cities across the country?

David Bacon

Mobilisations for protests at the FTAA summit in Quebec in April 2001 saw an incre
in the 'Teamster and Turtle kids' alliance that made the Seattle protests so successf

Resistance goes global

By the middle of 2001 resistance had touched five continents taking a variety of forms reflecting the local impact of neo-liberal policies and the strengths and weaknesses of specific labour and radical movements.

VIENNA, January 2000

How quickly did the spirit of Seattle reappear on the other side of the world? There was an enormous anti-fascist mobilisation in Vienna in January 2000. Around 250,000 people descended on Vienna in the bitter cold of winter. One small incident illustrates Seattle's potency. A young animal rights activist said that on the day the fascists entered the government he charged round to the Freedom Party's HQ with a bunch of friends. They occupied the office. He climbed onto the roof waving a banner. TV cameras gave instant publicity. That evening 20,000 people teemed into the Bauhausplatz calling for an end to fascist participation in government. Within 24 hours organisations were coming together to plan further action. He claimed that Seattle had been an inspiration and a model for direct action. There would have been a massive anti-fascist protest without Seattle having taken place. But the event in Seattle encouraged activists from all over Europe who teemed into Austria. Many would travel on to Millau, Prague and Nice.

WASHINGTON, April 2000 (A16)

The week of demonstrations against the joint IMF/World Bank meeting in Washington DC in April 2000 (A16) was the first very big explicitly anti-capitalist event to follow Seattle. It was strongly influenced by that event. The first meetings of the assembled coalition took place barely a month after and three months before Washington, DC. Discussion of Seattle was a regular feature on the A16 lists, with topics ranging from the actions of the Black Bloc (anarchists), the alleged lack of colour at Seattle,[2] to the involvement of the labour unions. The event itself was a great success. Around 30,000 people participated on 16 April and perhaps as many again in the events of the week leading up to it. It was smaller than Seattle yet some ten times as big as the 1998 demonstration against the same target (IMF/World Bank) in the same place. The absence of large cohorts of labour unionists explains the main numerical difference with Seattle, though it should also be pointed out that the Washington DC police chief luridly talked up the threat of violence beforehand. This probably deterred many sympathisers from attending on the day. After Seattle this factor must always be taken into account and, though the growing numbers prepared to defy such threats is immensely impressive, it sharply underlines the need for extending the range of activities beyond the set-piece mass demonstrations.

This lesson was drawn from another aspect of the DC event. Successful though it was in causing the conference some disruption and making considerable publicity in the media, the activities of the World Bank/IMF were not halted and neither could they be by any single mass demonstration or even a series of them. All major capitalist organisations carry on their work daily by other means including small unpublicised meetings and telecommunications facilities. The events in DC probably brought this understanding to all participants. That such activities are largely symbolic and are a means to draw people together in thousands is valuable in itself. To actually close down or disrupt functions is an added prize which encourages greater participation. It may also throw the institutions on the defensive where they may demonstrate their essential vulnerability by making apparent concessions to the demonstrators' arguments. This is what President Clinton did after Seattle and several officials of the IMF/World Bank have continued to do so since.

Eyewitness: Washington 2000

On Saturday 15 April I was illegally arrested and imprisoned for 23 hours, together with hundreds of peaceful protesters and at least a dozen innocent bystanders of whom I was one. As a consultant to the World Bank, a citizen of a developing country, and a person who has committed his life to the work of development, I was appalled by the conduct of the police and by the way the system works. As a consequence I am now far more sympathetic with the demands of the protesters and just a tad more cynical about the 'establishment'.

I was arrested with no explanation, no prior warning, and for no legitimate reason. I was standing close to the protesters because I disagreed with much I had heard them say in the media... I wanted to hear in person...to decide for myself whether their arguments were reasonable or not.

For all practical purposes, the police proved to be the greatest allies of the protesters...because they perfectly proved the point the protesters were trying to make in this march: poverty and suppression go hand in hand and lead to further social injustice. In my case, this first hand experience of American police and prisons was an enlightening, life-changing event that helped me to fully understand the sometimes incoherently expressed, but otherwise perfectly legitimate and profound arguments that I now firmly believe the majority of protesters were out to make.

Leon Galindo, Bolivian World Bank consultant

WINDSOR, June 2000

At Windsor, Ontario, in early June, there was a demonstration against a meeting of the Organisation of American States which activists saw as a further attempt to drive the neo-liberal agenda across the Americas. Canadian labour was involved with a big demonstration focusing upon NAFTA issues, which was followed by a direct action attempt to close down the meeting. Protesters were treated to heavy, even savage, policing with many arrests and threats of imprisonment against organisers. The organisation question came to the fore. At a certain point the direct action section was isolated and in serious danger of being smashed by superior police forces with the certainty of mass arrests. The socialist group intervened conducting a 'spontaneous' debate successfully persuading them to abandon their action and join the main march. Avoiding a 'massacre' meant avoiding likely demoralisation. People left feeling that the whole event had been a great success.[3] Another important feature of the Windsor event was the contingents from Central and South America which helped to strengthen links between anti-capitalist protesters in the North and those on the sharpest end of neo-liberal policies in the global South.

MILLAU, June 2000

From the end of June the focus of protest widened geographically from North America to Europe, Asia and Australasia. 'Seattle on the Tarn' was how the remote French town of Millau was referred to when 60,000 people travelled from across France and beyond to protest the trial of local farmers for dismantling the town's McDonald's. There were two days of exciting debate on globalisation and the means for defeating a system 'where people are sacrificed to the interests of the giant companies. It means freedom is destroyed in the interests of money'.[4] The scale of the protest in Millau was a strong affirmation that the new movement had taken root in Europe too. The event's success provided inspiration and impetus for the subsequent European demonstrations in Prague and Nice.

OKINAWA, July 2000

The G8 countries met in Okinawa in late July. Despite immense difficulties in travel and high intensity security 10,000 demonstrated against neo-liberalism and the continued occupation of the island by US forces. This event and South Korea in November underline most strongly the degree to which the new anti-capitalist movement has relentlessly targeted every public appearance of the agencies seen to be running the globalisation project.

PHILADELPHIA, July 2000 and LOS ANGELES, August 2000

The demonstrations in Philadelphia and Los Angeles at the presidential nominating conventions both continued to build the new movement. They were clearly hybrids. They included education, welfare, tax and political process reformers, and campaigners against the death penalty as well as the 'Seattle constituency', attacking corporate America for its scant concern for the environment, ecology of the planet, indigenous peoples and exploited labour. Both events were organised by coalitions of activists hostile to corporate America's values and practices, but crucially the scale of protest and the composition of protesters would not have happened without the galvanising experience at Seattle six months earlier.

These two demonstrations helped to keep momentum going, 'linking the nooks and crannies'[5] after A16, bringing more people into the movement. The coalitions formed to organise the days of demonstration, again drew people from a wide geographical area, especially important for the West Coast where the August event was the first mass activity since Seattle. The turnouts at both, of over 20,000, disappointed some activists but they were nevertheless impressive confirmations of the upward trajectory of the new movement. Both may have suffered from difficulties of maintaining campus organisation well beyond the end of the summer semester. And there was also the expected reluctance of national trade union leaders to risk bringing their members, especially to the Democratic convention. Already Ralph Nader was speaking to union members and achieving his first serious hearing after 30 years of campaigning. Damage to the Gore campaign was a primary consideration. Nevertheless the San Francisco Labour Council and many union locals did support the demonstrations.

Perhaps the best measure of change on the ground since Seattle comes from comparing anti-convention demonstrations in 2000 with those in the past. They were incomparably larger than any since Chicago 1968, and only the Republican convention in Detroit in 1980 (Reagan's nomination) had brought substantial numbers on to the streets at all since the 1960s. However, the biggest achievement of the rolling movement in the US was the Ralph Nader campaign. The vote he attracted of 2,750,000 was impressive considering the degree of hostility he engendered among Gore activists.

MELBOURNE, September 2000 (S11)

In early September the World Economic Forum's Asia-Pacific Summit met in Melbourne. This was the first test for the anti-capitalist movement in Australia. To the surprise of even some of the organisers 20,000 people turned up. It was overwhelmingly young (14-24 year-olds) including droves of high school students who walked out of school. Only three Australian unions endorsed the action, some union leaders actively counselling their members not to join in. Nevertheless many rank and file unionists did join the protest. Evidence has emerged since of a highly orchestrated politician-police-media conspiracy to undermine the protest by unsubstantiated allegations of intended violence by protesters.[6] It was the biggest turnout organised by the far left in Australia for a generation.[7]

Eyewitness: Melbourne 2000

Tens of thousands of Melbourne unionists have delivered a stunning blow to the legitimacy of the World Economic Forum and corporate globalisation, filling city streets with noise, colour and people.

The workers marched from Trades Hall in Carlton to the blockade's main base on

Queensbridge Road.

The marchers filled Swanston Street in downtown Melbourne, marching past the Nike superstore, chanting, 'Stop global sweatshops,' and 'The workers united will never be defeated,' before not only filling Queensbridge Road but also most of the nearby bridge across the Yarra River. Official estimates by Trades Hall put the crowd at 10,000, which seemed considerably understated.

The S11 Alliance had agreed to allow Trades Hall use of its stage for a platform, which featured some of the Australian union movement's most prominent leaders, including the Textile, Clothing and Footwear Union of Australia's Michelle O'Neill, the Construction, Forestry, Mining and Energy Union's John Maitland and ACTU president Sharan Burrow.

While rally organisers led loud chants of 'Fair trade, not free trade', both the sentiment from the massive crowd and the speeches from the platform were relatively free of protectionist tinge and full of support for the struggles of workers in the Third World.

Indonesian union leader Romawaty Sinaga, the international officer of the FNPBI (Indonesian National Front for Labour Struggle), received an especially warm reception. 'We want Australian workers to support Indonesian workers. We need your solidarity. We all, workers in Australia and workers in Indonesia, have common interests in stopping these people,' she said angrily, pointing at the conference venue across the road.

Sean Healy

PRAGUE, September 2000

The first announcement of an event in Prague in September was made on the internet in mid-May. From the start it was seen in Europe as a magnet for anti-capitalist activists. It was accessible from most parts of the continent. In Eastern Europe it gave an opportunity to check the penetration of anti-capitalist ideas in the former Stalinist sphere where in the wake of the fall of the Berlin Wall capitalism and the market had been hailed as the great hope. The IMF and World Bank went to Prague to wave the flag of neo-liberalism at a moment when enthusiasm for that project was in serious decline. Demonstrators went to Prague from every country in Europe, and from Brazil, Ecuador, Bolivia, Columbia, Nicaragua, India, Thailand, Canada and the US. Its international flavour was its most distinguishing feature. Large contingents travelled from Germany, Greece, France, Italy, the UK and Poland.

Despite massive harassment at border checkpoints and the airport, 20,000 people got to the centre of Prague participating in a series of disciplined illegal marches, threatened the closure of the conference centre and held three counter-conferences. Sean, from Newcastle, said, 'I was inspired by the internationalism—German, French, Italian, Polish, Turkish flying in from all angles, all for the same cause'.[8] despite the crude brutality of the Czech police.

Alice from INPEG reported, 'Our medical volunteers gave basic help to 350-400 people in the streets. Most of them had broken noses, loss of hearing, unconsciousness, injuries of face, head, neck, arms, breast, leg, complications from teargas or shock'.[9] The organisation and discipline in the face of such attacks marked a triumph of cooperation between often opposed political and human rights organisations.

The gathering was weak on official trade union representation, though from most countries there were many active trade unionists often representing their local branches. Boris Kagarlitsky saw Prague as a turning point. He wrote that the far left groups 'unexpectedly proved capable of not just uniting and working together on a European scale but showed that masses of young people are once again pouring into their ranks'.[10]

Monday

Arriving at Prague Airport all is quiet, just a few signs in the corridors showing IMF/World Bank delegates where to check in. As I wait for my bag, I pick up a free copy of the local English language business paper, which comments, 'Whatever happens this week, the argument now is not whether the IMF and World Bank should reform, but how.'

We set off into the city centre, to the INPEG information centre. INPEG is the umbrella organisation that has coordinated the protest. The centre is an old shop, full of people, leaflets, posters and flipcharts. Next to it is the Independent Media Centre. From there we make our way northwards by underground to the convergence centre. On our way I buy a rucksack in a local street market. The Chinese trader who sells it to me has a good understanding about what our demonstration is about. 'Banks rich, people poor,' he says.

At Strahov the Italian comrades, who turn out to be Ya Basta!, are preparing their equipment for tomorrow. More than anyone, they have had a struggle getting across the border. The authorities refused entry to four of them so they occupied the track for 20 hours.

Tuesday

Woken at 6am by an Italian comrade rousing the Ya Basta! contingent. Shortly afterwards an Irish activist blows the reveille to raise the rest of us. By 7am we are on the bus with our placards. To our surprise we get out of the underground at Namesti Miru without being challenged. The square has no more than a 150 there but a small steady flow is filling it. I talk with a young Lithuanian couple about why we are here. They are Green activists, campaigning on pollution issues, but are very interested in the bigger picture. They have spent two days hitchhiking to get here. We invite them for a cup of tea, discuss the politics of anti-capitalism and exchange addresses.

By 11am the square is getting very full. I reckon there are over 10,000 there. The International Socialist Tendency is probably the largest grouping, having organised a couple of thousand people. Then there are Ya Basta!, with over 1,000, all dressed up, the anarchists, the pacifists, the environmentalists, the debt campaigners such as Jubilee 2000, and large numbers who have come on their own or in twos and threes. A huge blue sphere says 'Balls to the IMF'. There is a pink tank, which refers to an action made by Czech dissidents before the Velvet Revolution. I particularly like the blue Warner Brothers logo you see in the cartoons: a blue shield with WB in it and above, 'That's all, folks!'

At 11.30am the three marches move off. The most impressive part of our march is made up of a large delegation of Greek trade unionists, including around 25 members of the telecoms union. The chanting is loud, ongoing and in several languages. Ya Basta! intend to break through the police lines. We intend to follow them. Our slogans include 'The World is not for sale', 'Hoch die Internationale Solidarität', 'The whole world is watching'. To judge by the huge press presence, this last slogan is true. After perhaps two miles we come within a couple of hundred yards of the police and the road bridge to the conference centre, renovated at a cost of two billion Czech crowns for the IMF/World Bank. The spirit is determined even courageous. Vinegar is distributed and we soak handkerchiefs and T shirts, to keep ready should we be teargassed.

Eventually, after four or five attempts at the front to break through, it becomes clear that we are not going to get any further. The 20 or so Darth Vader figures I can see 80 yards in front of me, standing on top of armoured cars equipped with water cannon, have hardly yielded an inch. There are more than a score of heavy police vehicles blocking the bridge. Underneath is a vast ravine, hard to get down and even harder to get up. Teargas and pepper spray have been used but it is clear that this was not the main reason why we could not get through. The bridge was impregnable.

We march back together in good order, several thousand of us. With the police concentrated fully around the conference centre we are free to march where we wish. We reach Wenceslas Square. At the top there is a large stone balcony from where a series of speakers, Alex Callinicos, Panos Garganas, a young Czech comrade and others, point out that the IMF conference has only been possible under the protection of precisely those police who 11 years ago were the force used to attack the student demonstrators who triggered the Velvet Revolution. This was the revolution which brought the political dissident Vaclav Havel to the position of president of the republic.

Wednesday

Settling in on the bus for the 24 hour ride home, the mood is upbeat despite the quite disgraceful coverage by many of the British papers which have tried to reduce the protest to the violent actions of an elitist group of stone-throwers.

The bankers have been on the defensive since the meeting at the weekend organised by Vaclav Havel bringing protesters and IMF/World Bank officials together. At this meeting the Seattle activist Walden Bello wiped the floor with his opponents. The decision by so many conference delegates on the Wednesday morning to stay in their hotels meant that the conference was closed down early.

The official agenda was meant to include a review of 'the international financial architecture', how the IMF and World Bank are set up and run, and an examination of how oil prices can be brought down and stabilised. In practice, James Wolfensohn, head of the World Bank and Horst Köhler, head of the IMF, were asked only about poverty in the Third World and the question of debt repayment. With these few measures alone, we succeeded in turning Prague into Seattle.

Geoff Brown

SERBIA, October 2000

There is a strong argument for including the revolution in Serbia as part of the European popular upsurge. Though its obvious target was the dictatorship of Milosevic, its impulses went much deeper than the removal of one man. It was a mass uprising involving tens of thousands of working people. Workers, alienated by years of increasingly authoritarian management and declining living standards, broadened their attack to include their factory bosses as well as their political ones. Another telling feature of the uprising was the absence of crude nationalist sentiment so much part of the Balkan landscape in the 1990s. Interestingly a core of them found their way to Nice in December to join that protest.

SEOUL, November 2000

In November 10,000 turned out against the meeting of the Asia-Europe summit. Led by the Korean Confederation of Trade Unions, the demonstrators faced off the strongest and most violent security presence of any of the set-piece actions in the year, 10,000 demonstrators were ringed by an armed cordon of 30,000 soldiers and police.

THE HAGUE, November 2000

Also in November some 6,000 protesters from 25 countries demonstrated outside the summit on climate change held in the Hague. The protesters built a dike around the conference centre 360 metres long, made of 70,000 sandbags to symbolise the gulf between politicians and lobbyists and the ordinary people who suffer from their decisions.

NICE, December 2000

Many of the activists travelling to Prague went to Nice in December. Many, like Kristin from Norway, went, 'to show I am against EU policies. I am against privatisation and undemocratic policies. They put profit before people. I want to unite with other people who think like me. I want to be part of this movement, the movement of hope and change'."Nice was a fantastic ending to a year of anti-capitalist activity. Endorsed by the CGT, in France and most of the other European trade unions it was likely to be big despite it being held in the depths of winter. Readily accessible to much of Europe, activists whetted their lips in anticipation. The top European politicians were heading to Nice with two big agendas: to extend the EEU to include much of Eastern Europe and Turkey, and to make easier the prosecution of neo-liberal policies throughout the area. In the event over 100,000 people travelled to Nice creating a monster demonstration, international and impressive. Peter from Norwich saw 'big delegations from Spain, Portugal, France, smaller size ones from Turkey and Greece, and Jake from Manchester added 'Slovenians, a Kurdish contingent, several Danish and Norwegian banners, from the large German unions and a contingent of Basques'.[12]

The demonstrators did not succeed in stopping the ministerial deliberations. Clearly 100,000 demonstrators could have blocked the conference centre, making a coherent meeting impossible. That is what a section of the demonstration wished to do. Despite repeated humiliations at the hands of government and, in the French case, a recent record of impressive fightback, it was a step too far for trade union bureaucracies and the rank and file was not yet ready to break ranks. The direct action contingents were unable to do it alone. Indeed questions were raised about a strategy the following day which separated 7,000-8,000 of the most militant activists off from the massed ranks of the unions to conduct a battle with the CRS (riot police) in isolation. This is not a criticism of those who stumbled through the teargas and batons to carry on the fight, but of the pre-event strategic discussion. Kevin from Bristol remarked, 'We have to find a way of fusing the two bits of the anti-capitalist movement—the direct action people and the workers in the unions. Anything else just plays in to the hands of the union bosses and the police'.[13]

Nevertheless the whole event was a striking success. Participants were of one voice in describing its inspiring nature. The sight of massed ranks of demonstrators from many countries in the same march with the same target was quite unprecedented, certainly in modern times. The anti-capitalist posters, banners and chants taken up by tens of thousands of people in unison would not be forgotten. Peter from Norwich wrote a week afterwards that 'the feeling of solidarity, fraternity and internationalism still makes my stomach churn with excitement. I really feel part of a growing, if still small movement. I feel the potential for it to grow, especially if everyone from across Europe took that spirit back home to their workmates, their campus, their community'.[14]

On the way to the march I made a note of the different countries people were from—there were loads of Italian **COBAS** and Spanish **CCOO** members with their flags, a bunch of Austrian trade unionists, loads of **ATTAC** members. The march itself was amazing. Talking to other comrades afterwards we all thought, albeit with no hard evidence, that it was bigger than the 100,000 that most people said. Not that 100,000 is bad!

After the march there was a big rally in the sports hall that was also used to put up loads of people who didn't have anywhere to stay. Susan George introduced it. She started by saying we should all be proud to have taken part in a protest twice the size of Seattle, that in the course of the last year this movement had shaped history, and that we had all been a part of that. She spoke very well and only added to everyone's excitement and sense of history about what we were doing.

The next morning we got up at 6am. Personally I'd hardly slept... On the way we found a shop where we grabbed a bite to eat and I grabbed two bottles of lemon juice for the scarves and bandanas we'd been hastily distributing. The 6.53am train was packed with comrades. It was only one stop to Riquier, where we got off and met the people already there.

As we marched towards the conference centre it became clear that the CRS were, after all, going to follow the same strategy as the police in Prague—hold the centre, don't spare the teargas—only more so. I was quite near the front (the Manchester delegation of about 20 having split into more handily-sized groups according to which part of the march people felt most comfortable being in) but I don't think I even saw the CRS before they bombarded us with gas. Most of the canisters were coming from straight ahead and landing quite close in front of us, but some of them were arching over the rooftops (or being shot off the roofs? I've no idea) and basically landing on our heads.

We carried on for a few hours. The fact that the cops were basically hunkered down and just using lots of gas meant we were fairly free to run around the streets, escaping one gas attack, to come at the conference centre from another direction.

Despite how unpleasant the gas was, everyone was in very high spirits, chanting (one of the favourites was the German 'Hoch die internationale Solidarität'—long live international solidarity), linking arms and urging each other on. If anyone got badly affected by the gas, there were always loads of people who'd look after them.

One thing that impressed me was the way all the organisations worked together. Another chant I liked was, 'Ce n'est que le début, continuons le combat' (this is just the start, continue the battle).

Jake Hoban

DAVOS and PORTO ALEGRE, January 2001

At the end of January this year a remarkable event took place—3,000 delegates from 1,000 organisations in over 100 countries opposing neo-liberal globalisation assembled in the southern Brazilian city of Porto Alegre. The World Social Forum (WSF) was born. Its mobilising call read,

Together we are building a great alliance to create a new society, different from the dominant logic wherein the free market and money are considered the only measure of worth. Davos represents the concentration of wealth, the globalisation of poverty and the destruction of our Earth. Porto Alegre represents the hope that a new world is possible, where human beings and nature are the centre of our concern.

The reference to Davos was central. On the other side of the world in Switzerland the World Economic Forum (WEF) was meeting for the 18th time. The contrast could not be starker. In Porto Alegre there was noise, dispute and diversity. The opening session was briefly interrupted by protesters shouting, 'Brazil, Africa and Central America—the fight for black rights is international!' Their demand for more space in the hundreds of workshops and panels was immediately conceded. Peasants, small farmers, women activists from campaigns in Argentina and Chile, trade union officials from South Africa, Nigeria, and Europe, environmentalists from Indonesia, the Philippines and North America, elected politicians from France, Spain and Albania, NGO officers from North America, Europe, Africa and India, students, and intellectuals rubbed shoulders with each other and disputed in over 400 workshops for four days. There wasn't a cop or soldier in sight. In Davos there was a chilly unity of bankers, financiers, corporate bosses, politicians, a small gaggle of trade union leaders from Europe and the US, and some leading figures from the UN. Their project was simple: how to most effectively prosecute the spreading of the free market to every corner of the globe. If there were disputes, we'd have to learn of them by rumour and gossip, for their deliberations were held behind closed doors, their meeting places guarded by armed police.

Point. Counter-point. Davos. Porto Alegre. The unity of opposites. A French TV organisation staged a live debate between the two. Davos's iron curtain was only slightly parted. The big players decided to preserve their anonymity. George Soros, the maverick speculator, Swedish capitalist Bjorn Edlund, and two members of the UN delegation spoke from a bare church hall. Soros said he wanted to reform capitalism, not destroy it. Edlund felt it was important to understand the role business can play constructively to make globalisation work. Malloch Brown from the UN believed it was critical to have a foot in both worlds, the world of economic globalisation as well as that of social reaction too. They were quickly under siege from the WSF delegation of 40. 'How many children did you kill?' Hebe de Bonfini, Mothers of the Plazo de Mayo, Argentina, asked Soros. Aminata Traoré from West Africa demanded that the Davos gang 'give the youth of Africa their futures back.' Trevor Wanek from Soweto felt that the only thing he had in common with Davos was the satellite link. Walden Bello put the matter succinctly: 'The best thing that can happen to the world is for the corporate executives, thousands of them in Davos, to be loaded into a spaceship and for that spaceship to take off and the world will be a better place for all of us. Thank you.'

The physical convergence of the discrete movements and organisations of Porto Alegre was forged on the streets. Their ideological diversity was expressed in the many workshops which took place and is evident in the inclusive nature of the Porto Alegre Call for Mobilisation (CFM) hammered out at the end of the event. 'We are women and men, farmers, workers, unemployed, professionals, students, black and indigenous peoples, coming from the South and from the North, committed to struggle for people's rights, freedom, security, employment and education. We are fighting against the hegemony of finance, the destruction of our cultures, the monopolisation of knowledge, mass media and communication, the degradation of nature, and the destruction of the quality of life by multinational corporations and anti-democratic policies. Participative democratic experiences—like that of Porto Alegre—show us that a concrete alternative is possible.'

John Sweeney, leader of the AFL-CIO union federation, said, 'The community of students, working people, environmentalists and people of faith demanding fairness around the globe is not "a backlash against globalisation". It is a new internationalism born from the crisis facing workers and their families.' A new internationalism is above all the meaning of the WSF at Porto Alegre. There will be a further meeting of the WSF in 2002. It is reasonable to predict that it will be bigger and even more geographically and organisationally diverse.

Eyewitness: Quebec 2001

'Nous vaincrons!' (We'll win!)
These were the ecstatic words of a young trade
unionist as he set out to march with his
contingent against the proposed Free Trade Area
of the Americas. Such confidence was on proud
display as over 80,000 people demonstrated in
Quebec City from the 21-22 of April 2001. During
these two days, workers in Quebec were joined by
their sisters and brothers from English Canada
and elsewhere. The mood of militancy was at a
fever pitch. Mass action was a compelling draw
for workers who have reaped little from the so-
called 'economic boom' of the past few years.

Without question, one of the most heartening
aspects of the Quebec City actions was the sight
of trade union militants mixing with anti-
capitalist radicals. Anti-capitalist youth were
certainly predominant in the 20,000 strong
protests that challenged the 4 kilometre security
perimeter barricading the talks over two days.
But trade unionists also figured in some of the
most spirited street battles seen in North
America since the Seattle protests against the
World Trade Organisation in November-December
1999.

Jaggi Singh—a popular anarchist militant
arrested for 21 days after the protests—took
pains to provide an accurate sketch of just who
was there. 'Oh sure,' remarked Singh, 'the anti-
capitalist youth, the punks, the students, the
Black Bloc... everyone one might expect were

right in the thick of things. But also present were the fuscia flags of CUPE (the Canadian Union of Public Employees), and the blue flags of the postal workers and auto workers.' Alan Zuege, a teaching assistant and CUPE 3903 member from Toronto's York University was at the fence: 'I have never seen anything like that before. We need tens of thousands of us there next time.' Chris Ramsaroop, an Ontario organiser for the Canadian farm workers' union, was even more succinct: 'People are trying to take back space that belongs to them.' Carol Phillips, director of the International Department for the Canadian Autoworkers Union, added that many of the trade unionists who didn't join the fight at the barricades should not miss their next opportunity. In an interview with the *Toronto Star*'s Thomas Walkom, Phillips said,: 'I don't think that will happen again... Now, we're no shrinking violets in our union; we do plant takeovers and that kind of thing. But this is different. Our activists are becoming more radical. This is what they're telling me,' she says. Phillips points out that Canada is supposed to host the July 2002 G8 summit in Ottawa. 'I'm sure we [the CAW] will be there,' she says. 'We won't be able to keep them away.' She goes on, 'I'm in my late 40s. I've worked inside government [she was former New Democratic Party premier Bob Rae's patronage advisor]. I've worked in the trade union movement. It's easy to become cynical. But this, this is real. This is a rejection of, I guess, capitalism.'

Joel Harden

May Day 2001

For more than 100 years, May has been a traditional day of demonstration for the socialist and labour movement. It must be recorded, however, that for decades it has not been an encouraging spectacle. In the Eastern bloc and China tens of thousands turned out, largely consisting of soldiers and school children who had no choice. In the West fairly demoralised groups numbering hundreds of the really committed shuffled round city streets for an hour to listen to Labour politicians and trade union leaders mouth platitudes.

In 2000 and 2001 the event has witnessed something of a revival. In many countries May Day has become a focus of the new anti-capitalist movement, a focus for mass demonstrations against the effects of World Bank/IMF policies. Last year and this in Britain thousands came onto the streets in London to be faced with enormous police mobilisations as the state struggles to obstruct the emergence of new activist coalitions.

The events of May 2001 in Britain and Australia have sharpened the debate on how best to bring effective pressure to bear upon the architects of capitalist excesses. It is almost certainly true that hundreds of thousands of demonstrators would have a much greater impact than the thousands who turned out on May Day. It is also true that any meaningful assault on the symbols of capitalist power like the stock exchange and the banks would be met by massive violence. A very much greater impact on capitalism would be made if mass demonstrations were accompanied by mass strikes.

Eyewitness: London, May Day 2001

Against a backdrop of mass police and press hysteria, around 8,000 people demonstrated in London on 1 May 2001. For weeks the media message coming from Michael Todd, assistant Metropolitan Police commissioner, was plain—the demonstrators were hellbent on violence, May Day was their excuse for burning and looting. The press was happy to churn this line out, and were delighted to find common voice with the likes of Tony Blair and Ken Livingstone.

The stories got more fantastic—protesters were trained in US camps, were due to be carrying samurai swords and bombs—all backed by Anita Roddick, owner of the Body Shop!

Thankfully, sections of the media started to question the plot. The numerous protests were, after all, called to make very serious points: against the destruction of the environment, Third World debt, homelessness, consumer culture, privatisation and sweatshop labour.

At 9am hundreds of cyclists formed a 'critical mass', bringing King's Cross to a standstill. There was a carnival atmosphere as people chatted and celebrated in the street. When the majority moved off towards Euston station the police attempted the first serious provocation of the day—penning in a few hundred protesters for a couple of hours.

At lunchtime a series of different protests formed. Students gathered at the University of London Union, LSE students marched from their college to the World Bank offices at Haymarket.

The largest gathering of the day was at the World Bank offices. Organised by Globalise Resistance, the demonstration highlighted the lack of movement on Third World debt. Swarms of people arrived and in the space of half an hour the protest numbered 1,500.

Police barricading and crowd control fell apart at the seams. A good-natured march then left towards the West End shopping centre of Oxford Street. Marching past countless boarded-up shops in a near deserted Regent Street gave the day a surreal air that quickly turned to bemusement when we arrived in Oxford Circus. Faced on all sides with lines of riot cops backed up by vans and horses there was no way out for the protesters. The south side of Regent Street (the point of our arrival) was then sealed in a similar way.

Confusion turned to astonishment as the police lines advanced on three sides of the blockade, squeezing everyone together. It was drizzling and cold. Many people had come out of work in their lunch breaks and were seriously under-dressed.

After a couple of hours the first announcement came: 'You are being detained to prevent criminal damage and a breach of the peace. Arrangements are being made for your release as soon as possible. Please remain calm.'

When repeated, the announcement met with derision and jeers, every half-hour. Fires were lit to keep people warm, chanting and joking kept up spirits. After a six-hour detention the police slowly started to filter people out of the area, searching, questioning and harassing everyone as they left.

Punished for daring to demonstrate, the protesters won the day. We put the issues at the centre of attention and the oppressive nature of the state was clear to anyone who can read a paper or watch the telly. Public sympathy swung from support for the police and New Labour to backing for the protests and their aims. The battle of ideas had been won on the day.

Guy Taylor, Globalise Resistance

Subcomandante Marcos' and the Zapatistas' fight against neo-liberal policies has been

Resistance on the sharp end

The development of resistance to the assaults of capitalism in North America, Western Europe and Australia is very impressive indeed. Even so, with some still rare exceptions, only a tiny minority have become activated. By contrast, there are several parts of the 'global south' where whole societies are in convulsion.

General or mass strikes have occurred in Argentina, Colombia, Ecuador, Bolivia and Honduras in Latin America, in Nigeria and Benin in Africa, and across the Indian subcontinent and China. There have been countless large strikes and popular protests in many other countries against the impositions of the international agencies. A conservative estimate suggests that in recent years there cannot have been less than 100 million people venting their fury with the results of neo-liberal agendas. They have acted with desperate bravery in the face of the unimaginable brutality of death squads, regular army and police. The scale of revolt in some places has literally embraced all but the state forces and those lackeys dependent upon them for their own survival.

Latin America has borne the brunt of the neo-liberal attempt to shape the world in its own image. The agenda of privatisation and de-regulation runs right back to the 1980s increasing poverty, child mortality and illiteracy in its bloody wake. Resistance goes back a long way too, sharpening in the 1990s with the Zapatista rebellion in Mexico, the Landless Rural Workers' Movement in Brazil, guerrilla armies in Colombia and provincial rebellions in Argentina. They were largely rural struggles in a continent where three quarters of the population live in cities. But in the second half of the 1990s the struggle became urban too. Massive strikes and blockades took place between 1996 and 1999 in Argentina, Venezuela, Uruguay, Colombia, Ecuador and Mexico.[15]

An excellent example, held up by others throughout this volume, has been the situation in Bolivia,[16] by no means resolved at the time of writing. In January 2000 the country was hit by the structural adjustment programme's demand for water privatisation. Workers with incomes of less than $100 per month faced an immediate price hike of $20. In the Cochabamba region incomes had already been forced down by the Bolivian government's complicity in the zero coca policy of the Clinton administration, an extension of Plan Columbia. The population simply came out of their homes, blockaded roads, marched on administration buildings, surrounded and occupied multinational company facilities and university campuses and struck demanding the termination of the privatisation scheme. The forces of the state reacted with bloody assaults on the demonstrators, killing and wounding large numbers of protesters. In April the government appeared to cave in, claiming to have removed the Bechtel Corporation of America's subsidiary the Anglo-Italian company International Water Ltd/Edison SpA from its claim on the country's water supply. Oscar Oliviera, the protest leader, said, 'For the first time in the history of Bolivia we have told the government "no" and made them back off from their destructive schemes for privatisation of our resources.'

The success of the mass campaign fed into a new summer/autumn protest on several fronts. The first was against the government's plan to build three military bases in the Cochabamba province with the assistance of a $1.6 billion loan from the US government, allegedly to police drugs traffic, but instantly spotted by the inhabitants as a response to their successful mass campaign. They returned to the streets employing the same tactics as previously. This campaign dovetailed with strike actions by teachers and doctors for pay increases and proper resourcing of education and health care against cuts in public services imposed by the Structural Adjustment Policies of the IMF. Again the government was forced to make concessions in both areas by the sheer determination shown by the workers in the face of intimidation and violence.

In Argentina resistance has also been on a mass scale, involving similar tactics to those in Bolivia. Here the impetus to the struggle has been a mixture of opposition to the government's new labour laws, cuts in social security and wage cuts—all a condition of a $7.2 billion IMF stand-by credit. Strikes started in December 1999 followed by mass demonstrations in April and May which included roadblocks in rural areas and a 24-hour general strike in June involving more than 7 million workers. In August teachers went on national strike against a 12 percent pay cut. The unrest festered on through the autumn, culminating in a further general strike at the end of November when factory workers blockaded motorways round Buenos Aires, forcing concessions from the government.

There was also militant action involving millions in Honduras, Paraguay, Peru, Ecuador, Brazil and Colombia, the latter in the front line of US policy to tame the rising anger of the people of Latin America. Under the mask of dealing with the traffic in drugs, the US administration is throwing money into re-tooling the military to shore up the corrupt regimes which are becoming increasingly isolated as they conduct warfare on all fronts against their own populations. What is truly remarkable is the level of resistance breaking out over the continent despite the fact that people are suffering the double assault of sharpening poverty and state violence.

So far the resistance movements show massive courage but few signs of developing a coordinated political leadership which can challenge the state coherently to maximise the gains made by protest. The Zapatistas showed enormous bravery and verve in leading the continent's new resistance in 1994. They became a shining example to the oppressed across the continent. In the early months of this year the movement gained enormous publicity for its march on Mexico City. Their obvious popularity clearly forced the new Fox government not to turn guns on them but to give the appearance of living with the movement. Yet the strategy they have employed has created for them a stalemate where they face integration through compromise or perhaps ultimate annihiliation at the hands of the Mexican military. Mike Gonzalez accurately expresses the impasse in their evasion of the question of power. 'It is a curious "quality" in a revolutionary organisation that it does not seek power. Their demands for land and the integrity of indigenous cultures are correct, as is their suspicion of the Mexican state. Yet, there is no space outside the system—globalisation does not tolerate free territories'.[17]

The electoral road in most countries is plagued by authoritarian constitutions and violence. In Venezuela Hugo Chavez, a social democrat who claims affinity with Fidel Castro, got an overwhelming endorsement in the July 2000 presidential election. In terms of a firm stand against the policies of the global institutions, to say nothing of the US, the result should be taken with extreme caution.[18] but as a confirmation of a leftward shift in the Latin American population it was very positive. In the same vein can be seen the success of the Workers Party in Brazil in October which won office in 17 of the 56 biggest municipalities including the financial capital, Sao Paulo. In September a national referendum organised by Jubilee 2000 and its affiliates saw nearly 6 million people vote against Brazil continuing its current (austerity) arrangements with the IMF.

Africa in 2000 saw a one-day general strike in South Africa in May against 'poverty, joblessness and the greed of capitalism', and a courageous electoral campaign against Mugabe in Zimbabwe, but the most significant event was the one-week general strike in Nigeria in June. A steep oil price rise was announced as part of an IMF structural adjustment package (removing all state subsidies). The main trade union federation called a strike. A massive response brought most urban centres to a total halt, enforcing a retreat on the reformist government of Obasanju.[19] The Nigerian action spread northwards to Benin where a one-day general strike took place on 12 June.[20]

Finally in this survey India was wracked by strikes throughout the year, the largest by power workers, starting in January in Uttar Pradesh. The year ended with a one-day national strike on 12 December. All were in opposition to the government's plan to privatise the electricity supply as 'required' by the IMF.[21]

Critical Mass cyclists converge on Kings Cross, London, early morning May Day 2001.

Genoa and beyond

The leaders of the G8 countries (Italy, US, France, Germany, Japan, Canada and Russia) will be holding their annual summit in Genoa this summer, 20–22 July. Last year they met in Okinawa where they wined and dined themselves to the tune of $780 million while doing nothing to address the increasing impoverishment of the majority of the world's population.

This year, they will be met on the streets of Genoa by tens of thousands of campaigners from all over the world. Tom Behan's eyewitness report from the Genoa Social Forum Planning Meeting below describes the international mobilisation which is taking place and what to expect when we get there.

From Britain, Drop the Debt and Globalise Resistance will mobilise more than 2,000 people from their organisations alone, many of whom will travel through the night on specially booked trains. Others will come by coach and car convoy from London, Brighton, Dublin and throughout Scotland.

Globalise Resistance's mobilisation for the event has taken place by leafleting, stickering, emailing and concentrating on big UK mobilisations and political meetings (union conferences, hustings and election meetings). Genoa has the backing of the following national trade unions: Unison, the GMB, the National Union of Journalists (NUJ), the Association of University Teachers (AUT), the Communications Workers Union (CWU), and the National Association of Teachers in Further and Higher Education (NATFHE). Many branches of these unions will have members on the overnight trains. Other organisation involved included the Socialist Alliance and the Church of Scotland Assembly.

Eyewitness: Genoa Social Forum planning meeting, 4-5 May 2001

The Meeting
About 250 people attended over the two days, with approximately 60 from outside Italy. The biggest single Italian grouping was probably the

autonomists Ya Basta!, particularly on the second day. Around 30 trade union activists came on the first day. Many of these were members of Communist Refoundation, whilst there was some likelihood that there were DS members (the Communist Party, the PCI, became the PDS in 1991 and DS in 1998), as well as a couple of Trotskyists. There were also anti-racists, environmentalists, feminists, lawyers, revolutionary socialists, students, union full-timers and intellectuals.

The non-Italians fell into three distinct groupings: ATTAC France; Drop the Debt from the UK, Germany, and probably elsewhere; plus a Globalise Resistance contingent from the UK. There were also representatives from the Austrian and German Communist parties, the French SUD union and trade unionists from Spain.

The meeting got off to a lively start when various people reported on May Day demonstrations around Europe, as well as the Greek general strike. Even more exciting, potentially, was the comparison made by people who had gone to similar planning meetings in Prague, held at a similar stage—they all said that things were looking much better for Genoa than they did for Prague.

There was some coverage in the local press, which was pretty non-committal. The national journalists attending a press conference on the second day, were nearly all obsessed about the possibility of violence. At one point a member of the SKA social centre in Naples sarcastically told them, 'After the beating we took at the demonstration in Naples in March, this time we're all coming with our own personal bazooka. This is what you want to hear, isn't it?'

The City of Genoa
Genoa has been a major port for centuries, but in recent years the number of dockers has been cut and a major steel factory has also shut down, and unemployment currently stands at about 12 percent. Maria Teresa, a housewife and council nursery worker, commented, 'It's been a city in great crisis, just like Liverpool. In 20 years the population has decreased from 900,000 to 600,000.'

What strikes any visitor to the city at the moment is the amount of building work going on—most of it related to the G8 summit. But as Antonio Bruno, a Communist Refoundation councillor in Genoa, complains, 'We've got drug addicts who are kept alive by donations from the local parish priest—because the government keep telling us there's no money.'

As Antonio Bruno said: 'We want to extend the underground line, but they keep telling us there's no money.' Maria Teresa explains why the refusal to fund and expand the underground is so frustrating: 'We've got the shortest underground in the world—it has two stops. We've been fighting to lengthen it for 11 years.'

Chiara, from the local Ya Basta! group, outlines other problems: 'Loads of military personnel will be put up in schools and hospitals— wards will even be closed to accommodate them. And most of the hospitals, including the city's accident and emergency departments, will be in the exclusion zone.'

One item of expenditure almost has a

bottomless pit in terms of finance: the government has currently set aside £33 million for security at the summit.

The summit area: the old town
In a way the architecture of the old town reflects what drives the anti-capitalist movement forward: inequality. In a few dozen metres you can move from breathtaking palaces such as the Palazzo Ducale (the summit venue) and the cathedral, to dark smelly alleyways in which some of the poorest people in Europe live.

What will happen to inhabitants of the old town will be a bit like what Palestinians suffer at the hands of the Israeli state, albeit with a much lower level of violence. People will only be able to move in and out of the 'red zone' with a pass, which will only be given to local residents.

There is an old Italian law, rarely enforced actively, in which all citizens must have a legal place of residence. The authorities appear to be preparing to use this law to depopulate the old town. Migrant workers employed on building sites created in order to beautify the district have been forced to leave their accommodation as they were not resident—and now perform the same work by commuting in from the outside. Even couples who have lived together for years or decades could be split up for weeks, if one of them hasn't already bothered to get official residence in the old town.

The unions and the question of a strike
There is a long tradition in Italy of general strikes. Indeed the first city-wide general strike in Italian history took place in Genoa exactly 100 years ago, in

1901. More important, and far more recent, was the general strike which broke the back of Berlusconi's first government in the Autumn of 1994. There were significant political strikes on 13 May 1999, the day allied planes left Italy to bomb Bosnia.

One excellent piece of news is that FIOM, the engineers' union, with a militant history similar to that of the miners, has supported the protests in July. So has the 'Work and Society' faction of the CGIL, linked to Communist Refoundation.

Most of the workers pushing for workers' demonstrations and strike action in July are in national rank and file groups, the most well known being Cobas. Translated as 'rank and file committees', these came into being in schools in 1986-88 as a breakaway national grouping to the left of the three official trade union federations. They also grew elsewhere in the public sector, particularly on the railways and in hospitals. However, over the last ten years there has been a process of fragmentation, with four or five competing rank and file groupings coming into existence, each organisation representing small numbers of workers—although railway workers are still frequently able to bring the whole national network to a halt.

But with the overall decline in strike levels, their isolation from the main union federations, and their fragmentation into competing groups, there has been a high level of demoralisation and mutual hostility in recent years. One worker remarked during the meeting, 'It is already a miracle that we're all together in the same place'—but such a statement can also be interpreted positively, in the sense that activists may be willing to bury their differences in view of the historic opportunity which Genoa represents.

One popular suggestion at the meeting was that groups of workers fighting multinationals should open the march on Friday 20 July. One suggestion was Danone workers from northern France. Another group could well be McDonald's workers from Florence, who recently won trade union recognition in the city's branches due to a series of strikes and protests.

Activists will need to engage with and overcome a high level of pessimism. As in Britain, workers have experienced a long series of closures, speed-ups etc, although in Italy workers have remained more combative than their British counterparts. The overall weakness perhaps is political, in the sense of being unable to fully understand the reasons for Berlusconi's expected victory.

One of the things that needs to be stressed in this context is that it was the centre-left coalition government, whose main party was the ex-Communist DS, which has been pushing and implementing neo-liberalism over the last few years.

An awareness of this can initially cause some degree of disorientation, but on the other hand there is a recent history (1994) which shows that Berlusconi can be beaten. And on a wider level, there is clear evidence that the anti-capitalist movement is growing, has started to gain victories, and is putting the ruling class on the defensive. One of the most important things to be argued is that the anti-capitalist movement represents an alternative to the current bout of pessimism and paralysis.

Tom Behan

Conclusion

One of the most exciting facets of charting the growth of this movement over the last 18 months has been the astonishing frequency and number of broadly anti-capitalist actions. A month has hardly passed without some event making the front page of the world's newspapers. We have only managed to tell the stories of the biggest, the ones receiving maximum publicity. Yet there have been dozens and dozens of local manifestations of the new mood of optimism for the struggle. And despite our best efforts, reporting of countless actions in Latin America, India, the Far East and parts of Africa has been slight. The internet has become a terrific tool for research of contemporary events and it can only improve as the movement grows. A network of correspondents has already been established with its strength in North America and Europe. People who pick up this book are encouraged to make contact: to join the web of global reporters.

John Charlton is a freelance writer and political activist living on Tyneside. He welcomes reports and comments on global struggles.
charlton@newcastle.u-net.com

Notes

1   This chapter will not revisit the events at Seattle which have now been covered many times. See, J Charlton, 'Talking Seattle', *International Socialism* 86, (Spring 2000); Kevin Danaher and Roger Burbach, *Globalize This* (Monroe, Maine, 2000); Janet Thomas, *The Battle in Seattle* (Golden, Colorado, 2000) and A Cockburn, J St Clair and A Sekula, *Five Days that Shook the World* (London, 2000).

2   'E Martinez, 'Where was the Color in Seattle?' in Danaher, above

3   Personal discussion with Canadian activists, July 2000.

4   P McGarr, *Socialist Worker*, 8 July 2000.

5   J Brecher, T Costello and B Smith, *Globalisation from Below: The Power of Solidarity* (Cambridge, Mass, 2000).

6   Dr B Barrett, report forwarded to the Office of the Omdudsman, Victoria, Australia, 15 November 2000.

7   Information on S11 supplied by David Glanz of the Australian ISO.

8   Sean K, Newcastle, personal interview.

9   Alice, INPEG, published on A16-international-planning@egroups.com

10 B Kagarlitsky, 'The Lessons of Prague', *International Socialism* 89, (Winter 2000).

11 Kristin, Norway, personal interview, 12 December 2000.

12 Peter, Norwich, and Jake, Manchester, personal interviews, 13 December 2000.

13 Kevin, Bristol, personal interview, 10 December 2000.

14 Peter from Norwich, as above.

15 L Selfa, 'Latin America: Rebirth of Resistance', *International Socialist Review* 10 (Winter 2000), examines the background critically.

16 Material on Bolivia garnered from www.1worldcommunication.org

17 M Gonzalez, 'The Zapatistas,' *International Socialism* 89 Winter 2000, p74.

18 In December Chavez planned to hold a referendum, the effects of which would be to draft a new labour law which would destroy freedom of association and collective bargaining replacing the independent trade unions with a government-sponsored institution.

19 Material on Nigeria, India, Benin and many other countries at http://x21.org/s26/struggles/nigeria

20 A detailed account of Africa is given by John Fisher elsewhere in this collection.

21 Labour Start is a source of strike reports from everywhere in the world.

CRS riot police block access to the courts of justice as protesters are tried for their actions at the EU summit demonstration in Nice, December 2000.

Where now?
Alex Callinicos

● ● ● ● ● ● ● ● ● ● ● ● ● ● ● ● ● ● ●

It is hard to believe that it is still less than two years since the great demonstrations in Seattle at the end of November 1999. The protests that precipitated the collapse of the ministerial meeting of the World Trade Organisation (WTO) also unleashed an avalanche of protests that show no sign of stopping. The most recent of those, against the Free Trade Area of the Americas (FTAA) summit in Quebec City on 20-21 April 2001, brought together in even larger numbers than at Seattle the 'Teamster-Turtle' alliance of trade unionists and largely student activists. Christophe Aguiton of the movement against financial speculation ATTAC commented, 'The demonstrations made one think very much of the days of May 1968 in Paris'.[1] Susan George is one of many also to compare the present movement with that of the 1960s, 'There has not been such a resurgence of activist energy since the Vietnam War'.[2]

But how are we more precisely to assess both the achievements and the limitations of this new movement? Its immediate practical effects have been real enough, but relatively limited. The demonstrations outside the Seattle summit gave the Third World delegates within the WTO meeting the courage to resist the demands of the US and the European Union (EU) for a new round of trade liberalisation. The protests in Prague on 26 September 2000 led to the general meeting of the International Monetary Fund (IMF) and the World Bank closing a day earlier than had been planned. The very threat of mass demonstrations prompted the World Bank to cancel its conference on development economics in Barcelona in June 2001. The international financial institutions (IFIs) are being forced to meet in more and more obscure venues to avoid disruption. Despite Western leaders' resounding commitment to 'democratic governance', the next WTO ministerial meeting, scheduled for November 2001, will take refuge from protesters in the desert autocracy of Qatar.

Significant though these achievements have been, the greatest impact of the movement against capitalist globalisation has been symbolic and ideological. After a decade in which many gave way to political despair, believing that the ascendancy of global capitalism was beyond challenge, Seattle demonstrated that collective action could still change the world. Moreover, the new wave of protests have been informed by a sense of totality, of the system itself rather than some specific aspect or institution being at fault. Other struggles whose immediate causes were apparently remote from the drive to impose neo-liberal policies globally have taken inspiration from the anti-capitalist protests. As discussed by Anne Alexander and John Rose in their contribution on the Middle East, Edward Said wrote of the Al Aqsa intifada:

> A turning point has been reached, however, and for this the Palestinian intifada is a significant marker. For not only is it an anti-colonial rebellion of the kind that has been seen periodically in Setif, Sharpeville, Soweto and elsewhere. It is another example of the general discontent with the post Cold War order (economic and political) displayed in the events of Seattle and Prague.[3]

This shift in consciousness has accompanied the emergence of more or less organised political milieux where a new left is beginning to take shape. In France *Le Monde diplomatique* and ATTAC have provided a model for opposition to neo-liberalism that has been widely imitated in continental Europe. In the US also a plethora of coalitions and campaigns have emerged to articulate the new anti-capitalist consciousness. Ralph Nader's presidential campaign helped to give a national focus to these movements in autumn 2000. As one supporter put it, 'Voting for Nader felt like a tiny step into a broader movement, an act that connected me with protesters in Seattle and Prague'.[4] Thomas Harrison summarised the main political thrust of the campaign thus:

> 'Plutocracy', 'oligarchy'—these were the words Nader used. Nader is no socialist—he is not even opposed to capitalism and the market as such. His rhetoric is very much like that of old-fashioned American Populism and Progressivism. But Nader's campaign relentlessly drew attention to the problem of class rule. Not since Norman Thomas in the 1930s has a prominent candidate for the presidency made this an issue and forced people to think about it.[5]

On a more modest scale, the Socialist Alliance and Globalise Resistance in Britain have brought together two overlapping constituencies—those inspired by the anti-globalisation movement, and Labour Party supporters disillusioned by the experience of the Blair government. This highlights the fact, mentioned by Adrian Budd in this volume, that in Western Europe the experience of the neo-liberal policies pursued by the social democratic governments elected in the second half of the 1990s has fed the growing opposition to corporate globalisation.

The IFIs and their apologists have been forced onto the defensive by mass demonstrations

This discontent is, moreover, finding ideological expression. Ten years after Francis Fukuyama proclaimed the 'end of history', new critiques of capitalism are emerging. These critiques have helped to articulate the protesters' understanding that the problem they are confronting is systemic. A variety of writers—some with a long-established reputation, others previously much less well known—have become the intellectual spokespeople of the anti-capitalist movement. Chief among them are perhaps Walden Bello, Pierre Bourdieu, Noam Chomsky, Kevin Danaher, Susan George, Naomi Klein, and George Monbiot. The result is a perceptible shift in the terms of debate. In a special report entitled 'Global Capitalism: Can It Be Made to Work Better?', *Business Week* argued:

It would be a great mistake to dismiss the uproar witnessed in the past few years [sic] in Seattle, Washington DC, and Prague. Many of the radicals leading the protests may be on the political fringe. But they have helped to kick-start a profound rethinking about globalisation among governments, mainstream economists, and corporations that, until recently, was carried on mostly in obscure think-tanks and academic seminars.[6]

The IFIs and their apologists have been forced onto the defensive. Both at Prague and at the World Social Forum at Porto Alegre Bello led teams that debated with representatives of global capitalism, including, in Prague, the heads of the IMF and the World Bank, and in both cases the hedge-fund wizard George Soros. The fact that the latter were willing to debate is remarkable. Moreover, both times they had a hammering. World Bank president James Wolfensohn was reduced to stuttering, 'I and my colleagues feel good about going to work every day.' After Bello had used a satellite television link to tell the business leaders attending the World Economic Forum in Davos that the best thing they could do for the planet was to blast off into outer space, Soros acknowledged:

> This protest movement is plugging into something that is widely felt. The methods they employ are not acceptable but they are effective—by their disruption they have created a concern that was not there before.[7]

As a result, the leading capitalist powers and the IFIs have been forced to make concessions. Some of these are purely verbal. The IMF and the World Bank have given the structural adjustment programmes that have done so much to increase Third World poverty the Orwellian name of 'debt reduction strategies'. The FTAA summit, while it met behind a fence to keep the protesters out, committed itself to reducing poverty in the American hemisphere. The new Mexican president, Vincente Fox, said, 'You cannot have genuine democracy in a society where there is so much inequality and poverty'.[8]

Somewhat more seriously, the IFIs are trying to engage non-governmental organisations (NGOs) in a 'dialogue' over their

'Company chairmen forced to cower behind police lines cannot help but be impressed by the strength of feeling and powers of organisation of people who might be ignored if they contented themselves with polite protest'
—*The Observer*

reform. This is part of a fairly blatant divide and rule strategy well explained by CNN reporter John King at Quebec City. He said that Western leaders were trying to develop a dialogue with some demonstrators so that when a minority 'engage in violence' they won't have tens of thousands of peaceful protest ers apparently supporting them and giving them legitimacy. The aim is to stop peaceful protesters from coming to future meetings.[9] A variation on this strategy was pursued by the Metropolitan Police when it sought, with the enthusiastic help of the media, to scare peaceful protesters away from the May Day 2001 demonstrations in London.

Some multinationals are also pursuing a strategy of 'dialogue'. As the *Observer* put it, 'Company chairmen forced to cower behind police lines cannot help but be impressed by the strength of feeling and powers of organisation of people who might be ignored if they contented themselves with polite protest'.[10] Sir John Browne, chief executive of BP, wrote recently, 'Business cannot fall into the trap of seeing NGOs as automatic enemies... In the long run, companies and NGOs are both agents of change... Our goal must be to put the two together, bringing different perspectives to bear on common issues'.[11] A similar effort to bring big business and 'civil society' together is involved in the Global Compact launched by United Nations secretary general Kofi Annan along with a number of leading multinational corporations.

This response reflects an understanding on our rulers' part that the anti-capitalist movement is a diverse one as well as the hope that they can exploit this by encouraging internecine conflict, incorporating the moderates, and isolating the more militant elements. On the whole the diversity of the movement is a source of strength: the sheer range of people involved—Christian anti-debt campaigners, environmentalists, trade unionists, socialists, anarchists, and many others—enhances the movement's moral authority and its capacity to mobilise. This diversity is reflected also in the variety of intellectual traditions within which the new critiques of capitalism are articulated—dependency theory, critical sociology, Green thought, classical Marxism and anarchism, autonomism, and so on. Michael Albert's and Colin Barker's contributions to this book illustrate how thoughtful representatives of different traditions are seeking to make them relevant to the new movement.

Only a fool would want to suppress this heterogeneity. It is evidence of a living movement. But it is necessary to be aware of the establishment's attempts to turn ideological and organisational differences into conflicts. One of the main reasons for producing this book has been that solidarity is more likely to be effective if it is informed by a critical understanding of the way in which the different issues that concern activists interconnect, reflecting how the capitalist system functions as a totality. Such an understanding will make it more difficult for the defenders of global capitalism to play us off against each other. It can also help us to focus our energies where they will be most effective. Orienting ourselves in this way requires us to confront certain key issues. Three in particular stand out: they concern strategy, tactics, and alternatives.

Strategy

There are in fact two important questions that need to be addressed here. The first concerns the movement's attitude towards the IFIs. Should the IMF, the World Bank, and the WTO be reformed or abolished? The crisis of the IFIs predates Seattle. The Asian financial crash of 1997-98 and the role of the IMF in imposing disastrous 'reform' programmes on Thailand, South Korea and Indonesia provoked a backlash against the neo-liberal 'Washington Consensus' that saw even fairly orthodox economists such as Jeffrey Sachs and Joseph Stiglitz join the critics' camp. Stiglitz was pushed out of his job as chief economist of the World Bank as part of a purge demanded by US Treasury secretary Lawrence Summers.[12]

NGOs campaigning against financial speculation, Third World debt, and environmental destruction have been faced with a dilemma. Should they ally themselves with spokespeople of what Stiglitz calls the 'Post-Washington Consensus'—critics such as Stiglitz himself, Sachs, and Soros, who call for reform of the IFIs and regulation of financial markets? Patrick Bond writes:

> Among the new social movements there are two fault-lines. One is a terribly dangerous tendency among the more conservative...NGOs and environmental groups—some even derisively called Co-opted NGOs or Co-NGOs—to cut pragmatic yet ultimately absurd and untenable deals with the establishment... The other is an ongoing debate over whether energy should be invested in helping Post-Washington Consensus reforms constitute a global state regulatory capacity—expanding upon embryos like the IMF and World Bank, WTO, United Nations and BIS [Bank for International Settlements]— or whether in contrast the immediate strategy should be defunding and denuding the legitimacy of current sites of potential international regulation so as to reconstitute progressive politics at the national scale.[13]

The most eloquent spokesperson for the latter strategy is Walden Bello. In a paper written with Nicola Bullard, he argues that a 'crisis of legitimacy now envelopes the institutions of global economic governance'. He warns against 'the soft corporate counter-offensive' designed 'relegitimise globalisation'. To counter it requires boycotting the efforts to develop a dialogue between the big corporations and 'civil society'. Furthermore, 'the time is ripe to press and build-up a global campaign for decommissioning or neutering' the IFIs and to 'extend the crisis of legitimacy from the multilateral institutions of global governance to the engine of globalisation itself: the transnational corporation'. Campaigners should stress 'the similarity between the mafia and the TNC'.[14]

Bello is probably the key strategic thinker of the movement against capitalist globalisation, and the broad thrust of his argument is absolutely correct. But it raises further questions. Any effective politics needs to decide who its friends and its enemies are. To start with the latter: against what are we fighting? Is it globalisation itself, as Bello tends to suggest? Or is it 'elite globalisation', as Kevin Danaher says?[15] Closely connected is the question of capitalism. Is the capitalist system itself the real enemy, as the term 'anti-capitalist' so widely used to describe the protests suggests? Or does the problem lie rather with the particular version of capitalism—what is often described as the free market Anglo-American model, as European social democrats tend to argue?[16]

These questions are obviously closely connected to that of the alternative, to which I return below. But there is also the problem of allies. Bello argues that campaigners against globalisation should ally with the Republican right against the IFIs:

> The motivation of the incoming Republicans in criticising the IMF and the World Bank lies in their belief in free market solutions to development and growth. This may not coincide with that of progressives, who see the IMF and World Bank as a tool of US hegemony. But the two sides can unite behind one agenda at this point: the radical downsizing, if not dismantling, of the Bretton Woods twins.[17]

But this seems like a very dangerous approach. As George W Bush's denunciation of the Kyoto protocol on climate change makes clear, the new Republican administration represents a shift to a more unilateralist policy by the US. The Republican right attack the IMF and the World Bank because they see such multilateral institutions as imposing unnecessary constraints on the self-assertion of US capitalism. This may be a stupid policy—the IFIs have in fact served Washington well—but the motivation seems clear enough: Bush and the Republicans want to strengthen the very multinationals that Bello rightly seeks to target. Moreover, from a purely tactical point of view, alliances with the conservative critics of globalisation will make the movement more vulnerable to the charge frequently made in the media that we are opponents of progress in cahoots with right wing protectionists like Pat Buchanan.

If the Republican right are our foes, our most important friend is the organised working class. Workers in North and South alike have been among the chief victims of capitalist globalisation—the former as a result of the endless restructuring and downsizing required to maintain competitiveness, the latter thanks to sweatshop labour and environmental destruction required by the relentless drive to cut costs. At the same time, the organised working class is set apart from all other oppressed groups by the collective strength that derives from the system's dependence on its labour. From France in December 1995 to South Korea a year later to many other countries since, mass strikes have played a key role in the resistance to neo-liberalism, as the contributions to this collection have shown.

Key to our rulers' divide and rule tactics is the effort to isolate the anti-capitalist movement from organised labour—the movement's success will depend critically on its ability to defeat these tactics

The decisive significance of Seattle, repeated on an even larger scale in Quebec, was the coming together of trade unionists and student and ex-student activists against capitalist globalisation. Key to our rulers' divide and rule tactics is the effort to isolate the anti-capitalist movement from organised labour. The movement's success will depend critically on its ability to defeat these tactics and to encourage trade unionists—the daily victims of neo-liberal policies of privatisation, deregulation, and public expenditure cuts—to widen their horizons and see themselves as the key agent in a process of universal emancipation.

Achieving this is a lot easier said than done. Kim Moody rightly stresses in his contribution the difficulties caused by the different social situations of 'rooted labour and footloose activists'. Moreover the conservative labour bureaucracies that dominate the trade union movement do their utmost to prevent their members from participating in anti-capitalist direct actions. All the same, even granted the enormous distance we have yet to travel, it still seems important to highlight the breakthrough that Seattle and Quebec City represented. The test ahead of us is to begin to demonstrate to rank and file workers the connection between their immediate preoccupations and the struggle against global capitalism.

Tactics

Here the most important issue is that of violence. This can be addressed at three levels. First, there is the morality of violence. Each year between 10 million and 12 million children die of diseases that could be easily prevented if the world's resources were fairly distributed. Capitalism killed those children as surely as if its agents had shot them.[18] This kind of structural violence vastly outweighs the minor episodes of stone or Molotov cocktail throwing in which some demonstrators have indulged at anti-capitalist protests—particularly when one takes into account the organised violence of the robocops deployed against them in Seattle and Prague and Nice and Quebec City, armed to the teeth with batons, riot shields, tear-gas, water cannon, rubber bullets, armoured vehicles etc.

Secondly, however, to be morally justified violence must be politically effective. Tactics should be aimed at including as many people as possible in mass action. Trashing McDonald's and the like can all to easily turn into a ritual performed for a mass media obsessed with portraying violence. Nor are all non-violent tactics inclusive. The highly publicised games that the Italian autonomist coalition Ya Basta! play with the riot police—witty and courageous though they are—tend to divide demonstrators into a minority of 'experts' set apart by their padded white overalls and the vast majority, who are reduced to the status of passive onlookers. But the entire history of mass struggles over the past two centuries, from the French Revolution to the overthrow of Stalinism in Eastern Europe and of apartheid in South Africa, shows that it is the sheer weight of numbers—particularly when this is combined with collective working class action—that forces change.

The third level at which the question of violence can be posed merges with the problems of strategy. Can the present system of oppression and exploitation be reformed, or is a revolution necessary? Some leading anti-capitalist intellectuals reject the goal of revolution. Susan George said at Porto Alegre, 'I regret that I must confess that I no longer know what "overthrowing capitalism" means at the beginning of the 21st century'.[19] But whether or not we agree that the real enemy is capitalism, campaigners against globalisation have to consider whether or not the bosses of the multinational corporations and their allies in control of every leading state in the world will peacefully give up their immense power and privileges. Given the repressive power that the state has mobilised against mere demonstrations, it is naive to imagine that any serious challenge to the system will not be met by what Marx called 'a "pro-slavery" rebellion'—the violent defence of the status quo. Once again, the only effective counter is mass action.

Alternatives

Increasingly within the movement the question arises: we know what we're fighting against, but what are we fighting for? For Bello it is 'deglobalisation', by which he means a return to the 'more pluralistic system of global economic governance' of the 1950s and 1960s based on the 1944 Bretton Woods agreement, when 'the East and south East Asian countries were able to become newly industrialising countries through activist state trade and industrial policies that departed significantly from the free market biases enshrined in the WTO'.[20] Bello makes it clear that he does not idealise the post-war global economic structure, and would like to improve on it, but he must all the same confront the difficulties with this alternative. Two stand out.

The first is that the 1950s and 1960s were indeed a period of global economic boom, but they gave way to a succession of world slumps that destroyed the Bretton Woods system and set the scene for the drive to neo-liberal policies that gave rise to the present movement. Bello is clear enough that capitalism has an inherent tendency towards crises of overproduction.[21] How would his revised version of the post-war-economic system avoid the tendency that ultimately destroyed the original? Secondly, the Third World industrialisation that did take place (in East Asia extending to the mid-1990s) was presided over by politically authoritarian and labour-repressive regimes. Clearly they do not represent an attractive model for a movement that seeks the radical extension of democracy.

Bello's slogan 'deglobalisation' acts in effect as a compromise formula that can be developed further in two directions. The first is what is sometimes called 'localisation', which would involve a radical decentralisation of the world economy and reliance on highly localised patterns of production and trade. George Monbiot is one of the most eloquent advocates of such an approach. The obvious dangers of this solution is that it would forfeit the genuine gains that the technologically dynamic and globally integrated capitalism of the present day has brought with it, and that it tends to idealise petty forms of capitalism that, because they lack the financial reserves and margin for manoeuvre of the big corporations, can be more exploitative than the large-scale version. Here the anti-globalisation movement dovetails in with the more radical Green opponents of industrialisation and the conservative critique of modernity.[22]

Bello's approach can be developed, secondly, into the attempt to develop stronger forms of international economic regulation. The model here is the use of the nation-state to control and civilise capitalism during the Keynesian era after the Second World War. The crisis of nationally organised capitalism in the 1970s and 1980s set the scene for the neo-liberal drive to remove all barriers to the global operation of capital. But key critics of neo-liberalism, particularly in Europe, seek once again to regulate capitalism, this time on the basis of international forms of economic governance. Pierre Bourdieu is, for example, one of many who believe that a reformed EU could act as an instrument of regulation, even though he acknowledges that the EU as presently constituted is an agent of capitalist globalisation.[23]

Here again we return to the question of whether existing international institutions can be reformed to serve more democratic and humane purposes. From a socialist perspective, this question must be answered in the negative. Capitalism is driven by the logic of competitive accumulation, for which both human needs and capacities and the structures and resources of the planet itself are mere raw materials to be used and consumed. Since capitalism is an evolving system, institutions come and go as its structure and requirements change, but the same anti-human logic drives it. The key question is then to develop a different social logic, where the aim is no longer to maximise profits but to meet human needs in an environmentally sustainable way and on the basis of democratic and collective control of the world's resources. This seems like as good a contemporary definition of socialism as we are likely to get.[24]

Of course, proposing a socialist alternative to capitalism poses questions both about the nature of this alternative and the strategy required to achieve it. But then the point of this essay, as of the book as a whole, is not to close off debate, but to contribute it. The problems I have identified are ones that anyone concerned with the future of the anti-capitalist movement must address, even if they offer different answers to the ones I have given here. The diversity of the movement and the debates it has provoked are signs of its vitality and of the brilliant future that lies ahead. As the first great critic of global capitalism wrote, we have a world to win.[25]

Alex Callinicos is a leading member of the Socialist Workers Party. He teaches politics at the University of York. His most recent books are *Social Theory*, *Equality*, and *Against the Third Way*. He is now working on an anti-capitalist manifesto.
atc1@york.ac.uk

Notes

1   C Aguiton, 'Les Mobilisations de
    Québec des 20 et 21 avril 2001 à
    l'occasion du sommet des Amériques',
    www.attac.org.
2   S George, 'Que faire à présent?', text
    for the World Social Forum at Porto
    Alegre, 15 January 2001.
3   E Said, 'Palestinians under Siege',
    London Review of Books, 14 December
    2000, p10.
4   *The Guardian*, 7 November 2000.
5   T Harrison, 'Election 2000: Infamy
    and Hope', *New Politics*, 8:2 (2001),
    p9.
6   *Business Week*, 6 November 2000.
7   *Financial Times*, 29 January 2001.
8   *Financial Times*, 23 April 2001.
9   Discussion of FTAA summit, CNN, 22
    April 2001.
10 R Cowe, 'The Acceptable Face of Anti-
    Capitalism', *The Observer*, 6 May
    2001.
11 J Browne, 'Time to Engage with
    Pressure Groups', *Financial Times*,
    2 April 2001.
12 R Wade, 'Showdown at the World
    Bank', *New Left Review* 2, 2001.
13 P Bond, 'Their Reforms and Ours', in
    W Bello et al (eds), *Global Finance*
    (London, 2000), pp66-67. Bond's
    paper is a useful summary of the state
    of debate on the eve of Seattle.
14 W Bello and N Bullard, 'The Global
    Conjuncture: Characteristics and
    Challenges', *Focus on the Global
    South*, www.focusweb.org, March
    2001.
15 K Danaher, 'Power to the People', *The
    Observer*, 29 April 2001.
16 See, for example, M Albert, *Capitalism
    Against Capitalism* (London, 1993), W
    Hutton, *The State We're In* (London,
    1995), and O Lafontaine, *The Heart
    Beats On the Left* (Cambridge, 2000).

17 'Is Bush Bad News for the World Bank?', *Focus on the Global South*, www.focusweb.org, January 2001.

18 Capitalism's chronic capacity to inflict disaster is set in a longer term historical perspective by Mike Davis in his brilliant book *Late Victorian Holocausts* (London, 2001).

19 S George, 'Que faire à présent?'

20 W Bello and N Bullard, 'The Global Conjuncture'. A certain nostalgia for the Bretton Woods system is characteristic of several contributions in Bello et al (eds), *Global Finance*.

21 W Bello, '*No Logo*: Brilliant, Flawed View of Contemporary Capitalism', on *Socialist Register* discussion group, www.york.ca/socreg/

22 For further discussion of 'localisation', see C Harman, 'Anti-Capitalism: Theory and Practice', *International Socialism* 88 (2000), also available at www.swp.org.uk/ISJ/. John Gray's *False Dawn* (London, 1999) is a good example of the conservative critique of globalisation.

23 See P Bourdieu, *Contre-feux* (Paris, 1998) and *Contre-feux* 2 (Paris, 2001).

24 For further thoughts on this subject, see A Callinicos, *Against the Third Way* (Cambridge, 2001), pp109-120.

25 K Marx and F Engels, *The Communist Manifesto* (London, 1998), p77.

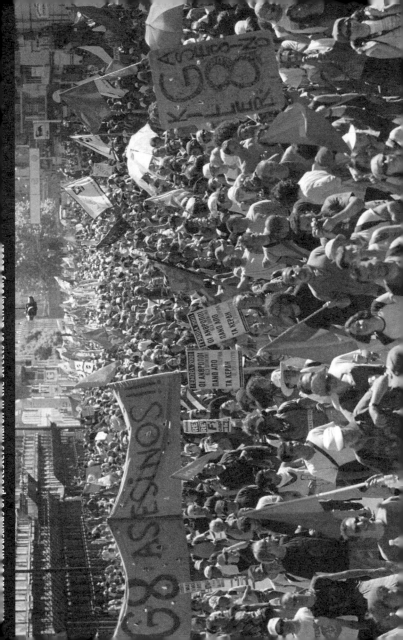

Afterword
Tom Behan

● ● ● ● ● ● ● ● ● ● ● ● ● ● ● ● ● ● ●

'This movement is unstoppable now in both rich and poor countries. We have seen nothing yet.' So said French activist José Bové after the Genoa demonstrations. His British counterpart George Monbiot agreed: 'Ours is, in numerical terms, the biggest protest movement in the history of the world.'

This short afterword will consider what was expected at Genoa, what actually happened, and what it means for the future of the anti-capitalist movement.

The expectations two months earlier (see pages 378-383) were that this would be a very left wing and working class series of protests. It was also hoped it would be a bigger mobilisation than the 20,000-strong Prague demonstration of September 2000. These expectations, and many others, were met—and vastly exceeded.

When the last edition of this book went to print, plans for Genoa were still being made. The Italian government spent some time negotiating with the umbrella organising committee, the Genoa Social Forum (GSF), and had made two solemn promises: (1) All major train stations in Genoa would remain open; (2) The EU's Schengen agreement, which abolishes border controls, would not be revoked. But a week before the summit began it was announced that Genoa's two main stations, Brignole and Principe, would be closed—forcing protesters to come in by road from several miles away. Silvio Berlusconi's government also announced it was revoking the Schengen

agreement, in the hope of being able to send large numbers of protesters back at the borders. Although a few individuals were sent
back, all large groups made it into Italy. Greek protesters had to literally fight their way onto Italian soil at the quayside in Ancona, but
they succeeded. Another success story was the Globalise Resistance
train from Britain, suddenly cancelled by the French government
three days before its departure, it was reinstated 24 hours later due
to pressure from French trade unions and ATTAC France.

So what happened when we got there? The GSF had organised its own public forum—seven full days of debates. Hundreds of
speakers came from all over the world, including Walden Bello,
José Bové and Susan George. The breadth, depth and vitality were
there for all to see—a far more interesting event than the eight
defensive men barricaded inside the Red Zone.

The first demonstration, in support of migrants and illegal
immigrants, took place on Thursday 19 July. Apart from migrants,
particularly Kurds, there were large delegations from the Italian
COBAS rank and file trade union organisation, ATTAC France, the
young communists of Communist Refoundation, and Globalise
Resistance. The police estimate was 50,000 protesters—the GSF
said later that 80,000 attended.

Friday 20 July was non-violent direct action day. The Red
Zone was surrounded from all directions by tens of thousands of
demonstrators. Up to 10,000 people marched in the west, organised by the CUB rank and file organisation. Thousands of Catholic
activists, feminists and pacifists congregated in three squares to
the north. In the south, thousands of people, mainly from ATTAC
France and Italy, and the Italian cultural association ARCI, congregated in Piazza Dante for several hours, and made two determined
assaults on the four metre high fencing. A joint march of 4,000, led
by Globalise Resistance, attacked the fence in Via Fiasella and
broke through in places before being hammered back by the teargas and water cannon.

The two marches in the east suffered the most police vio-
lence. The biggest march, about 15,000, was led by the autonomist
Ya Basta!, and was attacked soon after it left the Carlini stadium.
They fought the police off and continued, but retreated back to the

stadium soon after a 23 year old demonstrator named Carlo Giuliani was shot dead by the police in separate clashes nearby. The COBAS trade union federation had thousands of people assembling in Piazza Da Novi, including José Bové, when, after infiltration by Black Block, they were suddenly violently attacked by the police. Unable to establish any order, they abandoned their march.

The scale and ferocity of police violence dominated a mass meeting back at the convergence centre. There was real demoralisation and fear—leading unfortunately to Drop the Debt's decision not to march the next day. But in this meeting, and later on live television, the spokesperson of the GSF, Vittorio Agnoletto, made the following appeal: 'You've all seen what happened today on your televisions. So I'm asking all Italians to change their plans tomorrow. Get in your cars, jump on a bus or train, and come to Genoa.'

The most optimistic prediction for the Saturday 21 July march was 150,000, yet a magnificent 300,000 protesters came to Genoa. Tens of thousands suddenly decided to come out of a sense of solidarity and outrage.

The march was overwhelmingly left wing and working class. Communist Refoundation may have mobilised up to 100,000 people, and the FIOM engineering union claims to have brought 10,000 of its members. Equally important was the age range—80 percent of the protesters were under 30.

Old Italian songs such as 'Bella Ciao' and 'Bandiera Rossa' merged in with slogans in English first heard in Seattle. Local people threw flowers from their balconies, while some cooled protesters by showering them with buckets of water and streams from hosepipes. A few old people brought out the flags of their long defunct local branches of the Italian Communist Party and waved them, to huge applause. Many Genoese also opened their front doors to protesters trying to escape from baton-wielding police.

World leaders could no longer dismiss such a movement as a tiny radical fringe. Police violence against masses of peaceful protesters filled television screens worldwide. Tony Blair showed himself to be out of step with even the mainstream of British media when he commented, 'To criticise the Italian police is to turn the world upside down.' Journalists had seen, and even experienced, the extreme police violence for themselves.

Italy was certainly turned upside down over the next two weeks. Spontaneous demonstrations involving hundreds took place in Rome and Bologna just a few hours after Carlo Giuliani's death. Then, in an even stronger reaction, following the illegal police raid on the Indymedia centre on Saturday night, an amazing 60,000 people demonstrated virtually spontaneously in Milan on Monday evening.

Berlusconi's first comments on Genoa in parliament were full of smug self-assurance. But the anger and mobilisation continued. On Tuesday there were an incredible 50 demonstrations up and down Italy, all organised at 48 hours notice.

In his next speech Berlusconi's demeanour was described as 'ashen-faced'. Around the world journalists were still angrily denouncing their treatment at the hands of the Italian police. Protests were mushrooming abroad too—in the first week 124 demonstrations were held around the world in protest at police violence, including an occupation of the Italian embassy in Amsterdam. Bowing to all this pressure, Berlusconi sacked the deputy national police commissioner, the head of the anti-terrorism branch and the Genoa police chief.

Genoa has created the basis for a huge Italian anti-capitalist movement. Three days after the Genoa demonstrations 1,000 people met in Rome, listened to 50 speeches over five hours, and decided to set up the Rome Social Forum, a local version of the Genoa original.

The issue of violence has dominated discussion immediately after Genoa. The 'genuine' Black Block, should be engaged in discussion about tactics which provide for the possibility of police infiltration, violence and provocation. At the same time, we must not shift our focus from the violence of neo-liberalism which the police are protecting.

Luca Casarini, spokesperson of Ya Basta!, one of the groups which has tended to become 'professional demonstrators', recently commented on what he thought had changed after Genoa: 'To accept the logic of military clashes would be both crazy and political suicide. Our movement cannot match their military power. We would be crushed.'

Despite the live ammunition, armoured cars, helicopters, pepper spray, teargas, truncheons and water cannon, the movement came out of Genoa more mature, united and determined. And one of the key elements was strength of numbers—both in the sense that it makes it impossible to be dismissed as an irrelevant sideshow, and in the sense that it is almost impossible to drive 300,000 people out of a city.

The pressure continues to mount on world rulers. The next G8 summit will be held in the small Canadian town of Kananaskis in June 2002. Berlusconi wants to move the November 2001 FAO food summit from Rome to somewhere in Africa, as he wants to avoid another Genoa. At a WTO meeting ten days after Genoa, called to plan for the Qatar meeting scheduled in November, one envoy described the mood of the discussion as 'demoralising, discouraging, discomfiting and depressing'.

As Alex Callinicos has argued in the previous article, these victories have been hugely significant in a 'symbolic and ideological' way. To apply even more pressure, to take things to the next stage, we need workers in trade unions to begin to take strike action against neo-liberalism. Organised labour is quite literally the hand that feeds them—they bite it at their peril.

The signs that this is the direction we are going in are hopeful. Genoa showed that the 'Teamster-Turtle' alliance forged in Seattle is now a constant of the anti-capitalist movement— nobody was surprised or hostile to the fact that thousands and thousands of workers took part in all three days of protest.

After Genoa not only is another world still possible—the anti-capitalist movement has taken a big step closer towards it.

Tom Behan is a lecturer in Italian history and politics at the University of Kent at Canterbury. He has written extensively on many aspects of politics in Italy.
T.H.Behan@ukc.ac.uk

TO ORDER MORE COPIES OF THIS BOOK CONTACT

● ● ● ● ● ● ● ● ● ● ●

BOOKMARKS PUBLICATIONS LTD,
c/o 1 BLOOMSBURY STREET,
LONDON, WC1B 3QE
OR PHONE 020 7637 1848
OR ORDER ONLINE AT:
www.bookmarks.uk.com
publications@bookmarks.uk.com